Language in International Business

Language in International Business

The Multilingual Reality of Global Business Expansion

Rebecca Piekkari

Professor of International Business, Aalto University, School of Business, Finland

Denice E. Welch

Professor of International Business, Melbourne Business School, University of Melbourne, Australia

Lawrence S. Welch

Professor of International Marketing and International Business, Melbourne Business School, University of Melbourne, Australia

Edward Elgar
Cheltenham, UK • Northampton, MA, USA

Published by
Edward Elgar Publishing Limited
The Lypiatts
15 Lansdown Road
Cheltenham
Glos GL50 2JA
UK

Edward Elgar Publishing, Inc.
William Pratt House
9 Dewey Court
Northampton
Massachusetts 01060
USA

A catalogue record for this book
is available from the British Library

Library of Congress Control Number: 2014947024

This book is available electronically in the ElgarOnline.com
Business Subject Collection, E-ISBN 978 1 78471 099 6

ISBN   978 1 84844 989 3 (cased)
           978 1 78471 015 6 (paperback)

Typeset by Servis Filmsetting Ltd, Stockport, Cheshire

Contents

Foreword

KONE is a century-old elevator and escalator company with over 43 000 employees in more than 50 countries. For the first half of its existence, KONE was a domestic Finnish company, conducting almost all its business within Finland's borders. Starting in 1967, the company began expanding internationally until today Finland accounts for only 3 per cent of KONE's global business and less than 5 per cent of its personnel.

It has always been quite obvious to KONE's leaders, as it must be to this book's readers, that we could not function as a global company if we conducted business only in Finnish, a language spoken by barely five million (0.07 per cent) of the world's seven billion people. Coming from such a tiny population base, we have been forced throughout our company's history to confront the language issue, and the decisions we made have had a significant impact on our growth and success.

When KONE opened for business in 1910, the management and workforce were Swedish-speaking and remained so through the Second World War. The number of Finnish-speakers slowly increased as the company expanded after the war, but the changeover to Finnish as KONE's primary language was necessitated in 1967 when the company closed its old factory and headquarters in Helsinki and moved to a new facility 50 kilometers away. Many of the Swedish-speaking old-timers chose not to make the daily commute of more than an hour each way and were replaced by Finnish-speaking recruits from the countryside.

The construction of the new factory coincided with a determined push to expand business activity beyond Finland's borders. The domestic elevator market was too small to defend against attacks by large and aggressive multinationals. To survive, KONE had to gain footholds in new markets. By 1972, KONE had acquired subsidiaries in Sweden, Norway, Denmark, Austria, Canada and France, and was already publishing its annual report in English.

That same year in Copenhagen, KONE held its first international 'Top Management Meeting'. Simultaneous interpreters were brought in to facilitate the meeting, but at the end the participants were warned: 'Next year there will be no interpreters.' The meeting would be held in English, and everyone would be expected to function in that environment. Later that year, the first international management training courses were held in Finland, and the courses were exclusively in English. From that time on, English has been the official language of our company.

KONE's growth and internationalization took place primarily through the acquisition of existing companies. Each company brought its own language, culture, labour agreements, personnel practices and so forth to the growing KONE organization. To deal with this diversity, KONE followed a practice of 'local excellence & global support'. The global support functions naturally had to work in English, and mid-level managers in local companies were expected to be able to work in English when the situation called for it.

From the 1970s, all monthly, quarterly and year-end reports have been submitted to headquarters in English. Language classes were offered at the local company level. An English-language in-house magazine for all mid- and high-level managers was launched in 1982. By that time, KONE had added companies in Australia, Belgium, Brazil, Egypt, Germany, Great Britain, Hong Kong, Japan, Malaysia, Mexico, the Netherlands, the Philippines, Saudi Arabia, Singapore, the Soviet Union, Switzerland, the United Arab Emirates, the USA and Venezuela. For 'local excellence & global support' to succeed across such a wide spectrum, clear and accurate communication was needed.

KONE was an early adopter of computers (1964) and Internet technology (early 1990s), both of which called for a precise common language to describe everything from components and installation methods to business practices and the company's goals. The implementation of Enterprise Resources Planning (1996) further increased the pressure for working at almost all levels in a common language with common terminology.

The changes in operational practice were also reflected in the workings of the board of directors. Early board meetings were held in Swedish, followed by Finnish in the 1960s. Since the appointment of the first non-Finnish board member in 1996, board meetings have been held in English.

During the past decade, KONE has developed into a truly global company. We could not have made this difficult transition without a clear language strategy. Harmonized thinking and acting require a basis in harmonized language, which, in turn, helps determine our agility, productivity and responsiveness to market developments.

Antti Herlin
Board Chairman
KONE Corporation

Preface

This book arose from a meeting with Edward Elgar himself at Melbourne Business School on one of his many visits to Australia. When hearing about our work on language and international business, he immediately said: 'That's an interesting topic. Why don't you write a book about it?' After demurring and discussing this suggestion among ourselves, we decided to embark on a project that has taken far longer than anticipated. Now that the project has been finalized, we have to agree with Edward. There was a book to be written about how global expansion brings language into focus. We thank Edward for his encouragement and support.

Our interest in language arose from Rebecca's doctorate on organizational structural changes and inter-unit communication within a single multinational, the Finnish firm KONE. One of the results was the way in which the use of English kept being mentioned by interviewees, at all levels and in various subsidiaries of KONE. As a monolingual supervisor, Denice was struck by this emergent theme. When drawing this to Rebecca's attention, she was dismissive. How could language be an important issue? For someone fluent in multiple languages (Finnish, Swedish, Russian, English, Spanish and French), she took a little convincing that language was an issue worthy of pursuing. When Lawrence joined our discussion, we started to map out the various implications that arose from the thesis work. These early ideas, published in the *European Management Journal* in 1997, formed the basis of a research agenda that has continued, and remains an important part of our ongoing academic work. Reflecting on how the area of language research covered in this book has developed, we can no longer say that language is the forgotten factor in international business research. It has been gratifying to see the way in which language is now taken so seriously. No longer does language reside in the cultural 'black box', or as a peripheral area of cross-cultural management. The growing number of articles, conference papers and panel sessions, and special issues, has raised the profile of language as a topic in its own right.

International business scholars have come surprisingly late to the issue of language. After all, once a firm crosses national boundaries, at some point it tends to be confronted by the multilingual reality. Indeed, we have argued elsewhere that language is the essence of international business.

Scholars in other disciplines with a basic interest in language, such as linguistics and communication studies, have also become involved, placing their work into the context of international business. This is a natural fit for language specialists, reinforcing the value of foreign language research and teaching. As more firms confront the multilingual reality of global expansion, the demand for language-skilled individuals continues to rise.

While the audience for this book is likely to be mainly those working in international business, we recognize that colleagues outside the field may find some of the topics covered of relevance to their work, and it may appeal to a wide range of disciplines and functional specialists. We therefore explicate the core concepts and basics of topics coming under the international business umbrella to provide the setting for the treatment of language issues.

The scope of the book reveals that the issue of language is more than an area of scholarly research. There are practical considerations and consequences for those managing in a global context, and we show that many firms are taking account of language in their operations in creative ways, even developing explicit language strategies. We explore language at various organizational levels, and in areas including marketing, human resource management, and foreign operation modes. Thus we do not treat the internationalizing firm as a monolith. The role of the individual, both as a manager and as an employee, is highlighted throughout the book, recognizing that organizations do not have languages; people do. Our emphasis is on understanding and appreciating the complexity that the multilingual reality presents, rather than seeking to measure factors that magnify or reduce language distance.

This book could not have been accomplished without the support and encouragement of a range of institutions and individuals. First, we would like to thank the managers and staff of the various companies who have contributed time, availability for interviews and many insights that have contributed so much to our work on language. In many respects, this book is for and about them. Special thanks go to KONE, where Rebecca's research began. We appreciate their openness and their permission to use their name in our various publications. This openness is reflected in the attitude of top management. As an example, at the time of the doctoral defence in Helsinki, the foreign opponent, Professor Stuart Macdonald, asked the then KONE chairman: 'Rebecca's thesis contains some criticism of your management processes. How did you feel having this exposed in such a public forum?' The chairman replied: 'This is science. We support the work of the Finnish scientific community.'

We acknowledge the support of our home institutions, Aalto University, School of Business, and Melbourne Business School, University of

Melbourne. We are very grateful for the financial support provided by the Foundation for Economic Education and the HSE (Helsinki School of Economics) Foundation for this book. We wish to thank Catherine Welch for her insights and comments throughout this work; and to Ingmar Björkman and Douglas Dow for their support. Our thanks also go to our co-authors on the various journal articles and book chapters on aspects of language. We also acknowledge the many MSc students upon whose theses on the topic of language we draw.

   The contribution of Bea Alanko to this endeavour has been invaluable. She handled our many demands and the numerous practical challenges with characteristic cheerful efficiency and patience. The presentation of the figures and tables as well as the referencing and formatting in this book owe much to her expertise and dedication on this front. We would also like to thank Ludmila Velikodnaya for assisting in the formatting of the book. As well as Edward Elgar, we would like to thank Francine O'Sullivan and Ben Booth at Edward Elgar Publishing for their patience and resigned acceptance of the many moving deadlines. Of course, long-suffering family members, Lauri, Johanna and Tommi Piekkari, and Marina and Alexander Marschan are more pleased than most to see the book finished.

Rebecca Piekkari
Denice E. Welch
Lawrence S. Welch

1. Language and global business expansion

> We were exposed to five languages every day ... The official language of
> the authorities was Latvian, and 273 of the workforce and the local manag-
> ing director spoke Russian only. English was so to speak our working tool
> ... With some of the older employees and with our German suppliers we
> communicated in German ... and amongst ourselves [the Danish expatriates],
> we obviously spoke Danish ... the constant need for translation is of course
> very time consuming. I was very fortunate, however, my secretary and inter-
> preter, a young Latvian girl, was simply a linguistic talent. (Danish business-
> man's comment on his company's Latvian operation, in Jacobsen and Meyer,
> 1998, 11)

INTRODUCTION

To say that language permeates every facet of international business
would meet with little argument, especially from those involved in global
activities in any form. In the twenty-first century, as the globalization of
business proceeds, it is exposing companies to a wider and wider array of
the world's different languages. Despite the rise of technologies that are
ameliorating some of the demands of communicating across languages,
communication in the global village is becoming a more complex activity. Much of business still relies on social exchange, on person-to-person
interaction, which is difficult to sustain through automated translation
or through the use of professional translators. It has been estimated that
if two countries have a common language, trade between them will be 42
per cent greater than between two countries that do not (*The Economist*,
2012a).

Ready acceptance of the importance of language, however, is not the
same as understanding its role: where and how it is important; and what is
the range of its effects? As Maclean (2006, 1377) comments, 'Companies
deal with language issues every day, they cope, the world continues to turn.
How they do so, however, remains largely absent from the literature.' The
emerging work that attempts to redress this neglect is showing how an
organization can be rendered partially deaf, mute and blind because of

language effects, ultimately creating the silent organization (Lauring and Tange, 2010).

In this book, we delve into what goes on inside the internationalizing firm to reveal how language effects permeate activities across all levels of operation. We also explore the impact of language within and beyond firms and other institutions that are engaged in or impact upon international business activity. Thus we go beyond the obvious cross-cultural communication context. Instead, the book deals with language matters, or issues, that play an important role in furthering, or impeding, global expansion. By so doing, we aim to demonstrate how language matters in international business.

It should be noted that, throughout the book chapters, we use the generic term 'internationalizing firm' (rather than multinational corporation – MNC – or other such labels) to indicate that the language issue confronts all firms – small, medium and large. We also use the terms 'company' and 'firm' interchangeably, reflecting common use.

WHAT IS MEANT BY LANGUAGE?

Language is a term that would seem not to need a definition. As McCrum et al. (1986, 14) comment, 'There is almost no aspect of our lives that is not touched by language. We live in and by language.' However, in discussions about the role of language at conferences and seminars, a common question posed is 'What do you mean by the term language? Surely it means more than foreign languages?' As a response to such questioning, Figure 1.1 was developed to exemplify the various sides, or layers, of language used in the workplace:

1. *Everyday spoken/written language.* Normal social language, that is, everyday spoken and written language employed for interpersonal, inter-unit and external communication.[1]
2. *Company jargon.* So-called 'company speak', replete with acronyms, special terms and management process terminology specific to the company, which evolves over time. For example, a new employee from the Hungarian subsidiary of Eastman Kodak reportedly asked if there was an Eastman Kodak to English standard dictionary to help her deal with the specialized internal language she was encountering (Welch et al., 2005; see also Tietze et al., 2003).
3. *Technical/professional language.* As with company jargon, there is a coded language that is common within and between groups, and can be used to include or exclude others from a specific group – what

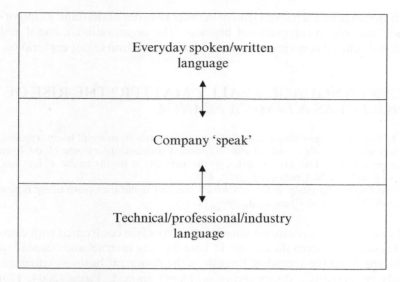

Source: Welch et al. (2005, 13).

Figure 1.1   Layers of language

Argote et al. (2003), term 'short-hand' and 'home-made' language (Nahapiet and Ghoshal, 1998; see also Hedlund, 1999). The intermingling of company terms with professional jargon can create barriers and compound miscommunication.

These layers of language are interconnected, as shown in Figure 1.1. In this book, we focus on everyday spoken and written language used within the workplace, though language is used more as an umbrella term. This reflects practice. For example, when an internationalizing firm transfers knowledge and information around its various global operations, there will be a mix of everyday language intermingled with company jargon and technical terminology.

Language, of course, is a key aspect of culture: it is inherent in a specific culture and also an embodiment of it: 'If language influences the way we behave and how we perceive things, it means that culture is also inherent in the language itself' (Claes, 1995, 99). But we deliberately take language out of what we have referred to elsewhere as the culture box. As Welch and Welch (2008, 341) argue, 'Language has an importance above and beyond the "embeddedness-in-culture" perspective.' This is not to underrate the importance of the cultural context. But we argue that there is a need to deal with language as a separate element in order to better understand its importance and role in international business. The organizational, social and national cultural contexts, however, remain a backdrop to our exploration.

DOES LANGUAGE REALLY MATTER? THE RISE OF ENGLISH AS A *LINGUA FRANCA*

> A living language is like a man suffering incessantly from small haemorrhages, and what it needs above all else is constant transactions of new blood from other tongues. The day the gates go up, that day it begins to die. (Mencken, 1919, cited by McCrum et al., 1986, 47)
> The English language is the sea which receives tributaries from every region under heaven. (McCrum et al., 1986, 11)

In presentations regarding language, we are often confronted with comments such as: 'Given the current IT context – the Internet and translation software – and the spread of English as the dominant business language, surely language is a disappearing problem?' Indeed, Tietze (2004, 176) notes that 'English is undisputedly the global lingua franca and serves as the communication tool of many intercultural encounters. This dominant position is also firmly established in the context of international trade and business.' It is telling that the Japanese e-commerce firm, Rakuten, has embraced English as its corporate language, to the extent of implementing an English-only policy in the Japanese headquarters. This was part of its efforts to become a truly global firm (*The Economist*, 2013c, 83).

There is ample evidence of the rise of English. *The Economist* has periodically commented on the role of English in international business. For example, in an article in the 22 December 2001 issue, it was estimated that 'over 85 per cent of all international organisations use English as one of their official languages' (p. 64). Earlier, in the 18 November, 2000 issue, *The Economist* reported 'Swiss multinationals, such as Swissair and UBS, conduct international business in English to save time and trouble' (p. 69). *The Economist* later commented on the results of a survey reinforcing the seeming dominance of English: in 1992, 44 per cent of UK executives surveyed indicated they were prepared to negotiate in a foreign language. Ten years later, only 28 per cent were prepared to do this (7 August 2004, 47). Perhaps an extreme example comes from a more recent article in *The Economist* (2013d, 12) about the interest in learning English in South Korea. Some parents have reportedly taken their children to an English-speaking country, or use the cheaper option of spending a summer in a specially created mock English village – called Gyeonggi English Village – where only English is spoken.

An article in the *International Herald Tribune* on Mongolia reports that the Mongolian prime minister at the time outlined the importance of English in a bilingual future for the country. 'We see English not only as a way of communicating, but as a way of opening windows on the wider world . . . With the English language, we can do outsourcing here, just like Bangalore' (Brooke, 2005, 2). It is not only the printed media that have been tracking the role of English. The *BBC News* reported that 'a recent survey showed that seven per cent of French firms used English as their main language' (8 February 2007).

It is pertinent therefore to look at the development of English as a *lingua franca* in international business. According to Mann (2004), the term was originally coined in the Middle Ages by traders operating from Mediterranean ports as a way of coping with the differing languages: 'In order to carry on the business of trade, they spoke a common "patchwork" language consisting of bits of Italian mixed with Greek, French, Spanish, and Arabic words.' Mann notes that modern English retains some of this original mixed vocabulary. Seidlhofer (2005, 339) views English as having become a 'contact language'; that is, used as a means of communicating with others from different first-language backgrounds. We can find evidence of this within modern multinationals. For example, Sørensen's (2005) survey of 70 corporations operating in Denmark shows that the companies did not use English as an overruling language, but more generally as a 'transit language' between various parallel local languages. Once documents in English arrived at subsidiaries, they were translated into the respective local languages.

As the above example illustrates, while English is widely used in international business encounters, it has not rendered the world of international business monolingual. On the contrary, language diversity remains an issue. Indeed, *The Economist* has stressed that language remains a major barrier to the achievement of true integration of the European Union, commenting that 'language has replaced work visas as the main barrier to mobility' (2013b, 49). Louhiala-Salminen et al. (2005) launched a new area of study in the field of international business communication called Business English as a Lingua Franca (BELF), which underscores the multilingual reality of today's business contexts (Ehrenreich, 2010; Kankaanranta and Planken, 2010; Louhiala-Salminen and Kankaanranta, 2012). Some of this research has examined the role of English in the internal communication of globally operating firms (Louhiala-Salminen et al., 2005), while other studies have investigated language use in external relationships such as sales negotiations (Planken, 2005) or distributor meetings (Poncini, 2003). As Nickerson (2005) points out, 'the communication event is often considerably more complex than the label of English

as *lingua franca* would suggest'. She explains that, in multinational settings, communication often takes place between non-native speakers of
English who may also use one or more other languages alongside English
(Marschan-Piekkari et al., 1999; see also Barner-Rasmussen, 2003). The
impact that non-native speakers of English are having on the use of the
English language is now an established stream of research in applied linguistics called English as a Lingua Franca (ELF), with its own dedicated
journal.

For many, language salvation has come in the form of the rise of English
as the global business language. Particularly for those from English-
speaking backgrounds, this can be offered as a justification for regarding
language as a peripheral management issue. But this is a sanguine view of
the evolution of language in international discourse. Further, the rise of
China as a global economic power means an inevitable rise in the importance and use of the Chinese language (or languages) as more firms enter
China and Chinese firms internationalize. It has been estimated that 'there
are currently 30 million people around the world learning Chinese as a
second language' (Erard, 2006, 2). This process is being reinforced by a
deliberate, funded government project to support the teaching of Chinese
across a wide range of developed and developing countries.

The rise of Mandarin will increase the diverse language demands of
international operations. For those drawing comfort from the role of
English as the language of international business, there is a troubling
future in store. A pertinent question to pose is: how would companies cope
if Mandarin overtakes English as a world language? The rise of China as
a twenty-first-century economic power will ensure that the English solution will be only partial. Of course, the rise of India will have some effect
in cementing the place of English. Inevitably though, other languages,
and even different versions of English, will have to be dealt with in the
language mix that goes with international business. Readers may be aware
of the efforts of nations such as France to protect their native languages
from the vocabulary inroads made by English, particularly as a result of
the global spread of information through films, music and the Internet. In
contrast, one of the strengths of English is its dynamism; it is a living language that happily incorporates words from everywhere, continuing the
tradition of the polyglot *lingua franca* of the Middle Ages. As Mann (2004)
relates, 'before English infiltrated the world, many of the world's languages infiltrated English'. They continue to do so. According to McCrum
et al. (1986), about 80 per cent of the English vocabulary is foreign born.

Another factor is the rise of social media, particularly the rapid adoption of Twitter. For some languages, such as Chinese, the number of characters needed to send a message via Twitter may be substantially reduced

compared to English. On a global basis, tweets written in English have fallen from about 67 per cent of the global total in 2009 to 39 per cent in 2012 (*The Economist*, 2012b).

LANGUAGE, COMMUNICATION AND INTERNATIONALIZATION

Moving across language boundaries brings additional communication challenges for internationalizing firms. How these are handled is an important part of the ability to operate as a global entity. In a sense, communication is at the heart of any organization, even more so as language groups are added. Increasingly, managers face the decision as to which language will form the basis of the everyday spoken or written layer of Figure 1.1.

In considering the impact of language, it is useful to set it in the context of the basic communication model depicted in Figure 1.2. This demonstrates how a sender transmits a message to a receiver through a chosen medium: such as face to face, via email or text message, or over the telephone. The effectiveness of the communication depends on the ability of the sender to accurately encode a meaningful, complete message; the selection of the correct medium or channel of transfer; and the ability of the receiver to decode and understand the message as it was intended. Despite the communication process's seeming simplicity, communication scholars have long recognized that it is fraught with impediments referred

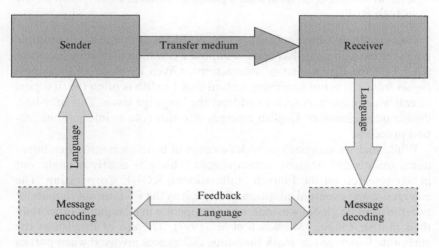

Figure 1.2   The basic communication model

to as noise, distortion and leakage – and this is even the case where senders and receivers share a mother tongue. The communication process is thus subject to many influences that determine its success. Text messaging, for example, has developed its own short-hand language, including symbols to denote moods.

We have added language to the basic model in order to illustrate how language may interfere with the transfer and receipt of the communication. If the receiver is unable to decode the message because of the language used, translation may be necessary. As we examine in Chapter 2, translation involving intermediaries plays a key role in effective communication across language barriers. Picture language may also play a part in assisting effective communication. Feedback is an important element, which is why face-to-face communication remains the preferred medium, particularly when there are language differences between sender and receiver. Body language is often used as a feedback element to gauge whether the receiver has understood the message, though this is also subject to cross-cultural differences.

Being exposed to a different language highlights communication challenges. The following comment by the co-founder of Jetpak, an Australian asparagus-exporting company, is illustrative. In an interview, explaining his operations in its major market, Japan, he remarked:

> You see, we're talking about a country [Japan] where you not only have a language problem but a *written* language problem. At least in Germany, sure, they speak German, but if you look at what's written, you can generally pick out some words, and understand what's going on . . . But in Japan, it's all bloody hieroglyphics.

One seemingly simple solution to the problems of operating in multiple language environments has been to impose a common corporate language (CCL) on the firm's internal interactions. Given its place as a business *lingua franca*, it is not surprising to find that English is often the first port of call when managers seek to address the language issue. This may be a deliberate decision, or English emerges into this role as internationalization proceeds.

While such an approach provides a range of benefits, it also often introduces unintended negative consequences. This was clearly brought out in our research on the Finnish multinational, KONE Corporation. The emergence and eventual adoption of English as the CCL meant that about two-thirds of its global workforce had to operate in a language other than their mother tongue (Marschan et al., 1997). The use of English as the corporate language can mask the subtle differences involved when parties are forced to operate in a second language. As Babcock and Du-Babcock

(2001, 376) argue, 'it is not only the languages that international business communicators speak', but also the language fluency of such communicators that matters. In her study of international teams, Kassis Henderson (2005, 75) noted that, although one visible 'surface' language was used to facilitate communication, team members continued to use diverse interpretive mechanisms derived from their respective native tongues. She claims that when English is used as the working language, parties engaged in the exchange are 'under the false impression that they are sharing the same context and the same interpretation'.

Communication matters are not confined to the internal interactions between units of the internationalizing firm. A range of external stakeholders is involved: various national and international bodies; customers, suppliers, trade unions, media organizations and lobby groups. The method of international operation is also a factor. For instance, firms using cooperative forms such as strategic alliances, or growing through a process of acquisitions and mergers, face additional communication challenges. Interaction with external parties is language-dependent. The literature on social networks demonstrates the importance of individuals in the building and maintenance of internal and external networks. We deal with these various aspects in greater depth in later chapters.

THE ROLE OF LANGUAGE IN THE STUDY OF INTERNATIONAL BUSINESS

Despite the often acknowledged importance of language, it has been a surprisingly neglected subject of research in international business studies. In some respects, the impact of language in international business courses has been trivialized through a focus in many textbooks on inappropriate literal translation of notices, advertisements and product names in different language environments. In such instances, language is used to illustrate cross-cultural communication issues, using well-publicized 'blunders'. For example, the *Sunday Times* (22 November 1992) published a collection of literal translations under the heading: 'Written English: but what does it mean?' Examples included an Acapulco hotel notice regarding drinking water that translated as 'The manager has personally passed all the water served here'. A Bangkok dry cleaner asked potential customers to 'drop your trousers here for best results'; and a Japanese hotel notice to guests: 'You are invited to take advantage of the chambermaid'. In the classroom, everyone has a laugh about the obvious error that should have been anticipated and catered for. Discussion then moves on to 'more serious' concerns relating to, for example, negotiations, buyer behaviour in the foreign market, and cross-cultural management. Thus language is virtually dismissed as a back-translation omission, or treated at a relatively superficial level.

This has not always been the case. Language was emphasized in early studies of internationalization by companies, as a component of so-called psychic distance, a concept roughly equivalent to cultural distance. Early international business scholars used psychic distance to explain an observed bias of internationalizing companies towards foreign markets that were culturally similar (see, e.g., Johanson and Wiedersheim-Paul, 1975). Psychic distance was defined as factors preventing or disturbing the flow of information between the company's home country and the target foreign market. These factors included differences in culture, including language. The bundling of language into the 'culture' box appears to have ensured that language became 'the forgotten factor'. However, lately there have been some attempts to separate out language from the bundle of components that comprise psychic (or cultural) distance (see, e.g., Dow and Karunaratna, 2006; Dow and Larimo, 2009).

Similarly, studies of a broad range of international business issues (such as foreign direct investment, joint ventures and international knowledge transfer) either ignore language as a factor or assume that, by including culture, it has been accommodated. A case in point is the ballooning research and publications on international knowledge transfer. One would assume that knowledge transfer would inevitably involve language as a key component in the successful transfer of knowledge and technology to the various units and stakeholders of a multinational. However, a review of articles published in international business journals such as the special issues in *Journal of International Business Studies* (2004) and *Management International Review* (2005) demonstrates how language is virtually ignored (Welch and Welch, 2008). Consequently, one could draw a general conclusion that language in and of itself does not warrant separate treatment.

The aim of this book is to provide evidence to the contrary. The emerging research on which we draw demonstrates that language has a range of important effects: impacting on processes of communication, the effectiveness of knowledge transfer, and even acting as an internal restructuring mechanism. Language can deliver power to individuals and groups (see Chapter 3), and shape the creation of powerful networks within and beyond the firm (see Chapter 5). Language impinges on how the internationalizing firm approaches human resource management (HRM), including staff transfers, expatriate performance in foreign assignments and the career paths of employees (see Chapter 6). These wide-ranging consequences, both positive and negative, are examined in detail in this book. We follow the way in which language is part of the inner dynamics of organizations operating in the international arena. As well, we go beyond the organizational context and trace language-driven interactions across organizations into different cultures and marketplaces.

LANGUAGE AND MANAGEMENT

George Green, chief executive of Hearst Magazines International, is reported to have said that: He doesn't need to speak anything other than English as he travels the world to meet with publishing partners, with the exceptions of Japan and China, where translators are used. I won't let anyone who works for me have a conversation in a language other than English when I'm around. (Kranhold et al., 2004, B1)

As is the case with academics, managers within internationalizing firms could be accused of insufficient attention to the language proficiency levels of their employees and effects of language on their multi-country and multilingual operations. Few have conducted audits of the language competence levels of their employees (Reeves and Wright, 1996). This is somewhat understandable, as language effects are not always obvious. They are often opaque, not readily seen, and employees do not necessarily draw attention to their impact as this can be seen to reflect negatively on their performance. In part, this is because it is individual employees who are often faced with the need to deal with language problems on the spot, and readily devise solutions without the language issue necessarily becoming obvious elsewhere within the company. Upper management levels can be easily screened off from the realities of different language effects that might provoke more substantive responses. In Chapter 2, we provide examples of just how inventive employees can be in coming up with solutions to translation demands in the workplace, beyond the purview of others.

Language aspects are often viewed by management as a mechanical translation problem. When confronted with foreign languages, the response is often to regard these as constituting merely a technical problem that can be readily addressed through the use of interpreters and translators, particularly with the continuing development of automatic translation software and related devices. While there is a valid place for these language aids, it is difficult to engage in social interaction and develop close ties through such media (Hagen, 1999). In other words, translation is not the same as social communication and, as we will discuss later, does not ensure the creation of social capital or networks. There is also the question of security of commercial-in-confidence material, as well as the problem that technical information may be inaccurately translated (Crick, 1999; Maitland, 1999).

Another way of seemingly removing the language problem is to view it as a selection issue: ensure that the company hires employees with the requisite foreign language skills and/or provide language training. As we will discuss in Chapter 6, it takes substantial time for a person to reach a level of operational fluency in another language, though the actual amount of time will vary depending on each individual's aptitude and motivation to learn. Firms face questions of whether to invest in the training of existing staff in the desired foreign language or whether to hire new staff with the appropriate language skills, assuming that such individuals are readily available. Either way, the company faces additional costs as well as the time constraint in achieving the necessary skills base. Hiring language skills may be possible if the internationalizing firm is establishing a 'greenfield' operation in a new market and is sourcing employees from the local area. In mergers and acquisitions, the acquirer inherits the set of language skills within the acquired organization (see Chapter 8).

THE ROLE OF THE INDIVIDUAL EMPLOYEE

While we stress the organizational context in our investigation of the role of language in international business, the issue is not only about organizations. Internationalizing firms are not in full control of individuals' utilization of their language skills for company purposes. As we explain later, language is part of individuals' human capital. Thus language as a resource for internationalizing firms is largely in the hands of their individual employees. Individuals make choices about whether, when and how they might employ any language skills they possess. They may choose whether or not to employ their foreign language skills for company benefit, or use them in a way that is contrary to company interests – in the same way that individuals make choices about whether and when to use knowledge and personal networks for company purposes (Marschan et al., 1996; Welch and Welch, 2008). Personal interests may dictate the type of action taken, while the ability to undertake any language-related tasks, such as translation, will be driven by the language skills and experience of an individual employee. Individual and organizational interests may coalesce, but this is not always the case, for example because of knowledge-sharing hostility (Michailova and Husted, 2003), the exercise of power (Marschan-Piekkari et al., 1999), lack of time (Marschan et al., 1997), or because the language task is outside and in addition to an individual's assigned job tasks. Thus, as Figure 1.3 illustrates, the reality for internationalizing firms is that foreign language use in and for a company is mediated or influenced by the individual.

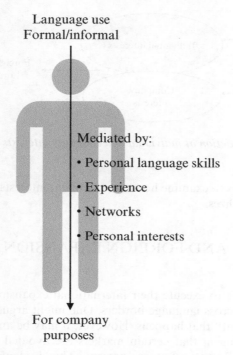

Language use
Formal/informal

Mediated by:

• Personal language skills

• Experience

• Networks

• Personal interests

For company
purposes

Figure 1.3   Personal factors influencing language use

Foreign language skills at the outset can create opportunities for an individual, at headquarters (HQ) or in different subsidiaries, which then lead to the creation of multi-country networks that the individual can call on for personal and/or company benefit over time. Alternatively, it may be through appointment to a position in a foreign language location that leads to an individual undertaking foreign language training, so as to perform the assigned job function more effectively, and the development of a related personal network. Internationalizing firms can shape the language development of individual employees through language policies and actions, for example in setting the language to be used in high-level international training programmes. In some cases, decisions with direct or indirect effects on language use are deliberate, but often they are not.

Individual and company drivers of language use overlap and interact in a dynamic process within shifting global contexts, as shown in Figure 1.4. Foreign language use is a complex by-product of individual and organizational interests as a result of this dynamic interaction. The aim of our

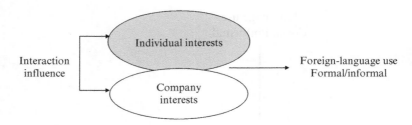

Figure 1.4   Interaction of individual and company interests

book, therefore, is to examine how these different interests play out as the firm internationalizes.

LANGUAGE AND FOREIGN EXPANSION PATTERNS

As firms continue to execute their international expansion strategies, at some point they cross language borders. One might argue that language is unimportant until that happens. However, it may be an implicit factor in decision-making in that certain markets are avoided because of the demands that different languages present. That is, language can be a silent influence even before a firm is confronted with the language barrier. It is well known from early studies into the impact of psychic distance that many firms are influenced by cultural factors in their selection of foreign markets. As noted above, language is part of psychic distance (Johanson and Wiedersheim-Paul, 1975). Of course, this is not surprising. International marketers feel more at home in foreign markets that have a common language. We now examine how language affects the internationalization process, and how individuals and firms respond to the challenges that it poses.

For a firm beginning international operations, going to a market where one's own language is used is one way of coping with the risks and uncertainties such a move entails. Staying within one's *language comfort zone* not only helps reduce psychic distance, but also has business advantages, particularly for firms in the early stages of internationalization. First, it is easier and cheaper to collect and process information pertaining to a foreign market that is using the same language as it removes the need for translation. Second, it is easier to build contacts and negotiate in one's mother tongue. Third, promotional activities, such as advertising, may be much cheaper to undertake. For example, promotional material from the home market sometimes requires little or no alteration for markets sharing a language. There are cases of firms being able to utilize advertising campaigns across markets that share a language, including television campaigns, although there are dangers in the assumption that language similarity equates with market similarity (O'Grady and Lane, 1996). Research in the UK found some exporters recruited foreign intermediaries as much on the basis of English fluency as on their selling ability (Crick, 1999).

It is not always, though, a conscious decision to select foreign markets on the basis of language or cultural compatibility. The exporting literature shows that frequently, in some studies overwhelmingly, the start into exporting is driven by foreign approaches (Bilkey and Tesar, 1977; Austrade, 2001). Often, individuals approach companies fortuitously, seeking to import their products or services or to act as agents in their own home market. Such approaches are more likely when the countries concerned have a similar culture and language. For instance, the Australian company, Ronstan, a leading global supplier of fittings for yachts and other marine hardware, had given no particular consideration to the possibility of exporting. However, in 1965 an order was received from Canada from a Canadian airline pilot who had become familiar with the products on visits to Australia and who saw a potential for them in the Canadian market. As Dow and Larimo (2009) point out, the size of a foreign market may prompt firms to hop the language barrier at an earlier stage as the prize of a large market beckons. However, if we take Australian firms' slow reaction to the potential that Japan offered, a large market *per se* may not be enough of a trigger for internationalizing firms to compensate for language and cultural barriers.

As Figure 1.5 indicates, the impact and timing of language effects on international expansion by companies in part depends on the starting point – that is, the home-country language base. By its very nature, global expansion ensures that the company eventually crosses the language barrier, though the point at which this occurs varies according to the home-language starting point and the growth strategies pursued by individual companies. What can be observed first is the impact of what we call the Empire and the Diaspora language paths.

The Empire Language Path

Colonial heritage brings together a unique combination of language, history, and economic and business ties. Empire brings language in its train: French in parts of Africa; English in countries such as India, Singapore, parts of Africa, and the Caribbean. Following the Empire

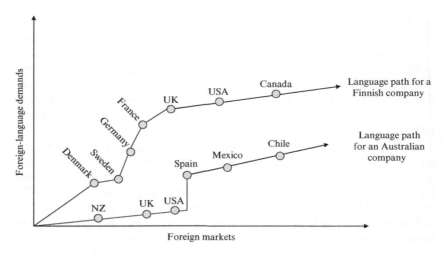

Figure 1.5   Hypothetical company patterns

route may be a mixture of conscious and unconscious factors operating to affect key decision-makers' perceptions that drive internationalization. Given the wider spread of English, companies from English-speaking countries can undertake expansion to a higher degree before encountering language barriers. To a certain extent, this pattern may even be extended to countries with high levels of English competence, such as the Netherlands, Denmark, Sweden and Norway.

Spanish is spoken in countries that once formed the 'Spanish Empire' and hence the heavy involvement of Spanish firms in Latin America. As White (1997, 13) states, 'Over the past few years, Spain has become the largest European investor in the region ... Spanish executives say this bias is explained by language and cultural ties, close knowledge of the countries involved, and a confidence in Latin America's future.' In a study of the determinants of the location decisions of Spanish multinationals over the period 1988 to 1997, Barrios and Benito-Ostolaza (2008, 14) separated language from its cultural link and found that 'Spanish FDI [foreign direct investment] abroad has been strongly influenced by language proximity'. This language path continues, but is also now operating in reverse. In US dollar value terms, mergers and acquisitions by Latin American firms in Spain exceed those in the opposite direction, with Latin American firms using Spain as a springboard to wider markets (*The Economist*, 2014).

Firms based in one Empire group can take advantage of other Empire languages, as the hypothetical path taken by the Australian company in

Figure 1.5 illustrates. It first enters the English-speaking markets, taking advantage of the cultural, including language, similarities and historical ties. Its UK operation may bring Spain closer due to EU interrelations at the business level and the firm decides to enter the Spanish market. Based on the market knowledge gained regarding the Spanish way of doing business, and exposure to the Spanish language, the firm may then feel confident enough to follow the Spanish-language path and expand into Mexico, given its geographical closeness to the US operation, and other Latin American countries such as Chile.

However, for a Finnish firm, coming from a language base of Finnish and Swedish, a conscious decision to expand only where Finnish or Swedish is spoken would restrict it to Sweden and Estonia, a country whose language is close enough to Finnish for a surface-level understanding. Given the small Russian-speaking minority in Finland, expansion into Russia is viable. However, Swedish provides the basis to expand across the Nordic region through what is referred to as Scandinavian language – a mixture of the Scandinavian languages, coupled of course with cultural commonalities (Marschan-Piekkari et al., 1999). Early Nordic research indicated a preference for Finnish firms to move into neighbouring markets first before moving to continental European countries and further afield, as indicated in the hypothetical path depicted in Figure 1.5. The simple business reality is that Finnish firms cannot rely on the use of Finnish beyond their home market. To some extent, this has been alleviated by the rise of English as a *lingua franca* and the fact that English has moved to the point of being an unofficial second language within Finland. This is particularly evident among younger Finns, who have grown up with a substantial use of English, through education and reinforced by exposure to English-based media such as MTV, the Internet, and the like. In other words, foreign market choices immediately force language questions to the forefront.

Diaspora Language Path

There is only limited early evidence of how language is, or may be, affecting the international expansion of Chinese firms. Some insight may be gained from the behaviour of overseas Chinese-owned firms in parts of East Asia that tap into the so-called 'bamboo network' of the Chinese Diaspora. During the nineteenth and early twentieth centuries, most of the Chinese who migrated from China during this period were from the southern coastal provinces of Guangdong, Fujian and Hainan. A study of these networks highlighted how dialect was a critical part of the connections formed throughout East Asia:

> Even today, ethnic Chinese may differentiate among themselves according
> to dialect, sub-dialect, clan and family, all of which are linked to their place
> of ancestral origin in China ... In this manner, the ethnic Chinese created a
> cohesive web of interlocking organizations and relationships that provided a
> firm and stable framework within which traditional society could be recreated,
> maintained, and developed and whose individual members could prosper far
> from home. (Backman, 1995, 2)

The study stresses how 'understanding the importance of dialects and
their distribution across East Asia is central to an understanding of how
ethnic Chinese business networks operated in the past, and operate in the
present'.

Personal networks are enabled by language, and as Backman's (1995)
study shows, the Chinese rely heavily on networks to conduct business.
An example cited in this work is the dominance of Teochiu speakers in
many sectors of South-East Asia's food trade. Thus the language picture
is somewhat complicated by the various dialects of Chinese (such as
Mandarin, Cantonese, Hokkien and Teochiu) used by the Diaspora, and
a Mandarin speaker dealing with a Hokkien speaker may have difficulties
tapping into the network. In a situation experienced by two of the authors,
overseas-born Chinese from three different South-East Asian countries
living close to each other used English on social occasions as one person
could not interact freely because he could only use Hokkien while the
others could only converse in Cantonese.

Using the networks and language benefits through the Chinese Diaspora,
Chinese firms may be able to extend the point at which the language
barrier is confronted in a major sense. Eventually, though, as with firms
using the Empire path, language differences have to be dealt with. The
sheer size and range of exports to, and other operations in, the USA mean
that internal English competence has to be developed. This can be very
dramatic in some cases – such as Lenovo's acquisition of IBM's personal
computer business (*The Economist*, 2013a). There have been examples of
the hiring of US overseas-born Chinese to head up Chinese operations in
the USA; and where members of the Chinese Diaspora have returned to
China, established businesses and then commenced international expansion from China. As we will discuss later in Chapter 6, the buying in of
language competence through selection decisions is a well-used response.

Of course, as the influence of China in the world economy and on global
trade and investment increases, there will be a reverse impact: firms from
other countries will be forced to develop Mandarin competence. As a
Chinese student in an MBA course in Beijing, conducted by two of the
authors, commented: 'English is difficult. It will be nice when Chinese
companies become so global that you will be forced to use Chinese.'

India is a different case. While Hindi and English are the official languages, there are 14 recognized regional languages, plus numerous local dialects. Given the official place of English as a unifying language within India, one could assume that Indian companies would be similar to those from other former British colonies and have the advantage of following the Empire path, with the added advantage of tapping into the global Indian Diaspora network.

While a Diaspora network can be useful for internationalizing firms, providing a powerful external resource to assist in penetrating foreign markets, it can be somewhat restrictive. Rapid penetration of a narrow segment in a foreign market can take the entrant firm only so far. At some point, it will still be necessary to move beyond the Diaspora network, crossing language and cultural barriers into the broader market context in order to grow. Elo (2013) provides the case of a Greek small and medium-sized enterprise that was able to use the Greek Diaspora to expand internationally into quite diverse markets, using only the Greek language. However, various difficulties arose due to the intensely personal nature of the networks established. This case highlights how reliance on language-based networks can be limiting, and can generate superficial internationalization.

Large Countries, Different Language Paths

Japanese firms face a similar language challenge to those from Finland, in that outside Japan there is limited scope to use Japanese. However, compared to Finland, the Japanese domestic market is large, and Japan holds a different geopolitical status. Such power bestows influence – not the least through buying power, which means that those seeking to sell into the Japanese market have to devise appropriate language solutions, such as the use of translators.

> Many Japanese firms have traditionally used trading companies to handle their international operations, thus effectively outsourcing the language issue. These large trading companies still play a significant role in Japan's international [business] activities, accounting for more than half of Japan's total foreign trade. (Welch et al., 2001, 197)

The choice of the UK for many early Japanese greenfield investments was strongly influenced by the ability to use English: 'Since most of the companies had production facilities in the US, the presence of production engineers with international experience and English language ability was regarded as critical' (Hood and Truijens, 1993, 54). In a study of Hong Kong exporters, Ellis (2000, 461) found, somewhat surprisingly, that 'more than two-thirds of early entries into the EU were to non-English

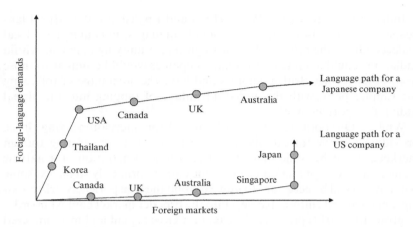

Figure 1.6   Divergent language paths of two large countries

speaking countries'. However, 'almost 90 per cent of these entries were
not initiated by the [Hong Kong] manufacturer'. Because of the lack of
requisite language ability, a party with the necessary language competence
had to intervene – that is, the EU buyer or a third party (such as a broker).

As Figure 1.6 illustrates, many Japanese firms have moved into English-
speaking countries, developed language and other cultural competences,
and then been able to continue an expansion path based on English-
speaking markets. Japanese firms have been able to move into countries
such as the Netherlands and Finland, due to the higher level of English
fluency found within such countries. Tapping into the English Empire
language path can provide certain *language economies of scale*.

On the other hand, as Figure 1.6 illustrates, US firms can follow the
English Empire path but movement into markets such as Japan will
mean a very steep jump in language demands. On the surface, the Empire
path can provide firms from English-speaking countries with a language
advantage, but, as we will later demonstrate, this may mask communication issues that affect performance. O'Grady and Lane (1996) argued that
familiarity can breed false confidence and carelessness, and termed this
phenomenon the 'psychic distance paradox'. Following along an Empire
path can produce false confidence, even hubris – what we would call the
paradox of language distance.

Previous research provides supporting evidence. Fixman (1990, 33–4)
indicates that, even when moving into non-English-speaking countries,
there can be a perception that foreign languages are not important:
'Most individuals whom I interviewed perceived foreign languages to
be of only secondary value for executives . . . One executive explained

that he really can "get by almost anywhere in the world without foreign language ability".' Tung's (1998) study found that respondents from the English-speaking countries of the USA, the UK, Canada and Australia deemed expatriate language skills as unimportant. In Figures 1.5 and 1.6, the mildly sloping line on the Empire language paths depicts subtle differences: versions of English and Spanish, for example, reflect the broader sociocultural, political and economic environments in which these languages are spoken. Thus, within language groups there may be still mild language barriers to cross. Further, Fixman (1990, 31) found that company size matters: 'Smaller companies, however, enter the global market place without the English-speaking networks to which their larger counterparts have access.' This constrained their ability to market products in foreign language domains.

In contrast, firms from countries such as Japan and Finland have to cope with foreign language demands from the earliest stages of international expansion. This means that they have to develop mechanisms, competence and procedures that assist in overcoming or at least managing language matters. It becomes a more basic feature of their approach to international operations. Nevertheless, all the hypothetical firms depicted in the above figures eventually have to cross the language barrier. To a greater or lesser extent, this unleashes a range of managerial actions such as language training, language-based staff appointments and the like, ultimately generating learning about the role of language that potentially can be leveraged in subsequent market expansion moves.

Foreign expansion paths are not exclusively language-determined. There is a complex interaction between foreign-market expansion and language paths. As with the role of Japanese trading companies for Japanese exporters, internationalizing firms are able to structure operation modes so as to minimize the need to operate in foreign languages, though this may not be the paramount driving factor in the decision of which mode to select. We take up these aspects in Chapter 8.

Obviously, firms do not have languages; people do. Individuals and their background experience, including foreign language competence, play a critical role in determining how language feeds into foreign expansion processes. This emerged in a study of 144 newly internationalizing Italian firms (Zucchella et al., 2007, 277). The authors looked at factors that drove the expansion and confirmed the importance of entrepreneurial characteristics, including educational background. Of these, knowledge of foreign languages was the most statistically significant variable affecting early internationalization. Discussing this result, they conclude: 'This [knowledge of foreign languages] is a pre-requisite for people who want to develop business contacts abroad and it helps in the formation of an international mindset.'

An individual may have the capacity to change the language path of an internationalizing company. There are examples in the literature of firms making decisions on which foreign markets to enter on the basis of the language background of key personnel. In one case, the company advanced the timing of its foreign direct investment in Europe because a member of staff was returning to his country of origin. Thus migrants may become *language bridge-builders* and promote language-driven internationalization. 'The migrant effect can operate at two levels: as key decision-maker, a migrant may select markets on the basis of former country familiarity; or the migrant as employee may trigger or confirm the attractiveness of a selected market, and language may be a major factor' (Welch et al., 2001, 194). These choices can be contrary to national psychic distance patterns.

In this introductory chapter, we have raised a wide range of issues connected with the impact of language on internationalizing firms. The remainder of this book explores how internationalizing firms respond to the multilingual reality of global expansion. We also include individual employees' responses and how these impact on what organizations are able to accomplish on the language front.

NOTE

1. Such as English or French, in contrast to discourses, which can be understood as 'framing devices, systems of shared meaning' used in speaking or writing about a particular subject matter (Tietze et al., 2003, 78).

REFERENCES

Argote, L., B. McEvily and R. Reagans (2003), 'Managing knowledge in organizations: an integrative framework and review of emerging themes', *Management Science*, **49** (4), 571–82.

Austrade (2001), *Knowing & Growing the Exporter Community*, Sydney: Austrade.

Babcock, R.D. and B. Du-Babcock (2001), 'Language-based communication zones in international business communication', *Journal of Business Communication*, **38** (4), 372–412.

Backman, M. (1995), *Overseas Chinese Business Networks in Asia*, East Asia Analytical Unit (EAAU), Canberra: Department of Foreign Affairs and Trade, Australian Government.

Barner-Rasmussen, W. (2003), *Knowledge Sharing in Multinational Corporations: A Social Capital Perspective*, Doctoral Thesis No. 113, Helsinki: Swedish School of Economics and Business Administration.

Barrios, S. and J.M. Benito-Ostolaza (2008), 'The location decisions of multinationals and the cultural link: evidence from Spanish direct investment abroad', Working Paper D.T.2008/04, Universidad Pública de Navarra.

BBC News (2007), 'French fury over English language', 8 February, international online version, accessed 6 March 2007.

Bilkey, W.J. and G. Tesar (1977), 'The export behavior of smaller-sized Wisconsin firms', *Journal of International Business Studies*, **8** (1), 93–8.

Brooke, J. (2005), 'Mongolians learn to say "progress" in English', *International Herald Tribune*, 14 February, 2.

Claes, M.-T. (1995), 'A case study of language overlap and cross-cultural communication problems', *Interface Journal of Applied Linguistics*, **10** (1), 99–111.

Crick, D. (1999), 'An investigation into SME's use of languages in their export operations', *International Journal of Entrepreneurial Behaviour and Research*, **5** (1), 19–31.

Dow, D. and A. Karunaratna (2006), 'Developing a multidimensional instrument to measure psychic distance stimuli', *Journal of International Business Studies* **37**, 578–602.

Dow, D. and J. Larimo (2009), 'Challenging the conceptualization and measurement of distance and international experience in entry mode choice research', *Journal of International Marketing*, **17** (2), 74–98.

The Economist (2000), 'Fifth tongue, fifth column?', 18 November, 69.

The Economist (2001), 'A world empire by other means', 22 December, 63–5.

The Economist (2004), 'Oh là là', 7 August, 47.

The Economist (2012a), 'The power of tribes', 28 January, 60.

The Economist (2012b), 'Twtr', 31 March, 66.

The Economist (2013a), 'From guard shack to global giant', 12 January, 52–3.

The Economist (2013b), 'English to the fore', 13 April, 83.

The Economist (2013c), 'Parallel worlds: a special report on the Koreas', 26 October, 12.

The Economist (2014), 'Shoe on the other foot', 25 January, 35–6.

Ehrenreich, S. (2010), 'English as business lingua franca in a German multinational corporation: meeting the challenge', *Journal of Business Communication*, **47** (4), 408–31.

Ellis, P. (2000), 'Social ties and foreign market entry', *Journal of International Business Studies*, **31** (3), 443–69.

Elo, M. (2013), 'How Diaspora networks make impossible possible? The internationalization story of one non-English speaking Greek SME', Paper presented at the 39th EIBA conference, University of Bremen, 12–14 December.

Erard, M. (2006), 'The Mandarin offensive', *Wired Magazine*, retrieved 8 May 2006 from http://www.wired.com/wired/archive/14.04/mandarin_pr.html.

Fixman, C.S. (1990), 'The foreign language needs of U.S.-based corporations', *Annals of the American Academy of Political and Social Science*, **511**, 25–46.

Hagen, S. (1999), *Business Communication Across Borders: A Study of Language Use and Practice in European Companies*, London: Languages National Training Organization in association with Centre for Information on Language Training and Research.

Hedlund, G. (1999), 'The intensity and extensity of knowledge and the multinational corporation as a nearly recomposable system (NRS)', *Management International Review*, **39** (Special Issue 1), 5–44.

Hood, N. and T. Truijens (1993), 'European locational decisions of Japanese manufacturers: survey evidence on the case of the UK', *International Business Review*, **2** (1), 39–64.

Jacobsen, M.K. and K.E. Meyer (1998), 'Opportunities in Russia: internationalization of Danish and Austrian businesses', Working Paper No. 17, Center for East European Studies, Copenhagen Business School, Copenhagen, Denmark.

Johanson, J. and F. Wiedersheim-Paul (1975), 'The internationalization of the firm: four Swedish cases', *Journal of Management Studies*, **12** (3), 305–22.

Kankaanranta, A. and B. Planken (2010), 'BELF competence as business knowledge of internationally operating business professionals', *Journal of Business Communication*, **47** (4), 380–407.

Kassis Henderson, J.K. (2005), 'Language diversity in international management teams', *International Studies of Management and Organization*, **35** (1), 66–82.

Kranhold, K., D. Bilefsky, M. Karnitschnig and G. Parker (2004), 'Lost in translation?' *Wall Street Journal* (Eastern edn), 18 May, B1.

Lauring J. and H. Tange (2010), 'International language management: contained or dilute communication', *European Journal of International Management*, **4** (4), 317–32.

Louhiala-Salminen, L. and A. Kankaanranta (2012), 'Language issues in international internal communication: English or local language? If English, what English?' *Public Relations Review*, Special Edition on Internal Communication, **38** (2), 262–9.

Louhiala-Salminen, L., M. Charles and A. Kankaanranta (2005), 'English as lingua franca in Nordic corporate mergers: two case companies', *English for Specific Purposes*, **24** (4), 401–21.

Maclean, D. (2006), 'Beyond English: transnational corporations and the strategic management of language in a complex multilingual business environment', *Management Decision*, **44** (10), 1377–90.

Maitland, A. (1999), 'The case of the misleading coffin', *Financial Times*, 17 June.

Mann, F. (2004), 'From lingua franca to global English', *Global Envision* (www.globalenvision.org) created 28 July, 2004; accessed 9 August 2010.

Marschan, R., D.E. Welch and L.S. Welch (1996), 'Control in less-hierarchical MNC structures: the role of personal networks and informal communication', *International Business Review*, **5** (2), 137–50.

Marschan, R., D.E. Welch and L.S. Welch (1997), 'Language: the forgotten factor in multinational management', *European Management Journal*, **15** (5), 591–8.

Marschan-Piekkari, R., D.E. Welch and L.S. Welch (1999), 'In the shadow: the impact of language on structure, power and communication in the multinational', *International Business Review*, **8** (4), 421–40.

McCrum, R., W. Cran and R. MacNeil (1986), *The Story of English*, London: Faber and Faber.

Michailova, S. and K. Husted (2003), 'Knowledge-sharing hostility in Russian firms', *California Management Review*, **45** (3), 59–77.

Nahapiet, J. and S. Ghoshal (1998), 'Social capital, intellectual capital, and the organizational advantage', *Academy of Management Review*, **23** (2), 242–66.

Nickerson, C. (2005), 'English as a lingua franca in international business contexts', *English for Specific Purposes*, **24** (4), 367–80.

O'Grady, S. and H.W. Lane (1996), 'The psychic distance paradox', *Journal of International Business Studies*, **27** (2), 309–33.

Planken, B. (2005), 'Managing rapport in lingua franca sales negotiations: a comparison of professional and aspiring negotiators', *English for Specific Purposes*, **24** (4), 381–400.

Poncini, G. (2003), 'Multicultural business meetings and the role of languages other than English', *Journal of Intercultural Studies*, **34** (1), 17–32.

Reeves, N. and C. Wright (1996), *Linguist Auditing*, Clevedon, UK: Multinational Matters.

Seidlhofer, B. (2005), 'English as a lingua franca', *ELT Journal*, **59** (4), 339–41.

Sørensen, E.S. (2005), *Our Corporate Language is English: An Exploratory Survey of 70 DK-sited Corporations' Use of English*, Master's Thesis, Aarhus: Aarhus School of Business.

Tietze, S. (2004), 'Spreading the management gospel – in English', *Language and Intercultural Communication*, **4** (3), 175–89.

Tietze, S., L. Cohen and G. Musson (2003), *Understanding Organisations through Language*, London: Sage.

Tung, R.L. (1998), 'A contingency framework of selection and training of expatriates revisited', *Human Resource Management Review*, **8** (1), 23–37.

Welch, D.E. and L.S. Welch (2008), 'The importance of language in international knowledge transfer', *Management International Review*, **48** (3), 339–60.

Welch, D.E., L.S. Welch and R. Marschan-Piekkari (2001), 'The persistent impact of language on global operations', *Prometheus*, **19** (3), 193–209.

Welch, D.E., L.S. Welch and R. Piekkari (2005), 'Speaking in tongues: the importance of language in international management processes', *International Studies of Management and Organization*, **35** (1), 10–27.

White, D. (1997), 'Return of the conqueror', *Financial Times*, 3 March, 13.

Zucchella, A., G. Palamara and S. Denicolai (2007), 'The drivers of the early internationalization of the firm', *Journal of World Business*, **42** (3), 268–80.

2. Translation

In a multilingual world, translation is an ever-present reality – in business, government, personal and social interaction, and communication. And it matters! Just ask Hilary Clinton, the former US Secretary of State. In an attempt to say, in a vivid manner, that the new Obama Administration was concerned to start afresh its relations with Russia, at a meeting with the Russian foreign affairs minister, Sergey Lavrov, Hilary Clinton presented him with a box that had a red button on the top, which he was invited to push. The idea was to symbolize a re-setting of the US–Russian relationship. She even suggested to him that they 'worked hard to get the right Russian word'. His response was blunt: 'You got it wrong . . . It should be *perezagruzka* . . . [not] *peregruzka*, which means overcharged' (Elliott, 2009, 22). The literature on language is littered with examples of inappropriate translations and their consequences – in part because of the inability to place a translated communication within its relevant cultural context, illustrating the reality that translation cannot be simply disconnected from culture (Welch et al., 2001). However, sometimes the translator saves political face: 'When a Hungarian leader receiving a ceremonial welcome in Sierra Leone was referred to as the President of Bulgaria, it was the interpreter who, without missing a beat, corrected the error' (Jaivin, 2013, 3).

Translation can be seen as a way of trying to cope with the demands of localization of languages. Indeed, the world of international business would shrink without it. Surprisingly, while there has been a recent upsurge of research on the role of language issues in international business studies, translation has received limited specific focus. It tends to be regarded as having been covered in, or subsumed under, the broader treatment of language aspects, not unlike the way language is often treated as simply reflective of culture in general. However, the emerging studies of language reveal enough about translation aspects to point to the need and potential value of a specific focus on translation as an activity and process, and its impact on the international operations of businesses (Marschan-Piekkari et al., 1999; Janssens et al., 2004; Kassis Henderson, 2005; Barner-Rasmussen and Björkman, 2007).

The increased translation demands, and their costs, of European Union (EU) expansion are illustrative of the continuing, even growing, need for translation in the world economy despite the emergence of translation-enabling technologies, such as machine translation, and the rise of English as something approaching a *lingua franca* in international business. With the inclusion of Croatian in 2013, there were 24 languages with official status in the EU, although the bulk of translation work involves the three main languages of English, German and French. However, in addition there are local languages, such as Catalan, that have been authorized for limited use within the EU. As a result, translation has become a major task for the European Commission, at a cost of about US$1.5 billion (*The Economist*, 2014).

As translation demands have increased globally, so have translation products in various forms. According to Common Sense Advisory, a research firm, 'the worldwide language-services business is worth $34 billion and it is growing fast, at about 12 per cent a year' (*The Economist*, 2012a, 64). Not surprisingly, the concept and characteristics of a translation market are now seriously examined, with consideration of various factors involved in the supply of and demand for translation services (Ferreira-Alves, 2012). In a global context, businesses and institutions such as the EU are not the only ones competing for high-quality professional translators. The rise of the so-called war on terrorism has led to a sharp rise in the demand for foreign language capable staff in military and intelligence services around the world (White et al., 2008).

The demands of translation and their effects are embedded in the broader context of the language influence on international business, and operate in a wide variety of situations. As mentioned in Chapter 1, a common approach to handling language diversity within multinational corporations (MNCs) has been to adopt a common corporate language (CCL), often, although not only, English. While this solves an array of diverse translation demands across the MNCs, it generates a set of new translation requirements associated with the need to move into and out of the CCL in different language environments (Marschan-Piekkari et al., 1999). Sørensen's (2005) survey of 70 corporations operating in Denmark shows that the companies did not use English as an overruling language, but more generally as a 'transit language' between various parallel local languages. Once documents in English arrived at subsidiaries, they were translated into the respective local languages. Thus, moving communication from one part of the internationalizing firm to another may require more than one act of translation. For non-English-speaking firms, such as those headquartered in Denmark, a document being sent from foreign subsidiaries to headquarters has to be first translated into the CCL, and recipients may then translate the document into Danish. In reverse situations, communications from headquarters may first involve a translation from Danish into English before being forwarded on to subsidiaries, where a further round of translation takes place. This may not be a straightforward activity when there are few subsidiary employees with the required level of fluency in the CCL. Inevitably, there are often many awkward aspects of these translation demands, potentially unleashing adverse consequences for the language and communication efficiency of the subsidiary and the firm in general, introducing problems such as distortion, filtration and blockage – with knock-on effects for managerial effectiveness (Marschan et al., 1997). The limited evidence indicates that translation is important for successful international business activity that encompasses multiple language domains. As such, it is deserving of greater research and business attention. Downgrading or ignoring the role and impact of translation as a front-line activity in international business may have deleterious effects for the companies concerned.

In this chapter, we undertake a thorough examination of the subject of translation, considering it as an activity and as a process. We consider how it is handled in the business context, its demands and costs (monetary and otherwise), and the potential effects that translation may have on the operations of internationalizing firms. Translation is a broad activity. It is not restricted to formal contexts involving professional translators, but also incorporates the wide range of informal, day-to-day situations, often by people who have no specific translation role. We use the term translation in an overarching way, covering both written and oral communication, though recognizing that translation is generally taken to refer to written communication whereas the interpreting function refers to oral 'translation' activity. In many business situations, there is often an interweaving of these two components to such an extent that the distinction between these two aspects becomes blurred and somewhat unhelpful. Further, as Jaivin (2013, 3) points out, 'The broad conception of translation that exists in English doesn't itself translate into all other languages.' In English, the word derives from Latin – *translatum* (that which is carried across): transferring something from one place or realm. She explains that in Hindi the process means to tell again (*anuvad*). The Japanese have different words for translation to indicate differences in quality, such as *setsuyaku* (humble, clumsy) to *chōyaku* (better than the original).

TRANSLATION AS AN ACTIVITY AND PROCESS

In the first instance, translation seems a relatively simple activity – what could be defined as the process of moving communication in any form (verbal or written) from one language to another. It may be activated

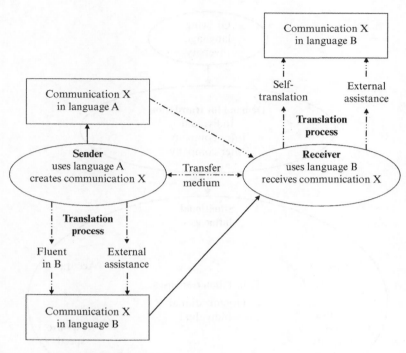

Figure 2.1   Translation model

automatically, for example through a translation software program. For a communication to be transferred effectively, one of the parties must convert the communication into the language of the other. As shown in Figure 2.1, this applies whatever the transfer medium – be it handwritten on paper, in electronic form, telephonic, or face to face. The translation could be undertaken on the spot through self-translation by the sender or receiver. Alternatively, the sender or receiver might call on external assistance in some form to carry out the translation activity. Once we consider these parts of the process, it becomes evident that translation may not be a straightforward activity. Moreover, as Figure 2.1 indicates, translation is far from a simple activity, even when only two parties are involved. Translation may be an onerous, daily task in many different localities for companies involved in international business operations. The Latvian example at the beginning of our first chapter highlights this.

Placed in the context of various international business situations, translation raises a host of issues, such as who should bear the cost of the exercise (see Piekkari et al., 2013). In international negotiations, there is the

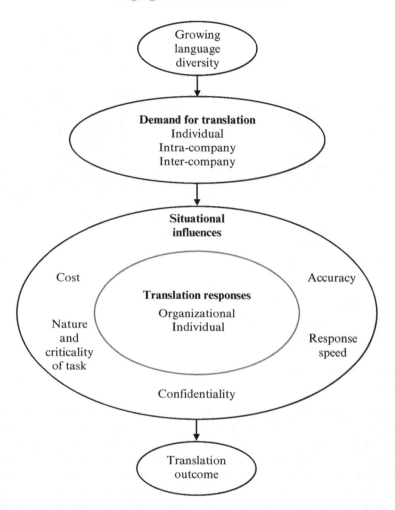

Figure 2.2   Influences on the translation process

question of whether translators should be involved to provide real-time translations during the negotiation process and, if so, where should they come from – from inside one of the negotiating parties or from an external provider of translation services? Such issues, detailed in Figure 2.2, are now discussed in more depth.

At a general level, Chapter 1 stresses the way in which international business brings with it growing language diversity, which inevitably influences the nature and extent of translation activity. As depicted in

Figure 2.2, translation demands can arise from various sources: individual clients seeking to transact business in their native tongue; other firms, including agents, government bodies, suppliers and the like; and through intra-firm communication and information exchanges. Whether and how these translation demands are met will depend on a range of situational influences.

SITUATIONAL INFLUENCES

Cost

Cost is obviously a constraining factor in the ability of a firm to provide a full range of timely translation services for its staff. The heavy demands and costs of translation across all EU activities are illustrative of how challenging this issue can be in a multilingual context, demonstrating that cost restricts the extent of translation undertaken. For example, the European Commission has estimated that translation accounts for about two-thirds of the cost of registering a patent in the different EU countries (*The Economist*, 2012b). This has raised questions about the 'economic efficiency of equal treatment for all languages' (Fidrmuc and Ginsburgh, 2007, 1351; see also Fixman, 1990). Many MNCs cover an even wider span of languages in their global operations than the EU, so it can be expected that they would face a similar range of demands and costs. It is an open question as to whether, or indeed how far, MNCs fall short of an optimal level of translation activity. For example, the extent of business lost because of a shortfall in translation activity may ultimately have a negative effect on profitability. Inevitably, choices have to be made regarding the allocation of what are bound to be limited translation resources relative to the tasks at hand.

One of the problems for internationalizing firms when dealing with the costs of translation is that their full extent is not always clear. In many instances they are in an overt, direct form, such as when external translators are hired or when there is a central language unit that operates as a cost centre: the costs are relatively clear and fully accounted for. However, much of the cost of translation is implicit or hidden (Welch and Welch, 2008; Piekkari et al., 2013). There are many instances where business is lost due to translation problems. In a study of Siemens, it emerged that mistranslation of relevant documents led to the failure of an attempt to win a project deal (Fredriksson, 2005).

The costs of translation, or mistranslation, in many cases may not be obvious, as in the above example of Siemens. For example, a poor buyer–seller exchange due to communication difficulties caused by language problems might lead to lost sales; or there could be extra demands on management time to undertake translation work that is unrecorded and unaccounted for. The high cost of translation in management time was evident in some instances in a study of the Finnish multinational KONE. Because the Taiwanese subsidiary manager was the most competent in the company language, English, he undertook the bulk of the translation work on key documents emanating from headquarters – despite the heavy demands on his time (roughly 50 per cent of his work time), and his admission that 'my English is not so good' (Marschan et al., 1997, 593). In a study of the Finnish MNC Outokumpu, one interviewee spoke about the extra time and difficulty – the cost – of having to use English in writing reports, of not being able to 'say things as you like'. Considering the translation option, he maintained that 'if you put other people to translate maybe the people translate exactly but the idea of the customer or the other problem they don't know' (Palo, 1997, 77). Maitland (1999, 19) comments that 'companies are often reluctant to hire experts because the costs [of translation] are considerable while the potential losses from bad translation are hard to measure'.

Internationalizing firms are often resistant to the notional costs incurred in improving translation efficiency, but these have to be compared with the 'orders lost, the misunderstandings, failed negotiations, frustrated meetings, poor internal communication and even blighted careers' that can result from lack of action on this front (Lester, 1994, 44). A study of the Nordic bank, Nordea, indicated that the bank was very concerned about costs associated with translation. The Nordea translation guidelines state: 'the costs involved in producing English [the corporate language] as well as simultaneous local language versions of a given text should always be taken into account by the person(s) responsible for ordering translation' (Piekkari et al., 2013, 779). It was evident in Nordea that managerial focus with respect to translation cost was related to the bank's central translation department. This department operated on the basis of cost recovery from all users. Informants in the study stressed that they felt constrained in the use of the central service because of what they saw as the high cost involved. This was one of the reasons that Nordea staff sought alternative solutions to their respective translation needs.

The type of translation activity also has a bearing on the nature and extent of costs – for instance, whether it involves documentation or person-to-person exchanges. Translation of documents may be assisted by machine translation. Documents tend to be in a more consistent form compared to personal exchanges, thereby reducing the translation time required. The transfer of tacit knowledge is generally considered to be more demanding and costly to transfer, and this is exacerbated when it involves translation activity (Roberts, 2000; Welch and Welch, 2008).

The 'language absorptive capacity' of the receiver is also a factor when communications or documents are sent in untranslated form. As Piekkari et al. (2013, 780) explain: 'Language absorptive capacity refers to the ability of a MNC to absorb and use information and knowledge that cross language boundaries – either entering or moving around the organisation.' High language absorptive capacity (ready availability and high level of language fluency of staff) reduces the need to resort to translation assistance and hence its cost. Buckley et al. (2003) report on the case of the Chinese international joint venture, Shanghai Bell, in which the transfer of knowledge initially was constrained by the lack of language fluency at the Chinese end. Shanghai Bell, established in 1983, was originally linked to Belgian Bell, but it was taken over by Alcatel in 1986. The company used a codified approach at the outset as its primary knowledge transfer strategy, assisted by the establishment of a documentation and language translation centre in China. The 'language issue . . . was addressed by the creation of a translation group, to convert materials from the parent into Chinese, for distribution to the relevant departments' (Buckley et al., 2003, 81). Low language absorptive capacity meant that codification was still a costly exercise.

Under the cost umbrella, there is the related question for internationalizing firms of whether to employ a sufficient number of translators, at considerable cost, so that the translation service can be provided internally, and at the direction of company management. Alternatively, should the firm outsource the activity to external providers? Some combination of these approaches is used by many firms. Limited evidence would seem to indicate that such decisions are not taken as part of a clear, overall plan but are taken more on a reactive, *ad hoc* basis as and when the need is seen to have emerged. At times, the need for translation cannot be fully anticipated as it is dependent, for example, on the actions and language skill level of external partners, customers and suppliers who may be operating in a different language. The development of machine translation and computer-based translation is undoubtedly lowering costs for many large-scale translation tasks, providing some relief in the face of rising translation demands (Hutchins, 2006).

Timeliness

Related to the cost question is the concern about how timely the translation should be. Having sufficient numbers of language-competent staff can be difficult and expensive, and there never can be enough to cover all translation contingencies. In many situations the most appropriate translation is immediate, so that the receiver of a communication can directly frame a response in the relevant language, as in many sales situations. This makes a demand on the salesperson to have the requisite language at a high enough level of fluency, or having a colleague on the spot to undertake the translation – as was evident in the Nordea study, conducted at its Finnish operation (Piekkari et al., 2013). As members of a service organization, Nordea staff often interacted directly with clients, some of whom preferred to operate in their own language or in English, as was often the case, rather than in Finnish. The service encounter typically required a prompt response. A bank customer, for example, could be waiting at the counter. Any delay could cause a queue to form, creating considerable pressure on the bank employee (see also Martin and Davies, 2006). In the Nordea study, informants stressed that the need for immediacy meant that drawing on the services of the formal central translation department was not feasible.

Immediacy is a particular concern in informal, social and other forms of person-to-person interactions that are such a critical part of international management and knowledge transfer – within and between companies – for example in training situations (Welch and Welch, 2008). Interpreters can be used in many international business situations where there is a lack of requisite language skills on the part of participants. However, social communication conducted through a translator is inhibiting. As we later discuss in Chapter 5, it does not ensure the creation of personal networks or social capital. Barner-Rasmussen (2003, 71) quotes the situation of a CEO of a major Finnish multinational: 'I can go to places where Finnish, Swedish, or English is spoken, but I can't go to France and speak to my people – it is of no use, really, because I don't speak French and they probably don't speak English.'

Accuracy

Connected with cost and timeliness is the issue of accuracy in translation. Highly precise or accurate translation can be expensive and take considerable time. For firms, therefore, a balance has to be struck between accuracy and the allocation of translation resources. In person-to-person situations, it may not be feasible to ensure highly accurate translation. Again there is the question of immediacy of response and it depends on the level of fluency of one or other of the parties to the cross-language exchange. In some instances, enough is translated for the meaning to become obvious, or at least adequate for the parties to understand the request or task involved. As we shall note regarding machine translation, the outcome may not be accurate, but sufficient for the purpose. However, accuracy is vital in instances such as those involving legal contracts or other official documents. Informants in the Nordea study related that in such instances there was a greater likelihood that the central translation department would be involved. Personal responsibility concerns tended to override the cost involved. For example, one informant commented: 'It takes a lot of time to do official and difficult translations, and on the other hand I do not want to take responsibility.' Another stated: 'If it should be official, then someone else has to do it . . . I would not do it since my job description is not translation services' (Piekkari et al., 2013, 778).

Another example comes from the US firm, Medtronic, which specializes in medical technology. The nature of its products means that many documents dealing with sophisticated technology, such as cardiac equipment, must be accurately translated into various languages. Responses have to be developed to deal with varied regulatory systems as a consequence of operating in 120 countries. 'A "multilingual core team" brings translation coordinators together with top managers from the company's marketing, technical communication, regulatory affairs and operations departments' (*Export Today*, 2000, L/8). Accuracy is vital.

Nature and Criticality of the Task

While translation in face-to-face situations may involve the need for a rapid response, it also allows adjustment and clarification in order to ensure that the message between the two parties is being transferred and understood, even though the language fluency may be limited. The informants in the Nordea study mentioned earlier 'stressed the difference between face-to-face encounters and the more formal translation involving important documents . . . The more the task concerned the written word, the more formal the task was seen to be' (Piekkari et al., 2013, 779). Those who lacked sufficient fluency and confidence in English would often turn to colleagues for assistance in handling the translation in face-to-face encounters.

Confidentiality and Information Security

Concerns about the security of confidential information and knowledge are an important factor in determining how translation is handled, particularly in terms of whether internal or external translators are used. This concern tends to be heightened in the international arena, with uncertainty about how security and confidentiality are valued and protected in foreign countries. Confidentiality matters to firms that are seeking to protect vital commercial knowledge from competitors – in areas such as intellectual property, strategic plans, foreign sales and market information. Because of these concerns, internationalizing firms frequently establish centralized departments to handle translation, rightly or wrongly expecting that confidentiality will be preserved.

In situations where external translation assistance has to be called on, firms sometimes approach this exercise by dividing the overall translation task and sharing it between different external translators. This will be accompanied by strict confidentiality provisions. An interesting example was the treatment of translators employed by the publisher when having Dan Brown's novel, *Inferno*, translated into various languages. The Danish translator reported his experience. He 'was locked in a London bunker, under the watch of guards, for five weeks . . . They [all translators involved] had to hand over phones and cameras and were denied internet access during the day and the manuscripts were locked up at night' (Steger, 2013, 31). The example also highlights the novelty and timeliness of the translated text, as discussed earlier.

However, taking the quest for security too far may compromise the consistency and reliability of the total work. Technical information, for example, may be inaccurately translated without full documentary material that explains how the part fits into the whole (Crick, 1999). Reported UK research indicates that 'only 8 per cent of UK translators were always told the intended readership and use of a document. One translator said he had been given a list of machine parts to translate but not told what the machine was' (Maitland, 1999, 19). The pressing need for rapid translation sometimes forces staff to look for informal routes – such as using friends or relatives – that may be irregular, but more trusted than unknown external translation services.

TRANSLATION RESPONSES

In Figure 2.2, we separate organizational responses from those made by individual employees, though these are not mutually exclusive. These various responses are further detailed in Table 2.1.

Table 2.1   Translation responses

Organizational responses	Individual employee responses
Language policy	Self-translation
Central translation department	Use of social networks
Computer-assisted translation tools	Seek organizational assistance
Outsource to external provider	Do nothing

Organizational Responses

Language policy

As mentioned earlier, the adoption of a CCL is one organizational response. However, language policy entails more than language standardization (for more detail, see Chapter 9). Aspects such as staff hiring, training and deployment may be incorporated as part of a language policy. Our illustrative examples uncover the interplay between national-level and company-level language policies that shape the ultimate organizational response. Furthermore, language policy may be an outcome of both top–down as well as bottom–up strategizing, particularly in smaller firms (Pohjanen-Bernardi and Talja, 2011).

Central translation department

At the EU level, the Translation Centre in Luxembourg was established to provide translation services for the numerous EU agencies, institutions and the like. For internationalizing firms, the establishment and use of such a centralized internal agency may be as a result of managerial recognition that its multilingual world requires effective translation as a base for company-wide communication. In the ELAN study, 27 per cent of respondents in larger firms indicated they had their own in-house language department (CILT, 2006). As noted above, whether and how the service is used depends on the situational factors identified in Figure 2.2, and employee actions. For example, one of the Nordea informants commented: 'I do not know where the translation department is situated and I do not know how to contact them' (Piekkari et al., 2013, 778). As in the case of the CCL, establishing a central service does not, by itself, ensure the desired outcome: effective translation performance.

Computer-assisted translation tools

Machine translation and computer-based translation memory systems (similar to spell-check software) are a work-in-progress. Machine translation has so far been shown to be of mixed quality, not able to deliver highly precise translation, but it can help to speed up human translation activity. Of course, technically accurate translation does not ensure that culturally appropriate meaning has been conveyed, and this is a difficult problem for the development of machine translation technology. Nevertheless, computer-assisted aids offer considerable hope of alleviation of the translation task. Even simultaneous translation by computer programs seems to be within reach. For example, though not perfect, one system allows both sides of a conversation in different languages to understand each other with the assistance of translated text on display (*The Economist*, 2013a).

The size and cost of, and growth in demand for, translation globally are major incentives for the continued development of technological solutions. However, at this stage they appear unlikely to fully replace the immediacy, cultural sensitivity and ability of skilled human translators to adapt in many informal and social situations where business deals are discussed and transacted. In fact, Hutchins (2006, 170) maintains that the 'aim of using computers for translation is not to emulate or rival human translation'. But this does not exclude an important role for machines in the translation of substantial documents (for example, in major projects) which represent a costly and lengthy task for human translators (Fixman, 1990; Hutchins, 2005). Machine translation is evolving rapidly, providing a useful first draft that translators can then hone to acceptable quality, assisting in speeding up the translation process, but also providing a partial understanding that is still useful in some fast-changing environments (*The Economist*, 2002). There are many situations where high-quality translations are not needed, and for many companies the consistency and speed of machine translation combined with translation memory systems are a significant factor (Hutchins, 2005, 2006).

In the Nordea study, respondents explained that a range of aids was available to assist in translation, such as translation software programs. These were apparently being updated as technological improvements came on stream. However, respondents considered that the tools were of varying degrees of usefulness. In some circumstances, computer-aided tools helped in achieving a rapid translation response, or in situations where high quality translations were not required. In other instances, they were seen to be of limited value. For example: 'I use the dictionaries and applications but they are pretty limited' (Piekkari et al., 2013, 778). The inability of technical assistance to provide the surrounding context of the subject being translated was stressed as a limitation.

Commenting on the EU experience, the Director-General, Lönnroth, has explained that 'our own system of machine translation is today mainly used to "gist" documents or to provide a rough text for further editing'. In addition, 'computer-assisted translation has become the rule. The documents to be translated are compared to similar texts in a huge repository of the Commission's translation memories, and recurrent sentences are immediately retrieved with their previous translations' (Lönnroth, 2008, 15). A range of associated measures, including the financing of research on language technologies, has meant significant progress in the Commission's development and application of new translation technologies to improve the efficiency, effectiveness and speed of translation processes within the EU. Without such developments, much of the EU's business would be stalled or the cost of translation would rise alarmingly. Nevertheless, despite the progress so far, there is little sign that the human role in translation will disappear, or even diminish. The globalization of businesses and human communication, in informal as well as formal situations, ensures that translation needs continue to expand and diversify.

Outsource to an external service provider
It is not feasible for globally dispersed firms to handle internally all translation demands. As a result, outsourcing of part of the translation task is inevitable. Even with a central translation department, the language variety and unprogrammed nature of many translation demands makes it difficult for translation staff to cover all languages, ready to respond at call to all translation requests. Many languages will simply not be covered internally, and will not be accessible via machine translation, especially those countries with little-used languages on a regional or global scale (for example, Icelandic, Estonian).

As Piekkari et al. (2013, 781) argue: 'Outsourcing operates as a pressure valve'. Translation demands can be so bunched that even central units have to resort to external assistance. Variation in translation demand was a factor in Oxfam's use of external translation services. At times, requests for translation assistance from its extensive global operations overwhelmed Oxfam's ability to respond, in spite of its preference for internal solutions (Lehtovaara, 2009). The head of Nordea's central translation system also indicated that external providers were used to relieve translation pressure in times of heavy demand. There is a company size aspect as well: smaller companies with no or a limited number of foreign subsidiaries are far less likely to have staff with relevant language skills as they expand globally, so that they need to resort to outsourced translation solutions (Fixman, 1990). In a study of Welsh firms (SMEs), of those in the small category, 32 per cent reported using translation services, while the comparable figure for larger firms in the sample was 69 per cent (Peel and Eckart, 1997).

A relatively new approach is the use of crowdsourcing as an external translation provider. Companies can invite interested translators to bid for a translation job. As such, this introduces a competitive environment. Experience has shown that this delivers a lower-priced translation service, although there is some question about the quality of the end product (*The Economist*, 2013b). There is also the issue of the security of commercial and confidential material, considering that those bidding through the crowdsourcing invitation may be unknown or even competitors seeking useful intelligence.

These issues emerged in a discussion with representatives of F-Secure, a Finland-based company, which provides cloud and Internet security services through over 200 agents in more than 40 countries around the world (company website). The service is the protection of customers' valuable content across mobile digital devices – for both private and business clients. More than 30 languages are involved, and most customers receive the service in their own language. This requires around 15 000 to 20 000 translation assignments per year. An in-house central translation department is supported by a global network of external professional translators. The head of F-Secure's translation department explained that the company deliberately avoided the use of crowdsourcing as the company could not control the quality, or depend on translators' commitment to the company's brand and what it stood for. He dismissed the cost advantages of crowdsourcing, preferring to invest in developing good, long-term relationships with reputable external translation providers. These relationships were buttressed by payment agreements and regular group meetings hosted by F-Secure.

Another issue related to outsourcing is its effect on the company's stock of language capital (see Chapter 5 for a discussion of the concept). In a sense, by externalizing part of the translation task, the firm creates an outside component of its language capital, that is, the ability to call on such service providers to deal with translation demands. Of course, the firm does not own the resource. However, it could be argued that, as in the F-Secure case, with strong continuing relationships built over time, the provider becomes tied to the firm, in a way achieving quasi-ownership. This is illustrated in Figure 2.3.

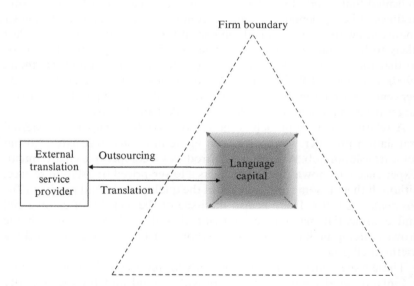

Figure 2.3   Language externalization

Individual Responses

Even with an effective, responsive, centralized translation facility, companies are still subject to the vagaries of translation responses on the 'front line', where immediacy often rules. Individuals are at the heart of any response to a translation demand, and how they react, sometimes in stressful circumstances, may be critical to internal company workflows and information exchange, customer and stakeholder relationships and the quality of the translation. The fluctuation in the demand for translation services makes it difficult for management to anticipate, plan and allocate language resources. A complicating factor is that much of what goes on is often hidden by a range of coping behaviours that individuals employ. In Table 2.1 we list the most common responses that emerged from the Nordea study (Piekkari et al., 2013). These represent a type of sequencing in responses for those confronted with a translation situation.

Self-translation
This is an obvious first step for those individuals who possess the requisite language competence and can move between the languages, often in an unconscious way. As a Nordea interviewee commented: 'I always first try to do the translation myself but . . . when I am not sure of something, I go to a colleague' (Piekkari et al., 2013, 776). Surprisingly, though, this response is rarely recognized by linguists, who tend to concentrate on the role of professional translation. Conversely, in the organization, because self-translation is occurring, formal responses such as a central translation department may not be seen as necessary. Translation simply gets done.

Obviously, self-translation allows for quick responses, but there are other positive aspects. For example, a Nordea respondent commented: 'It is good variety to sometimes receive foreign emails . . . It also gives me pleasure when I can use my language skills' (Piekkari et al., 2013, 776). There is also a confidence aspect to this: 'I often trust my own skills and the quality of my translations' (Piekkari et al., 2013, 713). For those who do not have the ability to self-translate, this may have a negative effect in that it can be seen as drawing attention to the lack of language skills in an environment where most colleagues are self-translating. This may also have a detrimental side effect because translation work is pushed on to others.

Use of social networks
In the work situation, it is rather obvious that individuals should turn to co-located work colleagues for assistance when faced with translation tasks that they feel unable to handle, or are unprepared to do, or simply do not have the time to do. Almost all the interviewees in the Nordea

study indicated that they sought help from their colleagues with translation tasks. Drawing on members of a network to accomplish work-related tasks has been the subject of research in other fields, such as industrial marketing (Hallén, 1992; Marschan et al., 1996). Obviously language commonality is essential to the development of networks. We cover social networks in more detail in Chapter 5.

Using members of a network can provide rapid and timely assistance, but this is not always the case. As one interviewee in the Nordea study commented, 'It takes time to complete a task in a foreign language since you have to ask someone who knows the language and wait for him or her to be available to help.' Those fluent in the relevant language can become a '*de facto*' translation department. The more requests from colleagues, the less time they may have to perform their normal work duties. This point was made by another Nordea interviewee: 'I get asked for help every day. I constantly have to look at documents and try to figure out what they contain and what they are about.' Linked to this was the concern that not helping out would affect the working relationship between colleagues: 'Sometimes I have to say that I'm busy right now and please look for some other ways to get the translation. However, it is not always such an easy task, because you want to be friends with the person asking for help' (Piekkari et al., 2013, 777). As Figure 2.4 illustrates, frequent requests for translation assistance on the one hand, as well as negative responses to such requests on the other, may cause relational stress and worsen the relationship between colleagues (Persons A and B in Figure 2.4).

If co-located colleagues are not available to help, then a wider search of members of a person's network may be activated. This could involve persons in another department, section or subsidiary; or external to the firm, such as friends, family members, and even a friend of a friend. As one of the Nordea interviewees explained, if she had difficulty in translating a communication, she would take the document or email home for her daughter to translate (Piekkari et al., 2013). Issues such as confidentiality were of lesser concern than task completion, though the trustworthy nature of the network could alleviate any concerns about information security.

The Nordea case raises an interesting issue. Much of the translation activity appears to be handled in an informal way, either by co-located network members or external trusted parties. In this sense, the social network is a key factor in the translation process and ultimately in the ability of the firm to respond to its global customers and global language needs. The *ad hoc* and informal nature of network usage poses a managerial challenge, as much is occurring with limited managerial oversight or control.

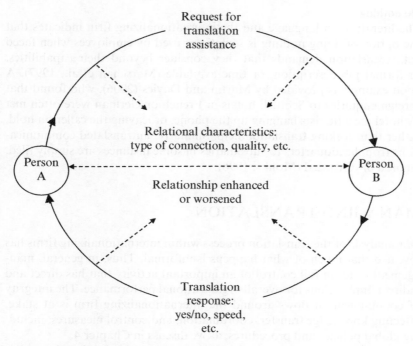

Figure 2.4   The relational side of translation

Seek organizational assistance

As indicated in Table 2.1, an alternative individual response to translation demands is to take a more formal route. Obviously, sending a request for assistance to the central translation department is one option, assuming that such a facility exists and can provide a response in sufficient time, and that the cost of using the facility falls within budgetary limits. Nordea interviewees indicated that organizational assistance was sought when the document concerned was important in a legal or contractual sense, or was too complicated, or was of strategic significance. Furthermore, new members of staff are more likely to revert to formal routes than existing personnel because they tend to lack the work-related networks that can be used for translation purposes. Another option is to seek official external assistance through a professional translation service. Again, this option would depend on budgetary limits, confidentiality constraints and timeliness.

A third option is for the individual to seek language training support if the requests for translation are such that it is justified on work grounds. It is also a longer-term solution for both the individual and the firm.

Do nothing
The literature on language and the internationalizing firm indicates that the option of doing nothing is sometimes used by employees when faced with translation demands that they consider beyond their capabilities, or formal job description, or time available (Marschan et al., 1997). A good example is provided by Martin and Davies (2006), who found that foreign enquiries to Scottish hotels in French or German were often met by hotel receptionists hanging up the phone, or leaving the caller on hold, rather than seeking translation help. Similarly, untranslated communications from headquarters to subsidiaries in some instances are simply filed, ignored or discarded (Monks, 1996).

MANAGING TRANSLATION

Our analysis of the translation process within internationalizing firms has revealed that much of what happens is informal. Thus, in general, management is not in full control of an important activity that has direct and indirect implications for overall organizational performance. The integrity of communication flows around the internationalizing firm is at stake, affecting knowledge transfer, coordination, and control measures, including global policies and procedures, as we discuss in Chapter 4.

It would appear from the limited literature and anecdotal evidence that companies develop translation policies 'along the way' as internationalization unfolds and various language pressures come to bear, giving rise to *ad hoc* solutions. At some stage, though, there are often managerial attempts to develop a more formalized or planned response, such as the establishment of a centralized translation entity. As will be discussed in Chapter 9, translation policy is often specified as part of broader language policy.

One of the problems in developing translation responses is that management tends to be one step removed from the front line where employees are dealing directly with customers who want to converse or send emails and documentation in a foreign language. At higher levels of the company hierarchy, there is not the same pressure for a rapid translation response in many of the tasks faced by top managers, such as research and reporting activities using foreign language sources, or in the preparation of strategy documents that require the input of material taken from foreign language sources. In such situations there is frequently time to use internal or external translation resources as well as the language skills of the upper-level managers themselves (self-translation). As a result, management tends not to see the translation pressures that confront those lower down the hierarchy, or the implications of the stress and coping behaviours employed by staff. For example, quality of output may be compromised by the urgency of the translation task, or the avoidance of the central translation department due to 'user-pays' directives that make its services prohibitive.

As we discuss later in this book, expatriate managers at foreign subsidiaries may be strong in the company language but have limited facility in the local language. Such managers are highly dependent on local translators' skills – often those of their secretaries – in order to function within the subsidiary, and to get their messages across in diverse situations. And local staff can change the content and intent of the information in a deliberate way through the translation process. Because of their limited fluency in Japanese, Nordic expatriates operating in Japan were found to place considerable importance on their bilingual secretaries as information sources. They experienced information being withheld or altered by Japanese managers. One expatriate president explained that 'information is filtered on the way' (Peltokorpi, 2007, 75). On occasions, expatriates can sense that their message is being altered even as they attempt to deliver a message, but there is little that they are able to do to change the situation, as the experience of an Australian in China demonstrates:

> An Australian employee of Otis (a US-based multinational elevator company) was sent to China on a quality control assignment – seeking to rectify problems with Chinese-produced component parts. In dealing with relevant Chinese personnel, he wanted to put across a strong message of how concerned the company was about the need to rectify the problems. However, he needed to use an interpreter, lacking as he did the requisite Chinese language competence. Nonetheless, it became obvious that the strength of the message was not being translated – it was being softened by the Chinese translator for the Chinese audience. (Welch et al., 2005, 15; based on Hamill et al., 2003)

A similar finding was reported in a study of technological knowledge transfer in a Japanese–Finnish strategic alliance (Fai and Marschan-Piekkari, 2003). A Finnish engineer, who did not speak Japanese, was sent to Japan to rectify a problem in product assembly and installation. The Finnish engineer communicated in English about the rectification and its rationale, and a Japanese engineer would translate for the Japanese service and maintenance engineers. As the work proceeded, it became clear that, during translation, the message had been adjusted. Rather than issuing general instructions that could be used in all of the 53 installation situations, the Japanese engineer was providing a more open-ended message. In making the translation more culturally appropriate, this engineer compromised the message, and the Finnish expatriate had to repeat his instructions at each specific installation (Fai and Marschan-Piekkari, 2003). These examples illustrate that globally operating companies become

major employers, users and trainers of translators, whether they see themselves in those terms or not. Similarly, their employees have embarked on
careers in which translation may become an important part of their job,
and have an impact on their career prospects.

As our opening illustrations reveal, in person-to-person interactions it
is relatively easy to convey inappropriate meanings, but also to correct
them, thanks to immediate translation and response situations. Again,
this represents a significant control problem for internationalizing firms.
How can they ensure appropriate translation in situations that are difficult
if not impossible to direct? This is reflective of the broader issue of the
place of language in the internationalization of firms and the management
of their operations. Appointment of translators on an *ad hoc* basis will
never provide the ability to cope with the multiplicity of cross-language
situations that employees will face in informal contexts owing to the sheer
volume of translation tasks. The use of external translators might provide
culturally appropriate, accurate translation, but this is bound to be primarily in formal settings, for example in official negotiations (Ribeiro, 2007).
Thus there is considerable potential for distortion, or 'noise' (Welch and
Welch, 2008) in the communication processes within MNCs and other
internationalized corporations that operate in multiple language contexts,
through the variety of translation avenues that participants utilize.

CONCLUSION

Our overview has shown just how important translation can be in the
international operations of companies. In fact, the globalization of business automatically increases translation demands. Customers demand
approaches in their own language, including the use of language options
on websites. Governments intervene in various ways to make translation
demands on foreign firms, such as in instruction manuals. Despite this,
translation is typically viewed as a minor, technical issue by managers
(Welch et al., 2005). To some extent, technology provides hope of substantial assistance in the translation process. As discussed earlier in this
chapter, computer-assisted translation tools are being extensively used
in assisting translation work. However, at this stage, they are not seen as
replacements for the human translation role.

Immediacy is a common demand on front-line staff, putting stress on
the language competence of staff, and on background recruitment, training and assignment policies of internationalizing companies. If anything,
skilled, professional translators have become even more valuable, but the
technical or legal nature of many documents, along with tacit knowledge

transfer around the firms, create an additional layer of complexity for the translation task and limit the ability to use translation professionals. A vibrant translation market that is partially international in scope has evolved, but firms are still loath to outsource the translation of what are seen as key documents.

REFERENCES

Barner-Rasmussen, W. (2003), *Knowledge Sharing in Multinational Corporations: A Social Capital Perspective*, Doctoral Thesis No. 113, Helsinki: Swedish School of Economics and Business Administration.

Barner-Rasmussen, W. and I. Björkman (2007), 'Language fluency, socialization and inter-unit relationships in Chinese and Finnish subsidiaries', *Management and Organization Review*, 3 (1), 105–28.

Buckley, P.J., J. Clegg and H. Tan (2003), 'The art of knowledge transfer: secondary and reverse transfer in China's telecommunications manufacturing industry', *Management International Review*, 43 (Special Issue 2), 67–93.

CILT (2006), *ELAN: Effects on the European Union Economy of Shortages of Foreign Language Skills in Enterprises*, Brussels: European Commission.

Crick, D. (1999), 'An investigation into SME's use of languages in their export operations', *International Journal of Entrepreneurial Behaviour and Research*, 5 (1), 19–31.

The Economist (2002), 'Tongues of the web', Technology Quarterly supplement, 16 March, 20–22.

The Economist (2012a), 'Legal language', 10 November, 64.

The Economist (2012b), 'Yes, ja, oui, no, no', 15 December, 58.

The Economist (2013a), 'Conquering babel', 5 January, 59–60.

The Economist (2013b), 'The workforce in the cloud', 1 June, 59–60.

The Economist (2014), 'Schumpeter: the English empire', 15 February, 57.

Elliott, G. (2009), 'President at charm's length', *Weekend Australian*, 25–26 April, 22.

Export Today (2000), 'Going global: one word at a time', 16, 3: L/8.

Fai, F. and R. Marschan-Piekkari (2003), 'Language issues in cross-border strategic alliances: an investigation of technological knowledge transfers', *Proceedings of the 29th Conference of the European International Business Academy*, Copenhagen, 11–13 December.

Ferreira-Alves, F. (2012), 'Translation companies in Portugal', *Revista Ango Saxonica*, **III** (Special Issue on Translation Studies), 231–63.

Fidrmuc, J. and V. Ginsburgh (2007), 'Languages in the European Union: the quest for equality and its cost', *European Economic Review*, 51 (6), 1351–69.

Fixman, C.S. (1990), 'The foreign language needs of U.S.-based corporations', *Annals of the American Academy of Political and Social Science*, **511**, 25–46.

Fredriksson, R. (2005), *Effects of Language Diversity in a MNC*, Master's Thesis, Helsinki: Helsinki School of Economics.

Hallén, L. (1992), 'Infrastructural networks in international business', in M. Forsgren and J. Johanson (eds), *Managing Networks in International Business*, Philadelphia, PA: Gordon and Breach, pp. 77–92.

Hamill, P., A. Liu and R. Wong (2003), *Otis Elevators*, MBA Project, Melbourne: Mt Eliza Business School.

Hutchins, J. (2005), 'Current commercial machine translation systems and computer-based translation tools: system types and their uses', *International Journal of Translation*, **17** (1/2), 5–38.

Hutchins, J. (2006), 'Computer-based translation in Europe and North America, and its future prospects', in *JAPIO 2006 Yearbook*, Tokyo: Japan Patent Information Organization, pp. 170–74.

Jaivin, L. (2013), 'Found in translation: in praise of a plural world', *Quarterly Essay*, **52**.

Janssens, M., J. Lambert and C. Steyaert (2004), 'Developing language strategies for international companies: the contribution of translation studies', *Journal of World Business*, **39** (4), 414–30.

Kassis Henderson, J. (2005), 'Language diversity in international management teams', *International Studies of Management and Organization*, **35** (1), 66–82.

Lehtovaara, H. (2009), *Working in Four Official Languages: The Perceptions of OGB Employees on the Role of Language in Internal Communication*, Master's Thesis, Helsinki: Helsinki School of Economics.

Lester, T. (1994), 'Pulling down the language barrier', *International Management*, **49** (4), 42–4.

Lönnroth, K.-J. (2008), 'Speech: efficiency, transparency and openness: translation in the European Union', Paper presented at the 18th World Congress of the International Federation of Translators, Translation and Cultural Diversity, Shanghai, 4–7 August.

Maitland, A. (1999), 'The case of the misleading coffin', *Financial Times*, 17 June, 19.

Marschan, R., D.E. Welch and L.S. Welch (1996), 'Control in less-hierarchical multinationals: the role of networks and informal communication', *International Business Review*, **5** (2), 137–50.

Marschan, R., D.E. Welch and L.S. Welch (1997), 'Language: the forgotten factor in multinational management', *European Management Journal*, **15** (5), 591–8.

Marschan-Piekkari, R., D. Welch and L. Welch (1999), 'In the shadow: the impact of language on structure, power and communication in the multinational', *International Business Review*, **8** (4), 421–40.

Martin, A. and S. Davies (2006), 'An evaluation of the language skills in Scottish hotels', *Journal of Hospitality, Leisure, Sport and Tourism Education*, **5** (1), 4–15.

Monks, K. (1996), 'Global or local? HRM in the multinational company: the Irish experience', *International Journal of Human Resource Management*, **7** (3), 721–35.

Palo, U. (1997), *Language Skills in Inter-unit Communication of an Internationalizing Company: The Case of Outokumpu*, Master's Thesis, Helsinki: Helsinki School of Economics.

Peel, M.J. and H. Eckart (1997), 'Export and language barriers in the Welsh SME sector', *Small Business and Enterprise Development*, **4** (1), 31–42.

Peltokorpi, V. (2007), 'Intercultural communication patterns and tactics: Nordic expatriates in Japan', *International Business Review*, **16** (1), 68–82.

Piekkari, R., D.E. Welch, L.S. Welch, J.-P. Peltonen and T. Vesa (2013), 'Translation behaviour: an exploratory study within a service multinational', *International Business Review*, **22** (5), 771–83.

Pohjanen-Bernardi, K. and K. Talja (2011), *Language Strategies in Finnish Small and Medium Enterprises*, Master's Thesis, Helsinki: School of Economics, Aalto University.

Ribeiro, R. (2007), 'The language barrier as an aid to communication', *Social Studies of Science*, **37**, 561–84.

Roberts, J. (2000), 'From know-how to show how? Questioning the role of information and communication technologies in knowledge', *Technology Analysis and Strategic Management*, **12** (4), 429–43.

Steger, J. (2013), 'A cog in Brown's machine', *Saturday Age*, 16 November, 31.

Sørensen, E.S. (2005), *Our Corporate Language is English: An Exploratory Survey of 70 DK-sited Corporations' Use of English*, Master's Thesis, Aarhus: Aarhus School of Business.

Welch, D.E. and L.S. Welch (2008), 'The importance of language in international knowledge transfer', *Management International Review*, **48** (3), 339–60.

Welch, D.E., L.S. Welch and R. Marschan-Piekkari (2001), 'The persistent impact of language on global operations', *Prometheus* **19** (3), 193–209.

Welch, D.E., L.S. Welch and R. Piekkari (2005), 'Speaking in tongues: the importance of language in international management processes', *International Studies of Management & Organization*, **35** (1), 10–28.

White, M.D., M. Matteson and E.G. Abels (2008), 'Understanding information behavior of professional translators', *Journal of Documentation*, **64** (4), 576–601.

3. Confronting language: the individual in the organizational context

In Chapter 1, we considered how language emerges as an issue for internationalizing firms. How this happens should not be expected to be consistent across all firms. National language, as we show through the use of hypothetical language paths, can influence how, where and at what stage firms confront the language issue. Once firms reach a substantial level and spread of international operations, however, it becomes more challenging to deal with language. In the following chapters, we will consider how management and individuals cope. We begin with a key managerial concern: how to maintain control, direction and coordination as the firm grows across borders, gathering languages as a consequence. We then consider how individual employees respond to the way in which management attempts to 'handle' the language challenge, particularly the imposition of a common corporate language (CCL).

MANAGERIAL CONTROL, DIRECTION AND COORDINATION

The then CEO of Accor – the French-based hotel and travel company – is reported to have said: 'Every morning when I wake I think about the challenges of coordinating our operations in many different countries.' This comment exemplifies the constant challenge for internationalizing firms: how to achieve the appropriate balance between overall control of their global operations and responsiveness to local market needs and pressures. Managerial action centres on the following four aspects.

1. *Communication and information flow*   It has been argued that companies are information organizations (Macdonald, 1996), in which case the internationalizing firm faces considerable challenges to ensure that information flows through its various communication channels

in a form that allows recipients to readily access and utilize it. As Marschan-Piekkari et al. (1999a, 425) maintain,

Communication flows within the multinational are an essential element of its ability to control and coordinate global activities . . . This is not an easy task: formal and informal channels are involved; information follows multiple directions . . . and is transmitted via a myriad of forms. The result is an intricate web of MNC information transfer.

As we have explained earlier, much of this information has to cross language borders. Indeed, Victor (1992, 15) stresses that 'perhaps no other element of international business is so often noted as a barrier to effective communication across cultures than differences in language'.

2. *Coordination of resources and activities across foreign markets* Internationalization involves establishing or acquiring new operations, introducing new products or services, and transferring technology, systems and processes. All of these aspects have a language component. As we will explore later, leveraging competencies such as knowledge and skills to sustain competitive advantage is recognized as important in the international management literature, though how and where language moderates an internationalizing firm's leveraging capabilities has received limited attention. Moving staff, with their language competencies, is an element of this.

3. *Consistency of procedures and performance goals* As the company grows, it invariably formalizes procedures as part of its formal control mechanisms. Standardizing performance evaluation, for example, is part of this process.

4. *Control and accountability* Control is usually achieved through formal reporting and budgetary accountability systems. Informal control mechanisms are also used, such as employee socialization into company norms and values and behavioural expectations – that is, building a unified corporate culture. The establishment of personal networks is often regarded as assisting informal control.

All these aspects are influenced in various ways by language, as highlighted in a study of Western-owned subsidiaries in Finland and China by Björkman and Piekkari (2009, 105). The findings show that 'subsidiaries with low language competence [in the shared language] were controlled to greater extent by centralization and formalization than units with high language competence'. Language appeared to act as a filter of control mechanisms, as illustrated in Figure 3.1.

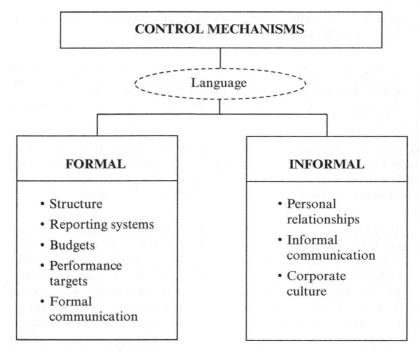

Source: Adapted from Marschan et al. (1996, 139).

Figure 3.1   Control mechanisms filtered by language

LANGUAGE STANDARDIZATION

A common response by firms when recognizing the way in which language is beginning to affect their international operations is to adopt a common corporate language (CCL) to assist in control, and to facilitate internal communication, reporting and information flow. We use the term 'language standardization' to describe this action. Thus language can be seen as operating at two levels: it filters the 'bundle' of control mechanisms noted in Figure 3.1; but it is also a type of formal control mechanism in itself, although managers will tend not to see it in those terms. Benefits commonly seen as flowing from the introduction of language standardization are:

- It facilitates formal reporting across and between the various organizational units that comprise the internationalizing firm. Information such as that contained in budgets, sales reports, performance targets and market forecasts needs to be in a language that may be readily accessed by various managerial and functional staff in different locations. A common language answers this need.

- It reduces the potential for miscommunication.
- It improves the ability of employees to access relevant company information such as technological developments, financial data, health and safety procedures and employment conditions.
- It enhances informal communication. This recognizes that information and knowledge are not always exchanged through formal means.
- It fosters a sense of belonging to a 'global' family. As part of an informal control mechanism, a common language can assist in building loyalty and commitment through a sense of identity with the global organization.
- It signals that the firm is internationally oriented. An example is provided by a manager of a Danish firm: 'When the corporate language is changed into English, it is to signal that it is an international corporation capable of carrying out global activities' (Sørensen, 2005, preface).

These benefits are reflected in the rationale for the use of English as the CCL provided to employees of the Finnish firm, Fazer Group:

> Building a common corporate culture requires a common language and terminology so that we will be able to easily share information and best practices and become a truly international and agile company. Having a common language will also enable active internal job rotation. (Fazer Group Language and Policy Guidelines, 1 January 2014)

English is now used for internal communication, but Fazer Group stresses that interaction with external clients and stakeholders will still be conducted in the relevant local languages.

In some cases, particularly those emerging from continental Europe, more than one language may be used. The German multinational, Siemens, for example, uses German and English; the Swiss multinational Nestlé uses four main languages (German, English, French and Spanish). For some firms, language standardization evolves over a period of time as global expansion brings with it different languages. In other words, it is not a conscious managerial decision initially, but at some point there is recognition of the need to formalize the CCL (or languages) for internal communications. The common language is often English by default, given its dominance, as we discussed in Chapter 1. In the Finnish multinational,

KONE, English was adopted formally only when its expansion path took it beyond the Nordic region. In this regard, a KONE manager commented that 'English has simply evolved by itself and it has become the natural language for internal communications: a practical solution with the increasing internationalisation of the company'. Harzing et al. (2011, 283) report the experience of one German firm. The interviewee commented: 'I think our company adopted English as the official corporate language only seven to eight years ago. That was in the vane of stronger internationalization.' On acquiring the personal computer division of IBM, one of the first managerial decisions of the CEO of Lenovo was to declare that English would be the firm's official language (*The Economist*, 2013).

The advantages of language standardization noted above seem logical and beneficial, but as with any international business decision, language standardization has managerial consequences, both planned and unintended. For example, those without a sufficient level of fluency in the CCL may be excluded from ready access to necessary information and can easily feel disconnected from the 'global' family. These aspects are borne out in a recent study of a German multinational. Swift and Wallace (2011) found that 90 per cent of respondents who were working in non-English-speaking countries needed to speak English, the CCL, in order to perform their work. However, varying levels of English fluency created work-related problems, such as performance in meetings. Respondents reported that a low level of English fluency resulted in misunderstanding, loss of efficiency, time needed to accomplish tasks, and problems in information exchange.

Managing language standardization poses distinct challenges. An interesting example is noted by Sulonen (2011, 69) in her study of foreign firms operating in the French-speaking Canadian province of Quebec. Stringent laws surround the use of the French language. Nevertheless, as one interviewee explained when asked if English was the corporate language: 'Yeah, you're right, but we don't say that. We don't want to have any trouble. But of course, everything is done in English . . . We try to keep it as low profile as possible.' Within KONE, instruction for new technical developments and products tended to be held in its centralized training unit in Finland, and these sessions were conducted in English, the corporate language. Obviously, only subsidiary personnel with sufficient English competence could attend. A Spanish manager commented that finding a suitable candidate to take part in these courses was problematical. A Mexican manager recounted similar difficulties, compounded by the fact that there was nobody who would come to Mexico and teach in Spanish (Marschan-Piekkari et al., 1999b).

In Chapter 4, we shall discuss the organizational aspects of language standardization. For the remainder of this chapter, though, we shall concentrate on how individuals handle it.

INDIVIDUAL RESPONSES TO LANGUAGE STANDARDIZATION

As mentioned above, KONE adopted English as the corporate language once it moved out of the Nordic language group and into the diverse language environment of continental Europe and the USA. In her study, Marschan (1996) reports that, for many employees, the necessity to operate in a second language – English – was a facilitator of and a barrier to their ability to communicate effectively within KONE. Drawing on data from this study and more recent work, it is possible to identify key responses or coping behaviours. How the individual responds to language demands will depend on many factors: for instance, fluency in the requisite language, work situation and immediacy or required response time. As Figure 3.2 illustrates, these can range from avoidance (passive or active) through to forms of acceptance, as we now detail. Further, these responses can be formal or informal, and undertaken over a short or longer time period.

Attempts to Avoid

Individuals exhibit various types of what we term avoidance behaviour, such as ignoring (passive) or seeking ways to minimize the personal burden

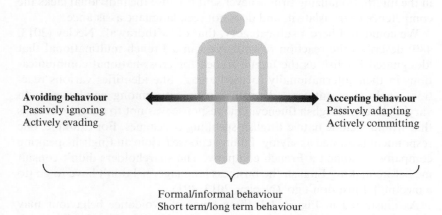

Avoiding behaviour
Passively ignoring
Actively evading

Accepting behaviour
Passively adapting
Actively committing

Formal/informal behaviour
Short term/long term behaviour

Figure 3.2   Individual responses to language demands

of language standardization (evasive). When confronted with formal communication from headquarters or another subsidiary unit in the corporate language, individuals without the requisite language competence might simply disregard it. In their study, Harzing et al. (2011, 284) found cases of 'selective, but persistent, resistance against the adoption of English as a corporate language'. They provide an example related by a German manager in the Japanese subsidiary of the German multinational: 'There are a couple of areas and functions where English as the official corporate language is still deliberately ignored.' He admitted that he did not discipline staff for this passive response, and even at times encouraged them 'to reply in Japanese'. At the extreme, passive avoidance could mean throwing a document into the wastepaper basket, or deleting the email message.

Another passive response may be to note the communication or report but file it away, not bothering to have it translated and distributed. A manager in KONE's Spanish subsidiary unit explained: 'We should receive this [corporate] information in Spanish so that it could be used here. I have a lot of information about maintenance here in these folders, but I don't have time to translate it into Spanish. At present, I can't read it, nor understand it or use it' (Marschan et al., 1997, 593). In a study of Irish subsidiaries, Monks (1996) reports how the Irish HR director of a French bank admitted that, as all documents and policies received in the Irish subsidiary were written in French and not translated, they rarely paid them any attention. One wonders how important the information was that the individuals ignored. The consequences could be serious for company operations and performance. A further hidden danger is that important information that an individual should be transferring to others in the internationalizing firm is never sent because the individual lacks the competence to translate it, and does not seek language assistance.

We could add here a sub-category, that of 'withdrawal'. Neeley (2013, 480) describes the reaction of employees in a French multinational that 'designated English as the lingua franca for cross-national communications in their internationally focused areas'. She identifies various reactions such as resentment, distrust and anxiety among employees with varying level of English fluency. One response was not to attend meetings that would include native English-speaking colleagues. For example, one respondent is quoted as saying 'I didn't choose to join an English-speaking company – I joined a French company. The shareholders didn't consult me before making English the business language. If I don't have to go [to a meeting], I just don't go' (Neeley, 2013, 491).

As illustrated in Figure 3.3, these types of avoidance behaviour may result in what can be called an *information black hole* in the subsidiary concerned. Some of the information flowing into the subsidiary disappears.

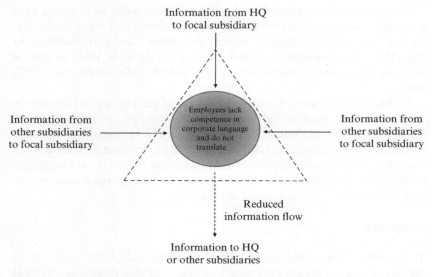

Figure 3.3   Language-based information black hole

As Peltokorpi (2007) found, expatriates in Japan who lacked Japanese language skills were not only cut off from interaction with their department managers, but received filtered information, and relied on bilingual secretaries to find out what they should have been told. Likewise, some of the information that should flow out never reaches the internationalizing firm's wider communication network. Passive behaviour, then, can be viewed as a type of filtering system, blocking or distorting information flows.

The 'actively evading' behavioural response in Figure 3.2 can be seen as a more subtle form of avoidance. One example is when individuals identify 'language contacts' in other parts of the multinational. The intention is to create a language alternative, parallel to the corporate language, which allows them to continue to use their own mother tongue for communication and information purposes. In effect, it means that individuals can avoid the necessity to become fluent in the corporate language. For example, a middle-level manager in KONE's Spanish subsidiary explained:

> One of the things [my bosses] did already some time ago was to visit units and factories in Europe to get to know the people. They went and looked for personal contacts, for people who would speak Spanish over there. In the KONE [internal phone] directory they marked the people whom they got to know personally. These are the people whom we contact when there are some problems. [The network is small, but it truly works . . .]

This action also extended to formal activities such as training pro-grammes: 'At present, we send people for training to France and Italy, because the communication is easier with them than with Finland. In Italy, the Italian language is rather easy for the Spanish, [and] in France there are quite a lot of people who speak Spanish' (Marschan et al., 1997, 594).

As this action illustrates, people find ways of getting around barriers in order to operate, even though such behaviour may run counter to formal managerial direction. While it is possible to live in a parallel language universe for some time, eventually the necessity to interact with others will force these individuals to confront the need to use the corporate language. In this sense, individuals are following their own language paths, similar to those of firms, as we discussed in Chapter 1.

Acceptance

At the other end of the scale, individuals may accept the necessity to operate in the corporate language and adapt to this reality in different ways and to varying levels of commitment (see Figure 3.2). Often this may be forced upon the individual who might otherwise be passive. A German manager in Siemens explained that 'even though English skills were not his strength, he was "simply forced" to use the language' (Fredriksson, 2005, 82). It may be that the specifics of the task or job are such that ignoring the formal communication is not an option. It may be that the person needs to use the corporate language to communicate beyond the immediate task environment. Communicating with other subsidiary units or headquarters will require the use of the formal corporate language. This is borne out by a case study of the merger experiences of two Nordic firms – Stora Enso and Nordea. Both were dealing with the outcomes of cross-border mergers and the adoption of English as their corporate languages. 'In both com-panies, individual work profiles differ to a great extent as to the need for English . . . In both companies, there were employees who did not need any English at all and there were employees who communicated almost totally in English' (Louhiala-Salminen, 2002, 150).

Faced with the need to deal with language standardization, research indicates various behavioural responses, as detailed below.

Using Work Colleagues on Hand as Translators

As outlined in Chapter 2, a common response is to have a work colleague – in the immediate work context – act as a translator. A KONE Italian middle-level manager related his experience: 'Other people use me for international communication. I would hope that the communication could be delegated to a larger number of people [as] . . . sometimes I'm the only reference person in all the office due to language problems' (Marschan et al., 1997, 594). A similar approach was identified by Nurmi (1995, 89) in her study of Nokia. A Finnish expatriate working in Nokia's German subsidiary commented: 'I notice that it was easier for a German to ask me to call Finland for him than [he] call Finland directly. Often I was acting just as a middleman.'

Using Expatriates as Language Nodes

The KONE case study revealed the critical role played by expatriates as communication conduits. Of course, this can only be the case if the individuals concerned are bilingual – in the corporate language and local language – especially after the expatriate has moved to another posting or back to headquarters. As a Mexican middle manager described, 'Basically, I can communicate directly with [Mr X in Finland]. He is a person who speaks perfect Spanish, which has facilitated enormously the communication' (Marschan et al., 1997, 594). This particular individual had been an expatriate in Venezuela in the late 1970s, during which time he became fluent in Spanish. He was transferred back to Finland and later held a senior management position at KONE headquarters. During an interview, this person explained how knowledge of his Spanish competence spread to the Spanish subsidiary after he acted as a Spanish interpreter for a delegation from the Spanish subsidiary visiting Finland. His language nodal role was confirmed during interviews with managers in Spain. As one manager commented, 'since this person speaks Spanish, the communication is very direct with him. He is the start of everything . . . [and] he passes us on to other persons [if necessary]' (Marschan-Piekkari et al., 1999b, 386).

Another example is provided by Harzing et al. (2011, 285). An interviewee described how Japanese expatriates working at the German headquarters became language nodes: 'The person from Japan is the contact person for the Japanese. This is exactly his function. In parallel, this person can develop himself by improving his language capabilities or building up personal networks.'

In such instances, language nodes facilitate what is referred to as back channelling: using personal contacts to assist in acquiring information or exerting influence without following the formal communication route. The difference here is that the relationship is language-based. Louhiala-Salminen (2002, 142) provides an example of this in her study of the merger between the Finnish bank Merita and the Swedish bank Nordbanken. The corporate language became Swedish. One interviewee explained: 'we had a Finn here [in Sweden] the first year . . . and he was the channel for communication, so we heard a lot about what was going on in Helsinki, and we understood that this [the use of Swedish] was an . . . issue.'

Language nodes may also be considered as intermediaries. They play an important bridging role but, at the same time, become others' coping mechanisms, sometimes allowing individuals to delay the need to learn the corporate language. For instance, in a study of Wärtsilä, a Finnish multi-national, Lahtinen (2000, 93) reports the experience of Finnish expatriates in the Italian subsidiary. One interviewee remarked: 'It's so difficult that [some locals] speak such bad English [the corporate language] and write even worse, so that I have to write everything and [information] passes through me.' Another commented that 'they don't ask me to [write reports for them] but I have to, they don't get done otherwise'.

Using Internal Networks

The use of expatriates as language nodes is an example of a broader process of personal network building within an internationalizing firm. Over time, individuals build relationships, forming a social network that can be utilized for work-related purposes. These relationships are formed through various contact mechanisms – for example, training programmes, regional and functional meetings, sales promotion activities, technical interchange, subsidiary or headquarter visits, and formal staff transfers. All are language-dependent. We return to this topic in Chapter 5 where we discuss the role of language in network development, utilization and maintenance.

Learn the Company Language

Introducing a corporate language automatically introduces pressure on individuals throughout the internationalizing firm to acquire competence in the mandated language. An obvious response is for the individual to undertake language training. Such an activity indicates a high level of acceptance and even commitment. Individuals may be strongly motivated by the benefits seen to accrue from possession of the corporate language. An example is provided from a study of the Ukrainian operation of SimCorp, the Danish financial software multinational, which used English as its corporate language. Ukrainian employees viewed SimCorp as offering them interesting and challenging work, as well as interaction with, and visits to, the Danish headquarters. These benefits were strong motivating factors for improving their English competence. English-language courses were offered at company expense (Benito et al., 2013).

How the individual reacts to language standardization will depend on where the individual 'sits' within the firm. Is the individual employed by the parent company – either in headquarters or in a unit within the parent country? Or is the individual employed by a subsidiary or affiliated unit? What is the job level (that is, managerial or operative) and in what capacity (as a production engineer, accountant, salesperson etc.)? It is reasonable to expect that a top manager be fluent in the CCL, while a person working in a factory in a subsidiary may not be under such pressure. The former CEO of the Swedish/Swiss multinational, ABB, was adamant that 'every manager with a global role *must* be fluent in English [ABB's corporate language], and anyone with regional general management responsibilities must be competent in English ... we are adamant about the language requirement – and it creates problems. Only 30 per cent of our managers speak English as their first language' (Taylor, 1991, 94). A similar reaction is reported by Fredriksson et al. (2006, 417). A top executive is quoted as saying, 'language skills are very important. The higher one gets on the management level, the more language becomes a must.' In such situations, it is difficult for managers not to respond to the language requirement.

Fluency in the corporate language is linked to promotion and wider job opportunities within the internationalizing firm. In other words, it is in the person's self-interest to invest in language acquisition if they wish to have a career within an international company. It becomes a matter of individual choice. The more competent one is in the corporate language (usually English), the greater the chances of advancement. Language opens up the possibilities to attend training programmes offered in the corporate language, to build networks, and to be posted on international assignments. All these are important to having an international career. Not learning the corporate language restricts one to a domestic-only career path, as Figure 3.4 shows.

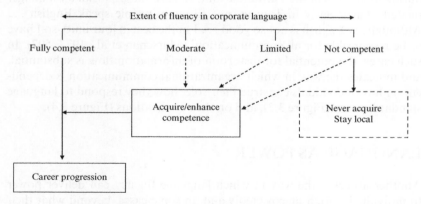

Figure 3.4   Individual choice related to language requirement

Learning the language can be on an informal basis at the individual's initiative and expense. However, in larger multinationals, corporate language training is often provided by the organization, sometimes through external providers and outside normal working hours. The onus is on the individual to make use of this facility. These issues are explored in greater depth in Chapter 6.

Language Standardization is not a Managerial Panacea

What the above section highlights is that the decision to standardize language may, on the surface, seem to accomplish the objectives determined by top management. However, individual responses to language standardization indicate that by itself a CCL does not remove the language barrier. Communication still can be impeded, for example, at the subsidiary level. Global expansion brings additional languages into the 'family'. Language standardization therefore requires more individuals to switch between languages in their day-to-day working life, thus increasing the potential for miscommunication. Some comments from the KONE study are illustrative. An Austrian technician commented: 'The problem with Finland is that they speak English, but not as their mother language. And we speak English, but not as a mother language. There are many errors in translation and there may be some problems' (Marschan et al., 1997, 596). Another example was provided by an operative from the German unit: 'Once I phoned [Italian unit] and the call took 30 minutes because [the chief designer] was not able to speak English and I am not able to speak Italian. So the secretary had to translate what I said to him and backwards again' (Marschan et al., 1997, 596). An even more telling example emerged during interviews in the Taiwanese unit. A Taiwanese subsidiary manager related: 'Particularly in Taiwan, not so many people speak English . . . Although my English is not so good . . . I'm the best in [our unit], so I have to be responsible for all communication' (Marschan et al., 1977, 593). In such cases, the potential for distortion of information flow is substantial, and indicates the way in which organizational communication is dependent on how individuals construe their role, how they respond to language standardization (Figure 3.2), and on their motivations (Figure 3.4).

LANGUAGE AS POWER

Another aspect is the way in which language fluency can deliver power to individuals, often unexpectedly and, in some cases, beyond what their formal status or job description would normally involve. Research has long recognized the way in which possession of critical information can provide an individual with a source of expert power: controlling knowledge flows and enabling the establishment of critical contact networks (see, e.g., Mintzberg, 1983). Language competence provides an opportunity to act as a communication gatekeeper. Indeed, from a study of a merger between the Swedish Nordbanken and the Finnish Merita banks, Vaara et al. (2005, 595) identify ways in which 'language skills become empowering or disempowering resources in organizational communication, how these skills are associated with professional competence, and how this leads to the creation of new social networks', becoming what the authors term 'circuits of power'.

Given that a large proportion of company information is sensitive, using external sources to assist with translation is often not an option for those who lack the requisite language skills. This places the employee in an unusual position: being privy to information that would not normally come to him/her. Imagine what it must have been like for one of the individuals in the KONE 1996 study, posted as an expatriate to the Mexican subsidiary in a middle-management level. He found that his language skills placed him in a somewhat unique position – the only person in the small subsidiary who spoke all three relevant languages: Finnish, English and Spanish. The subsidiary manager, an expatriate from the Italian subsidiary, had poor English skills (the corporate language) but spoke Spanish. The Finnish expatriate explained: 'I am the only one who maintains the contacts abroad. When I have to leave the office some jobs will have to be postponed until I return. There is nobody to [ask] a question in English [elsewhere in KONE]' (Marschan-Piekkari et al., 1999a, 431). Thus this manager was in a powerful position with regard to information flowing to and from the subsidiary, including sensitive information he was being asked to translate for his superior and colleagues. Sensitive information could include strategy documents, performance appraisal and management reports, budgets and targets.

The above example illustrates that it is not just competence in the corporate language that matters, but the set of languages that an individual may possess. The weighting placed on certain languages is context-driven in terms of the degree to which a set of languages delivers power and influence. Figures 3.5 and 3.6 are a convenient way of depicting combinations in a given subsidiary context.

The Finnish middle manager mentioned above exemplifies Position 1 – the holder whose language set delivers a powerful communication nodal place. The subsidiary manager was effectively in Position 4. There was another Finnish expatriate in the Mexican unit who was able to speak Spanish but had poor English skills – thus in Position 5. This individual

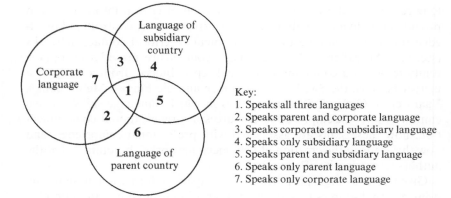

Key:
1. Speaks all three languages
2. Speaks parent and corporate language
3. Speaks corporate and subsidiary language
4. Speaks only subsidiary language
5. Speaks parent and subsidiary language
6. Speaks only parent language
7. Speaks only corporate language

Source: Adapted from Marschan-Piekkari et al. (1999a, 432).

Figure 3.5 Language combinations

had significantly reduced language power compared to his compatriot in Position 1, with implications for performance and involvement at a broader global level, as he explained: 'The only international meeting I have participated in was among all subsidiary quality managers. I could not fully participate because of my limited skills in English' (Marschan-Piekkari et al., 1999a, 432).

Another example is the case of the Chinese joint venture operation of Bayer, a German pharmaceutical multinational, established in 1995 (Hou et al., 2003). As is often the situation for companies entering a new market, Bayer placed heavy reliance on German expatriates in managerial and other key positions, but as they had limited language skills of both Chinese and English, they were replaced gradually with local staff. German expatriates without fluency in Chinese, not surprisingly, had posed a range of communication problems, which had spilled over into perceptions of arrogance by local staff. The study found that an important change came when a Chinese-born German was appointed as head of the key pharmaceuticals division. He had obtained his doctorate in Germany, worked at Bayer's German headquarters, and was fluent in German, English (the corporate language) and Chinese (his mother tongue). Improved communications resulted from this appointment. The difference between this situation and that of KONE's Mexican operation is that in Mexico language power rested with a middle manager, whereas in Bayer, the CEO had both position power and language power.

The other side of the power 'coin' is that lack of fluency in the corporate

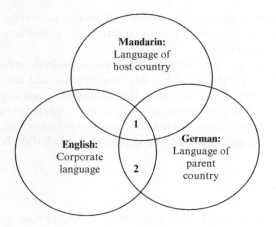

Key:
1. General Manager Pharmaceuticals speaks all 3 languages.
2. Plant Manager Pharmaceuticals speaks parent and corporate languages.

Source: Hou et al. (2003).

Figure 3.6   Language combinations in Bayer

language can have a disempowering effect and even cause some individuals to feel isolated. As we shall discuss in Chapter 5, language standardization can lead to the creation of 'in-groups' and 'out-groups' based on language competence (see also Barner-Rasmussen and Björkman, 2007).

IMPLICATIONS FOR INTERNATIONALIZING FIRMS

The preceding discussion reveals how individuals, as possessors of language competence, can influence how the organization deals with the language challenge. The Bayer and KONE examples demonstrate how the language set of key managers influences their abilities to control their subsidiaries. Having all the relevant languages can place a subsidiary manager in a much more powerful position. In the Bayer example, the German managers who did not speak either Chinese or English found it difficult to operate effectively. Once management changed, however, there was a perception among local Bayer China employees that nothing could be hidden from the new language-competent expatriate. In other words, it became harder to 'hide behind the language'. Of course, how the dynamics play out in terms of managerial control will depend in part on the composition of the top management team in a particular subsidiary and its mix of language competences.

In this chapter, we have concentrated on individual responses to the effect of the imposition of a CCL – what we have termed language standardization. Chapter 4 will consider the managerial and organizational perspectives on language standardization and other language-related effects of global expansion, such as organizational structure, knowledge transfer, international teams and headquarter–subsidiary relationships.

REFERENCES

Barner-Rasmussen, W. and I. Björkman (2007), 'Language fluency, socialization and inter-unit relationships in Chinese and Finnish subsidiaries', *Management and Organization Review*, 3 (1), 105–28.

Benito, G.R.G., O. Dovgan, B. Petersen and L.S. Welch (2013), 'Offshore outsourcing: a dynamic, operation mode perspective', *Industrial Marketing Management*, 42 (2), 211–22.

Björkman, A. and R. Piekkari (2009), 'Language and foreign subsidiary control: an empirical test', *Journal of International Management*, 15 (1), 105–17.

The Economist (2013), 'English to the fore', 13 April, 83.

Fredriksson, R. (2005), *Effects of Language Diversity in an MNC*, Master's Thesis, Helsinki: Helsinki School of Economics.

Fredriksson, R., W. Barner-Rasmussen and R. Piekkari (2006), 'The multinational corporation as a multilingual organization: the notion of a common corporate language', *Corporate Communications: An International Journal*, 11 (4), 406–23.

Harzing, A.-W., K. Köster and U. Magner (2011), 'Babel in business: the language barrier and its solutions in the HQ–subsidiary relationship', *Journal of World Business*, 46 (1), 279–87.

Hou, J., R. Jiang and P. Li (2003), *A Study on the Implementation of Bayer's International Strategy in China*, MBA Project, Bejing: Mt Eliza Business School.

Lahtinen, M. (2000), *Language Skills in Inter-Unit Communication of an Internationalising Company*, Master's Thesis, Helsinki: Helsinki School of Economics.

Louhiala-Salminen, L. (2002), *Communication and Language Use in Merged Corporations*, Working Paper W-330, Helsinki: Helsinki School of Economics.

Macdonald, S. (1996), 'Informal information flow and strategy in the international firm', *International Journal of Technology Management*, 11 (1/2), 219–32.

Marschan, R. (1996), *New Structural Forms and Inter-Unit Communication in Multinationals: The Case of KONE Elevators*, Doctoral Thesis No. A-110, Helsinki: Helsinki School of Economics.

Marschan, R., D.E. Welch and L.S. Welch (1996), 'Control in less-hierarchical MNC structures: the role of personal networks and informal communication', *International Business Review*, 5 (2), 137–50.

Marschan, R., D.E. Welch and L.S. Welch (1997), 'Language: the forgotten factor in multinational management', *European Management Journal*, **15** (5), 591–8.

Marschan-Piekkari, R., D.E. Welch and L.S. Welch (1999a), 'In the shadow: the impact of language on structure, power and communication in the multinational', *International Business Review*, **8** (4), 421–40.

Marschan-Piekkari, R., D.E. Welch and L.S. Welch (1999b), 'Adopting a common corporate language: IHRM implications', *International Journal of Human Resource Management*, **10** (3), 377–90.

Mintzberg, H. (1983), *Power in and around Organizations*, Englewood Cliffs, NJ: Prentice-Hall.

Monks, K. (1996), 'Global or local? HRM in the multinational company: the Irish experience', *International Journal of Human Resource Management*, **7** (3), 721–35.

Neeley, T.B. (2013), 'Language matters: status loss and achieved status distinctions in global organizations', *Organization Science*, **24** (2), 476–97.

Nurmi, T. (1995), *Expatriate's Role in Influencing the Communication within Multinationals: The Case of Nokia Telecommunications*, Master's Thesis, Helsinki: Helsinki School of Economics.

Peltokorpi, V. (2007), 'Intercultural communication patterns and tactics: Nordic expatriates in Japan', *International Business Review*, **16** (1), 68–82.

Sulonen, J. (2011), *International Organizations in the Linguistic Context of Quebec*, Master's Thesis, Helsinki: School of Economics, Aalto University.

Swift, J.S. and J. Wallace (2011), 'Using English as the common corporate language in a German multinational', *Journal of European Industrial Training*, **35** (9), 892–913.

Sørensen, E.S. (2005), *Our Corporate Language is English*, Master's Thesis, Aarhus: Aarhus School of Business.

Taylor, W. (1991), 'The logic of global business: an interview with ABB's Percy Barnevik', *Harvard Business Review*, **69** (2), 91–105.

Vaara, E., J. Tienari, R. Piekkari and R. Säntti (2005), 'Language and the circuits of power in a merging multinational corporation', *Journal of Management Studies*, **42** (3), 595–623.

Victor, D.A. (1992), *International Business Communication*, New York: HarperCollins.

4. Language and international management

In Chapter 3, we discussed the language effects of global expansion, with an emphasis on the individual. In this chapter, we extend the analysis to the organizational level, focusing on key aspects that expose how language intrudes into the internal functioning of the internationalizing firm. These aspects include organization structure, headquarters–subsidiary relationships, communication and the ability to transfer knowledge throughout the various parts of the firm.

There are inherent dilemmas confronting the internationalizing firm: how to balance the needs of the global entity and those of its local operations; and how to maintain unity (integration) yet be responsive to the diverse and often conflicting demands of operating in different national environments (differentiation). Chini et al. (2005) use the concept of the headquarters–subsidiary trench to describe the differing perceptions, expectations and dependence among the various parts of the internationalizing firm. Management is also concerned with maintaining overall strategic direction and preserving the firm's own unique characteristics. As noted in Chapter 3, language standardization may assist in fostering a sense of corporate identity. As one of the respondents in the original KONE study commented, speaking English, the company language, made him feel 'international' and 'KONE' (Marschan et al., 1997, 595). However, having to operate in diverse language and cultural settings may work against this drive for unity. This constant tension provides the backdrop for considering how language affects the relationship between the various parts of the internationalizing firm, as illustrated in Figure 4.1.

ORGANIZATION STRUCTURE

Management literature consistently includes the organization's structure as an integral component of its control architecture. As mentioned in Chapter 3, the overarching concern is the need to maintain and hold relevant parties to account. Macdonald (2004, 64) explains succinctly, 'Control is fundamental to the manager. There is no point making

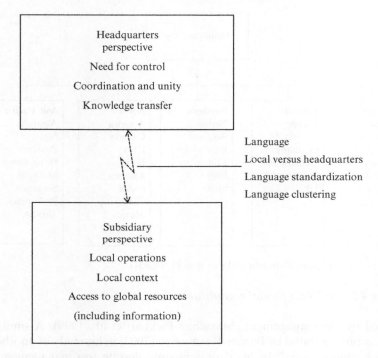

Headquarters
perspective

Need for control

Coordination and unity

Knowledge transfer

Language
Local versus headquarters
Language standardization
Language clustering

Subsidiary
perspective

Local operations

Local context

Access to global resources

(including information)

Figure 4.1   Differing perspectives

decisions if there is no assurance that the decisions will be carried out.'
Control and communication are therefore fundamental to the management process, and language is central to this.

The structure shown in the organization chart (Figure 4.2) depicts the
formal allocation of authority, responsibility and accountability, and how
the various units are linked together. The organization chart also shows
formal communication and reporting lines. Perhaps one of the most surprising outcomes of research into the Finnish multinational KONE was
the way in which language acted as a 'counter-structuring agent'. At the
time of the study, KONE was following a strong regional structural form,
as depicted in Figure 4.2. However, this structure did not accurately reflect
the organizational reality. The KONE German and Austrian subsidiaries
had a common mother tongue and thus tended to interact more between
themselves, becoming a 'language cluster'. There were other such language
clusters – English, Scandinavian and Spanish – that shadowed the formal
structure. As a consequence there was what we term a 'shadow structure'
that lay behind the formal organization chart, something not necessarily

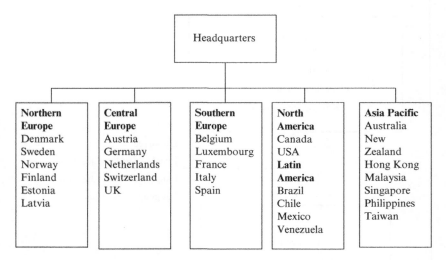

Source: Adapted from Marschan-Piekkari et al. (1999, 434).

Figure 4.2   KONE's formal organization chart

noticed by top management (Marschan-Piekkari et al., 1999). A similar conclusion was found by Barner-Rasmussen (2003) in his study of another Finnish multinational. In his case company, despite top management's endorsement of 'multilinguality', a shadow structure emerged around Swedish, reflecting the personal preferences of key decision-makers, although there appeared to be some convergence towards English.

Language connections of various clusters generated a different structural arrangement to the formal geographical/regional lines, as Figure 4.3 shows. In an operative sense, these language clusters facilitated rather than impeded communication and knowledge flows between the respective units, and had an impact on performance outcomes through the sharing of resources. Language acted as a form of glue, uniting certain subsidiaries.

Going around the language standardization barrier to create a new way of organizing, however, had potential negative consequences in that language clustering could mask other language-related issues from top management. For instance, cross-subsidiary interaction could reinforce regionalism, forming silos rather than a unified global whole – a primary managerial objective. Communication between language clusters tended to be impeded. There was also a lessening of motivation for those within language clusters to learn the common corporate language (CCL).

Figure 4.3 also demonstrates what we term 'language distance': fluency in the relevant languages influenced perception of closeness to, or remoteness

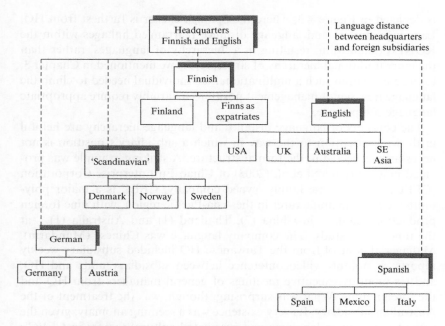

Source: Adapted from Marschan-Piekkari et al. (1999, 434).

Figure 4.3 Shadow structure based on language in KONE

from, the organization's centre – its headquarters (HQ). The concept of language distance parallels that of psychic distance, which we discussed in Chapter 1. As KONE is a Finnish-based multinational, those speaking the parent language were at the apex of the multinational language tree and thus closest to HQ due to ease of access to information and frequency of interaction, of course assisted by geographical closeness. Of course, this was dependent on also being fluent in English, the CCL. Not unexpectedly, subsidiaries in English-speaking countries are positioned in Figure 4.3 as close to HQ due to the high proportion of English competence among local subsidiary employees. Due to historical and cultural connections, the Scandinavian cluster is also positioned closer, just behind the Finnish and English clusters. Many Finnish employees have some competence in Swedish and therefore understand what is referred to as Scandinavian (a polyglot of the Nordic languages). Nordic subsidiary units also had a relatively high number of employees competent in the corporate language. In contrast, interviews with KONE employees in the Spanish-speaking units revealed fewer with English competence and these perceived themselves as more distant and disconnected from the organization's centre. This is depicted in Figure 4.3, where the Spanish cluster is furthest from HQ. Language clusters and language distance rearranged linkages within the KONE organization, resulting in a 'hierarchy of languages' rather than the more traditional hierarchy of structure. As we mentioned in Chapter 3, to progress within such a multinational, an individual needed to climb the language tree: senior management positions invariably require appropriate language competence.

The concepts of language distance and language hierarchy are helpful in drawing attention to the way in which a subsidiary's position is not necessarily reflected in the formal structure. A striking example was provided in a study by Ni et al. (2003) of Chiao Fu Enterprise Corporation (CFEC), a Taiwanese family-owned company. CFEC is a major polyurethane foam manufacturer in the Asia-Pacific region, with nine foreign production plants – in China (7), Thailand (1) and Australia (1) – at the time of the study. The company language was Chinese (Mandarin). Managerial control from the Taiwanese HQ included subsidiary weekly reports; a monthly videoconference between subsidiary units and HQ; and six-monthly executive meetings of general managers from HQ and the foreign units. What was surprising, though, was the treatment of the Australian subsidiary. Its very existence was a seeming anomaly, given the role of the Chinese language and associated cultural factors in CFEC's international operations and future expansion plans that focused on what the CEO termed the 'Chinese cultural region'. However, CEFC was taking advantage of the large Chinese Diaspora population (see Chapter 1): the Australian subsidiary was established as part of its initial overseas expansion in 1990 when it acquired businesses in Australia, Thailand and China. Despite this early start, the Australian subsidiary did not appear in the formal organization chart in 2003, creating what could be termed a 'ghost structure' (Welch et al., 2005). Moreover, it operated with relative autonomy for ten years, under a succession of Australian rather than Chinese managers. The main reason given for this arm's-length approach was the lack of suitable employees who had Mandarin competence, coupled with management's perception of high cultural distance between Taiwan and Australia. In 2000, concerns about control over the Australian operation led to a family decision to take a more hands-on approach, resulting in the appointment of the wife of the CEO to oversee the Australian operation, holding jointly the positions of subsidiary and finance manager. While this appointment increased HQ's control over the Australian operation, it did not remove the language problem in general within the Australian subsidiary, due to a continuing lack of fluency in Mandarin (Ni et al., 2003). According to the company website in 2010, the Australian subsidiary is now formally recognized. It is no longer the ghost.

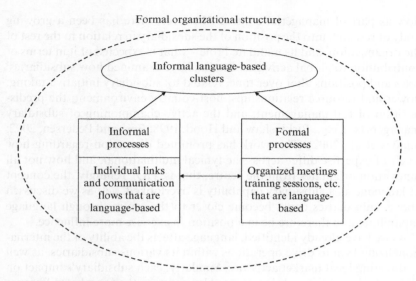

Figure 4.4   Language and structure

The formation of shadow and ghost structures illustrates the importance of connections that allow employees to overcome more formal barriers – in this case the language barrier – that otherwise impede work flows. As shown in Figure 4.4, the informal language-based clusters develop through formal as well as informal processes, such as the combined training programmes between KONE's German and Austrian units. Of course, the formal organization structure drives many of the control and coordination mechanisms. However, informally based, person-bound connections may develop a life of their own, complementing formal managerial arrangements in ways not seen by top management, creating quasi-structural forms. That people communicate and cooperate within these informal structures in a productive manner may further explain why top management can appear somewhat oblivious to language problems within their global operations.

HEADQUARTERS–SUBSIDIARY ROLES AND RELATIONSHIPS

To a large extent, what has been written on headquarters–subsidiary relationships takes the perspective of HQ, and language standardization is a reflection of such an orientation: a tool to assist reporting and information flow as part of managerial control. However, there has been a growing body of research into the position of the subsidiary in relation to the rest of the organization, and its mandated role – what is expected of it in terms of contribution to global activities. Studies have examined how subsidiaries' roles and positions alter over time, related to: subsidiary initiative-taking; power and resource relationships; host-country environment; the predisposition of top management; and the active championing of subsidiary managers (see, e.g., Birkinshaw and Hood, 1998; Foss and Pedersen, 2002; Simões et al., 2002). This work has prompted discussion regarding how levels of expertise differ across the typical multinational, and how not all innovation originates from the centre, that is, HQ. Tellingly, the concept of language as a subsidiary capability is overlooked, yet, as we discussed above, subsidiaries could become closer to the centre through language capabilities and therefore be in a position to exercise more influence.

As we have already identified, language affects the ability of the internationalizing firm to drive operations within its various subsidiaries, as well as directing local market activities. Similarly, each subsidiary's impact on HQ is mediated through language. The question then is what difference does language make to inter-unit relationships and factors such as subsidiary autonomy and embeddedness in the local context? Figure 4.5 illustrates that the language competence of subsidiary and HQ staff influences the ability of various parts of the multinational network to effectively connect and operate as an overall entity. This can be a key factor in the extent of subsidiary autonomy. A lack of corporate language competence at the subsidiary level becomes a communication barrier between it and HQ. This constrains the ability of HQ to control subsidiary operations, but also limits the ability of the subsidiary to affect HQ attitudes, strategy and general operative procedures towards the subsidiary. Lack of relevant language skills thus can be seen as a two-edged sword – delivering some autonomy through what we have called 'hiding behind the language', but at the expense of the ability to influence the subsidiary's destiny in the global context. The potential consequences of effectively granting too much autonomy to a subsidiary were vividly revealed in the experience of KONE with its managerial approach to a newly acquired Italian subsidiary. KONE's top management had taken a hands-off approach, placing faith in the efficiency of its formal financial reporting, budgeting and control system. There was little informal oversight, partly due to poor language skills (little Italian in the Finnish HQ and poor English skills at the Italian end). The resultant poor communication isolated the subsidiary. In 1995, top management discovered deliberate accounting errors in its Italian units that significantly overstated their profitability (Marschan, 1996).

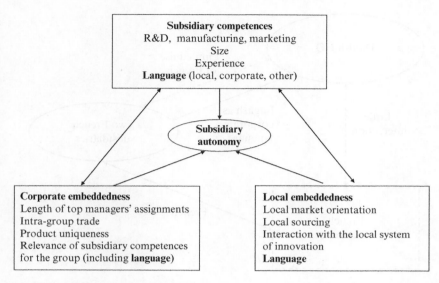

Source: Adapted from Simões et al. (2002).

Figure 4.5 Inserting language as a determinant of subsidiary autonomy

With different effects, a similar situation is recounted by Andersen and Rasmussen (2004) in their study of Danish firms in France. One of the case companies was a Danish construction machinery firm with two French subsidiaries and about 130 employees. The company used English as its company language, but only had one person at HQ that could speak French (see Figure 4.6). The French employees were uncomfortable about operating in English, and could not speak Danish. As Andersen and Rasmussen (2004, 240) commented:

> The lack of communication with the French market from the headquarter in Denmark makes the firm extremely vulnerable to sudden changes in the market. Information is mostly given in the form of orders and options and any unrest in the market – which is not seen in the stock of orders – is not observed by the managers in Denmark.

Here, language prevented HQ embeddedness at the local level, by default assigning more power and hence autonomy to the French units with regard to the French market within which they were clearly embedded. Thus, ignoring the moderating effect of language in work on subsidiary autonomy raises questions about the explanatory power of some of the studies dealing with such issues.

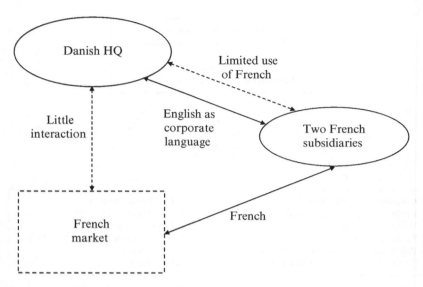

Figure 4.6   Language as a moderator of embeddedness

The use of expatriates as a control mechanism, along with the transfer of technical and commercial know-how, is well recognized. As such, their ability to achieve these expected outcomes is often dependent on effective communication skills, including of course the appropriate languages (CCL and the local language). However, research suggests that expatriate selection is weighted more towards technical and managerial expertise, with language skills given lower priority – an issue we shall return to in Chapter 6. It is therefore not uncommon to find expatriates isolated due to a lack of subsidiary language. In other words, they may be embedded in the corporate network but excluded from the local environment.

The language oversight is more striking given that much of the integration-differentiation literature connected with headquarters–subsidiary relationships addresses the degree of local embeddedness required in order to achieve corporate strategic outcomes within the local market (see, e.g., Prahalad and Doz, 1987). For instance, the greater the need for product adaptation to suit local consumers, the more likely the subsidiary will be given greater autonomy. Again, the issue becomes one of HQ needs versus local sensitivity in terms of decision-making. However, managerial control tends to remain paramount, reinforcing reliance on formal mechanisms (which, as the KONE Italy case demonstrates, may give rise to a false sense of security), or on language standardization that can actually conceal vital market information, as shown in the Danish–

French example. Of course, language is not the only operative factor in terms of subsidiary isolation or autonomy, but it powerfully reinforces perceptions of distance from the centre.

It should be pointed out that language affects all the company's units, not just those located in foreign countries. A study of Siemens, the German multinational, showed that the movement to adopt English as its CCL created challenges for those working with the German domestic units as well as at its Munich-based HQ. The inadequacies in English skills among the German workforce limited communication with other parts of Siemens' global operations. At HQ, 'almost everyone was able to speak English [but] the English used was "pigeon English", very simple and short in order to get things done . . . [beyond HQ] in Germany, apparently some parts within the subsidiaries still exist where language skills are not needed but such places are becoming scarcer' (Fredriksson, 2005, 82). What this study's findings suggest is that, as globalization proceeds, and interaction between various units increases, it becomes more difficult to avoid encountering the need to have some facility in a corporate language even when seemingly 'safe' in the multinational's home country. That is, the individual's choices we discussed in Chapter 3 shrink as the need for language fluency is pushed lower and lower down the organization's hierarchy.

Our concept of a shadow structure is useful in explaining how subsidiaries can create alliances in order to obtain resources and influence their positions within the global family. A subsidiary strong in the corporate language can emerge as a powerful player among its counterparts. A subsidiary that has a strong link to HQ through language can be a language intermediary for other units that are disconnected by language differences, including the company language. Take a hypothetical French multinational that uses French as its company language, depicted in Figure 4.7. Its three Asian subsidiaries – China, Australia and Singapore – have limited or non-existent fluency in French. However, only the Singaporean subsidiary can communicate freely with both the Chinese and Australian subsidiaries, as a lack of Chinese fluency on the Australian part and lack of English on the Chinese part creates a barrier.

By acting as a language intermediary, the Singaporean subsidiary in Figure 4.7 supports the development of a subsidiary bloc. Without managers able to communicate in the language of the parent, in this case French, subsidiaries can hide behind the language. While such tactics can result in isolation for an individual subsidiary, an alliance with similar subsidiaries provides some 'safety in numbers', provided they can communicate effectively among themselves. The danger is that, if one subsidiary acts as the language intermediary for others, then that subsidiary holds considerable power and may engage in gatekeeping behaviour. The Singaporean unit's

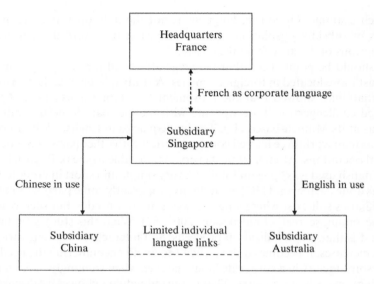

Figure 4.7   Language-based subsidiary links

power would be maintained if it had individuals fluent in French, the company language. While it could not hide behind the language, its gate-keeping capacity with respect to the other two units remains intact. We can only speculate here due to the lack of empirical evidence on this issue, though our central argument that language matters for effective inter-unit communication holds.

For the HQ in France, disconnection from subsidiary units can produce a range of behaviours that run counter to its strictures, circumstances that language standardization aims to avoid. Thus, at some point, our hypo-thetical firm will have to either invest heavily in French language training across all its subsidiaries, or adopt English as the company language. Even then, as we consistently show in this book, this does not eliminate communication barriers. The Chinese subsidiary would still require an English training focus, supplemented by recruitment of English-speaking staff.

A study by Barner-Rasmussen (2003, 89–90) highlights the problem of communication between subsidiaries' employees at lower levels of the hierarchy, particularly in production and operation departments. In one of the case companies, Barner-Rasmussen reports that, during interviews:

> down in the hierarchy, discussions of [differing] accents gave way to descriptions of how language blocked out departments and functions. Aki, a Finnish middle

manager who together with his colleague Jukka was responsible for coordinating two of his Finnish units' functions with equivalent functions in sister units, said 'No-one from [a Dutch unit] contacts our production [department] directly because they know the language skills aren't really there. Similarly, the Swedish units, don't . . . contact them either. Our biggest communication problem at the moment, if we're talking about internal communication, is this one [Swedish sister unit] . . . for production, there is nobody there [in Sweden] right now who can contact our production directly.' [Aki adds, referring to the Swedish sister unit] 'Their quality foremen only speak Swedish and [the people on the factory floor] in our quality department only speak Finnish. So there's the problem – that either Jukka or me always has to act as a go-between.'

Another example comes from a study by Palo (1997, 86) of Outokumpu, the Finnish mining equipment multinational. Horizontal communication emerged as a subsidiary–subsidiary issue, again particularly in the production departments. For example, communication between the Finnish and Spanish units was impeded due to the lack of fluency in the company language. While managers were usually fluent in English, this was not the case at lower levels. As a result, direct contacts between production staff were very restricted. Yet production lines in Pori (Finland) and Zaratamo (Spain) are similar, and closer cooperation could benefit both mills, and in this way also product and process development could be enhanced.

Our treatment of headquarters–subsidiary relationships has shown how language is a key aspect in the formation of formal and informal connections between parts of the internationalizing firm. It is somewhat telling that the role of language has been ignored in the body of research dealing with these issues. We find this a curious anomaly. One of the key processes in inter-unit interactions is that of knowledge transfer. Internationalizing firms depend on the ability to move information and knowledge around the organization. The importance of language in knowledge transfer seems obvious but, again, it has been a forgotten factor, as we now go on to demonstrate.

KNOWLEDGE TRANSFER AND LANGUAGE

In their now seminal work, Kogut and Zander (1992) stressed the basic function of a common language in allowing communication and exchange as a foundation for international knowledge transfer. Hedlund (1999, 11) similarly observed that: 'For knowledge to be exchanged and combined, there has to be a shared medium of communication. People have to be able to make sense to and of each other. One aspect of this is shared spoken general language.' Nahapiet and Ghoshal (1998, 254) went further, arguing that a shared language may provide 'a common conceptual apparatus for evaluating the likely benefits of exchange and combination'. In this context, language is viewed as a component of corporate identity within which knowledge can be more readily transferred (see, e.g., Phene et al., 2005). Cohen and Levinthal (1990) include a shared language as part of prior related knowledge when defining their concept of absorptive capacity, but there is scant elaboration on this issue. In general, reference to the basic role of language in knowledge transfer receives little if any consideration and exploration in empirical studies, including those who follow Kogut and Zander's work. Even Nonaka's much-cited work that draws on research on Japanese firms is curiously quiet on the impact that language issues have on communication and knowledge flows (see, e.g., Nonaka and Takeuchi, 1995).

Knowledge comprises two components: tacit and explicit knowledge (Nonaka and Takeuchi, 1995). Howells and Roberts (2000, 20) define tacit knowledge as 'disembodied know-how, which is acquired by the informal take-up of learned behaviour and procedures. Explicit, or codified knowledge . . . can be written down in the form of a document, manual, blueprint or operating procedure.' There must be some form of articulation, making the knowledge explicit, in order for it to be transferred. Articulation can involve non-verbal communication. For example, demonstration – the show-how aspects of knowledge transfer – is normally accompanied by some verbal instruction. Explicit knowledge is transferred in codified form, such as words, technical drawings and graphics. One of the aspects of knowledge transfer stressed in the literature is that codified knowledge, to be useful, inevitably calls upon tacit knowledge (Welch and Welch, 2008).

Another key point is that knowledge requires interpretation at the individual level. This is recognized in much of the thinking about the concept of absorptive capacity: the ability to recognize, accept and apply new knowledge that has been transferred into an organization from elsewhere (Cohen and Levinthal, 1990). Language is part of absorptive capacity but it is primarily reliant on individual competence. A study of three joint ventures in China by Buckley et al. (2005, 56) found that language was a constraint on knowledge transfer. Once managers attempted to move knowledge to the shop-floor level, foreign-language competence was at a very basic level: 'As a result, all documents relating to such workers needed to be translated into Chinese, which delayed the process of knowledge transfer and increased transfer costs.'

Given the above, it is easy to see the connection between the basic communication model (Figure 1.2) and knowledge transfer. Indeed, as Figure 4.8 shows, one can superimpose knowledge transfer on the basic communication model. Explicit knowledge transfer, such as technical

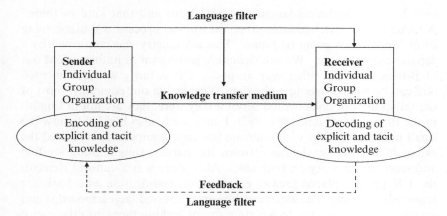

Figure 4.8   Language and knowledge transfer

specifications, will generally be translated into the corporate language for global distribution with the expectation that further translation will occur if a subsidiary uses a different language. In other words, the ultimate receiver may not have the corporate language competence to utilize the knowledge being transferred. As Buckley et al. (2005, 48) note: 'Knowledge transfer requires the use of language and communication to enable articulation in order to promote assimilation.' Further, the first receiver may not translate, thus stopping the transfer process, as we exemplified earlier in this book. The first receiver can be an individual within a department or unit that is apart from the ultimate end-user within the subsidiary. Whether this action is deliberate or not, translation, by its very nature, alters the original text or message (Janssens et al., 2004). There is an equivalent process at the sender's end leading to a final encoded form for transmission. Further, as Figure 4.8 illustrates, if the receiver responds to any message, inevitably language intrudes during the feedback process with potentially equivalent encoding and decoding issues.

Knowledge transfer becomes even more complex when a parent company has only partial or no equity in the relevant foreign units, and they do not have a common language (see Chapter 8 for a fuller discussion of equity arrangements). This is a situation where it may not be possible to mandate adoption of a CCL for internal communication. For example, Lam (1997, 992) contrasts the sender behaviour on the two sides of a Japanese–UK international joint venture. One of the UK interviewees commented: 'I think we have supplied more information that J-firm has, but in most cases, there is no reluctance to supply information. The only barrier is technical language, translations and that kind of thing.' Another UK interviewee summed up the transfer process as 'Little coming from Japan, a lot going to Japan'. This asymmetry was confirmed by a Japanese interviewee: 'We are definitely getting more [information] out of B-firm, than the other way around ... It is fairly well-documented and can be passed over just like that. Whereas, in our company, most of the things are not documented. Even if they were, they are not in English in the first place' (Lam, 1997, 992). Lam's study also highlights how the small number of those with requisite language competence restricted the extent of personal exchange between the parties, thus limiting sending and receiving capacity on both sides. Also, there was a cultural element: the UK partner placed greater emphasis on codification as a basis for knowledge sharing. The Japanese, however, stressed tacit knowledge and interpersonal exchanges, to a certain extent locking them into the use of the Japanese language rather than codifying knowledge into English to facilitate knowledge transfer.

KNOWLEDGE TRANSFER PROCESS

In our discussion so far, we have considered the impact of language on knowledge transfer within the broader context of communication. We now focus more particularly on knowledge transfer itself and the way in which language plays into this process – that is, the various factors that drive the movement of knowledge around the internationalizing firm. Figure 4.9 portrays how the interplay of language and the seven drivers influence knowledge transfer. The feedback loops stress its processual nature.

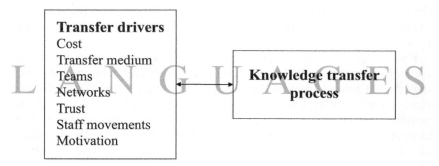

Figure 4.9   Language and the knowledge transfer process

Knowledge Transfer Drivers and Language

We identify seven main drivers: cost, transfer medium, teams, networks, trust, staff movements and motivation (see Welch and Welch, 2008). These transfer drivers are not mutually exclusive, and influence managerial choices and actions regarding how, what, when and where knowledge is transferred throughout the organization.

Cost

In simple terms, knowledge transfer is constrained by cost. We argue that language costs are part of this picture. The knowledge transfer literature tends to treat the transfer of tacit knowledge as more costly than explicit or codified knowledge transfer (see, e.g., Roberts, 2000). One of the reasons that tacit knowledge is generally considered to be more expensive to transfer is the imperative of face-to-face interaction. Hedlund (1999, 12) argued: 'The fact that much individual as well as organizational knowledge is tacit requires interaction to be intensive and extended in time for demerging, merging, and remerging of knowledge elements to be possible.' However, as we outline in Chapter 2, the cost of translating documents is not insubstantial.

Costs associated with language codification are exacerbated when there is a concern to check for equivalence and cultural sensitivity, particularly during back-translation (Janssens et al., 2004). As Buckley et al. (2003, 81) report, the Chinese international joint venture, Shanghai Bell, was forced to establish a special centre for documentation and language translation because of the perceived low absorptive capacity of the joint venture, which had inhibited the transfer of technology. Materials were translated into Chinese for distribution to relevant departments. While documents and other codified knowledge seem easier to transfer, as Lamberton (1997, 77) observes, 'codification, because it is not a purely technical matter, but involves human and organizational capabilities, runs up against limits of affordability'.

Some companies may elect not to translate, or do so only on a limited basis. While this may achieve some savings, there is often a range of hidden costs associated with such an approach; for example, staff denied access to new knowledge, or misapplying new technology. As we note in Chapter 2, the development of dedicated software only partially relieves the cost of translation, and can introduce distortion through aspects such as cultural insensitivity.

Transfer medium

Recently there has been an explosion in the media through which knowledge is transferred. Traditional forms have been supplemented by advances in communication technology that allow large volumes of data and information to be instantly accessible. One could debate how effective these developments are in terms of knowledge transfer, but whatever the medium used, language intervenes. In some cases, incomprehensibility may be introduced in short-hand message forms, such as Twitter.

Despite the new technological developments, people still prefer to conduct a range of business activities face to face. The continuing and even growing use of international business travel attests to the importance of face-to-face interaction. Internationalizing firms continue to place great emphasis on the need to gather staff together in formats such as meetings, training sessions and the like as a basis for knowledge sharing (Welch et al., 2007). Participation in such gatherings is, naturally, language dependent. This is illustrated in Lahtinen's (2000, 80) study of the Finnish multinational, Wärtsilä's Italian subsidiary. One interviewee commented: 'How many times I could have gone to Finland to discuss, to participate in meetings and I never go [because] I don't understand [English, the corporate language].' A study of research and development (R&D) centres in 14 large multinationals by De Meyer (1991) found that socialization was the most important mechanism used to improve inter-unit communication. The multinationals involved used training, temporary assignments and constant travelling as socialization tools.

As we shall discuss in Chapter 5, effective interaction depends on relationship context and relationship development as precursors to the transfer and absorption of knowledge (Johannessen et al., 2001). Take the case of the Norwegian firm, Moelven, a global player in the timber industry. The development of its Russian operations in the early 1990s, initially through importing, involved building personal relationships with key individuals in Russia:

One manager from the purchasing department responsible for imports commented: 'Personal contacts were so important that during the first three years [of] dealing with the Russians, I had between 50 and 100 trips to Russia, talking to suppliers and maintaining the personal networks.' (Welch et al., 2002, 227)

Further, Roberts (2000, 434) notes:

Given the importance of tacit knowledge as a factor enabling the assimilation of codified knowledge, face-to-face contact may well be a prerequisite for the transfer of much codified knowledge. In addition, the establishment of a level of trust to facilitate the exchange of knowledge also favours co-presence and co-location.

Face-to-face contact cannot yet be fully reproduced by information and communication technology, particularly in terms of its 'richness, variety and scope'.

Teams

A mechanism to assist in knowledge transfer is the use of cross-border teams whose members may be drawn from various business and functional units across the MNC. Work teams differ from groups in that they are more task-directed, self-regulated, legitimized by management, and formed for a specific objective and timeframe. Team members may work in a virtual environment, supplemented by face-to-face meetings, conference calls and intranet communication. When carefully managed, they can be a highly focused solution to a range of issues and problems, as well as powerful mechanisms of international knowledge transfer, given the varied contributions of team members, their diverse networks, and sometimes multiple languages (Harvey and Novicevic, 2002).

The question of course is whether people from various national backgrounds can operate effectively in teams when their expectations are shaped according to different underlying philosophies. In fact, research indicates that formation of international teams does not necessarily result in harmony, cooperation and successful task outcomes. Values, attitudes and expectations of team functioning differ, and mutual respect and trust are necessary to develop the required spirit of cooperation for effective team functioning (Tenzer et al., 2014). Schweiger et al. (2003) interviewed senior managers, team leaders and team members in various European and Japanese multinationals. They found that a shared team performance focus was critical. Cultural differences – in language, demeanour, values and norms – impeded the speed of work, particularly during the early stages of the team's formation. One multinational in their study – Air Liquide – deliberately formed teams on the basis of nationality – French or significant experience of working in France – in order to avoid complexity.

What is emerging from this body of research is an observed pattern where members drift into groups within multinational teams on the basis of their mother tongue because of the ease of communication – another form of language clustering. For example, Barmeyer and Mayrhofer (2008, 34) report on the experiences of a merger between German, French and Spanish companies that chose English as the corporate language within the newly formed merged entity. However, the reported study concentrated on the interplay of the German and French units. 'Little by little, the collaborators find themselves in informal *national* [sic] groups: the Germans with their German counterparts, the French with their French colleagues. At this point, communication and cooperation seem to come to a halt.' Illustrating another way in which language may influence knowledge transfer, from her study of MNCs in France, Kassis Henderson (2005) found that, even when teams operated in a common language (English), language diversity affected interpretations and socialization processes. These were 'hidden obstacles' in team performance and knowledge sharing. Further, when teams are composed of native and non-native speakers of the corporate language, tensions can be created over the perceived non-recognition of the difficulties of communicating in a second language (Glaister et al., 2003).

Hambrick et al. (1998, 198) maintain that language, while interacting with other cultural components – such as values, cognitive schema and demeanour – has a distinct influence on the functioning of international management teams. They conclude that 'a low degree of common language facility [will] generally . . . impair group functioning, hampering the exchange of information and trust'. Even in instances where there is a high degree of common language facility, not every team member will exhibit the same degree of confidence or ability to communicate complex ideas in a foreign language. Moreover, 'language not only reflects social context, it may also influence social interactions within teams' (Chen et al., 2006, 688). Thus culture and language do not always simply overlap.

Teams operating within the subsidiary context may become isolated from the rest of the multinational, with negative consequences for access to and transfer of relevant, useful knowledge, thus reducing the subsidiary's absorptive capacity (Hedlund, 1994; Zellmer-Bruhn, 2003; Mahnke et al., 2005). Knowledge can easily become locked within a subsidiary-based team, thereby restricting sending capacity. Further, language is a factor that can cause subsidiary team isolation. 'This is why expatriates with the required language competences (local and corporate) can play such an important role in breaking down subsidiary team isolation and thereby ensuring knowledge transfer in both directions' (Welch and Welch, 2008, 349).

Informal global teams may emerge due to staff interaction in the normal course of international operations. For example, Goodall and Roberts (2003), in their study of a European-based oil multinational, found that expatriates working on projects in different countries developed into a highly socialized, networked team. However, while the global team supported knowledge sharing between expatriates, it acted as a barrier for locals who did not possess the appropriate languages – 'English and corporate speak' – and this restricted knowledge sharing with the locals.

The above discussion highlights how language reinforces other mainly cultural differences that affect team dynamics and performance. Language differences can be an initiating force for team breakdown. The use of a

CCL may not be the panacea that top management expects when looking for ways to enhance knowledge sharing and transfer via global teams.

Networks
The role of networks and interpersonal relationships in facilitating knowledge transfer is well chronicled in the literature. It is often referred to as the know-who aspect (Hansen, 2002). As Reagans and McEvily (2003, 240) stress, 'Informal interpersonal networks are thought to play a critical role in the knowledge transfer process.' Informal networks are not always obvious, but are used extensively, in some cases contrary to the formal direction of top management (Marschan et al., 1996). Informal networks act like a powerful underground movement, providing members with quick access to a large pool of potential knowledge. This is often referred to as back channelling, as people access network contacts to facilitate information flow and knowledge sharing. Further, research shows that it is not just direct personal connections that are important. The wider indirect connections in a network may also be brought into play. For example, an associate in another unit could provide direction to the source of required knowledge that is known to this associate's broader network (Hansen, 2002). We discuss the issue of networks in more detail in Chapter 5.

Trust
Trust is recognized as a critical component in the operation of networks and relationships (Young and Wilkinson, 1989; Kassis Henderson, 2005). 'There is an inherent perception of reliability and veracity of knowledge disseminated from sources that are seen as trustworthy. Trust also mediates or alleviates concerns about how knowledge and information is to be used, and encourages disclosure and sharing of knowledge' (Welch and Welch, 2008, 350; see also McEvily et al., 2003). Research indicates that trust is particularly important in the transfer of tacit knowledge (Dhanaraj et al., 2004). For trust to be established between the sender and the receiver of knowledge, a relationship has to be built. Teamwork is enhanced by the development of trust, but this depends on a degree of face-to-face interaction (transfer medium) over time. However, these factors are connected to having a shared language as a basis for effective inter-unit communication that enhances information and knowledge flow and knowledge sharing. The importance of language for the development of trust has been confirmed in a study of 310 inter-unit relationships of multinational subsidiaries. 'Results show that language fluency related significantly to shared vision and perceived trustworthiness in both the Chinese and Finnish subsidiaries' (Barner-Rasmussen and Björkman, 2007, 105).

Staff movements
Moving staff around the global enterprise has been a well-used mechanism, part of the show-how and know-how aspects of knowledge transfer. For example, Alavi and Leidner (2001) regard staff transfers as more effective for highly context-specific knowledge distribution as they allow access to the routines and tacit knowledge of others. Motorola (China) used 'extensive short term movements internationally in order to personalise knowledge' (Buckley et al., 2003, 79). However, there is no absolute guarantee that employees will be effective knowledge transfer agents. Taylor's (1999, 864) study of Japanese expatriates in Chinese subsidiaries found that the Japanese expatriates tended to 'focus on their jobs rather than seek to cross-fertilize management knowledge and practice'. A similar finding is reported by Marschan-Piekkari et al. (1999), where technical staff assigned to international subsidiaries of the Finnish multinational, KONE, concentrated on the project, stayed for a short time, and had relatively limited interaction with local staff. This restricted the transfer of knowledge to local staff. Lack of local language fluency was the major constraint. Likewise, Welch et al. (2005) relate a number of examples of language-related problems encountered by those on short-term international assignments, such as having to work through interpreters, who modify the messages to cater for local audience sensitivities or, in cases where the corporate language is used, a varied level of local competence constrains receptivity.

Motivation
Motivation has been shown to be an important influencing factor in knowledge transfer. There may be reluctance, even hostility, to knowledge sharing by individuals and groups (Szulanski, 1996). For example, Michailova and Husted (2003, 63), based on their study of this issue in the Russian context, reported: 'Russian managers strongly expressed the view that they should always be more knowledgeable than their employees.' The interviewees considered that the opportunity cost of sharing was high. In addition, people tend to be reluctant to share knowledge in situations of uncertainty. As Nielsen and Ciabuschi (2003, 36) explain: 'In times of business restructuring and resulting job reductions, people tend to protect their intellectual capital (knowledge).' The motivation to share is even further reduced when language difference is involved.

RECONFIGURATION AGENT

Language has the potential to interpose in myriad ways and at different stages of the knowledge transfer process. Language determines aspects such as who has the information and knowledge, whether and how it is articulated, when and if it is shared, and in what form. It affects sender transfer capacity, recipient absorptive capacity, as well as the drivers identified in Figure 4.9 above.

As Welch and Welch (2008, 355), stress, much of existing knowledge transfer literature tends to concentrate on organizational-level processes, including unit-to-unit transfer. However,

> much of what is transferred occurs at the individual level . . . language competence may deliver power to certain individuals within the company but there is no certainty about how this power will be used. An individual may be constructive and use the relevant language competence to facilitate knowledge transfer. Alternatively, the actions may be that of a powerful gatekeeper who modifies and frustrates the transfer process.

Considering the individual level is therefore important, as we discussed in Chapter 3, given that the individual can play an important, sometimes covert, role in reconfiguring the knowledge transfer process.

Language is simultaneously an active agent in the knowledge transfer process itself, as well as an influence on the background set of determinants. We argue that language affects the total organizational system within which knowledge transfer takes place. Also, the shadow structure concept indicates how language influences subsidiary clustering and inter-unit communication; that is, it acts as a reconfiguration agent. In Chapter 5, we extend this idea through an examination of how language may drive and reconstruct social networks.

CONCLUSION

The focus of this chapter has been on the ways in which language affects the internal functioning of the internationalizing firm, often with important consequences. For example, a study by Hamill et al. (2003) of Otis Elevators, the US-based competitor of the Finnish firm KONE, highlights this. Engineering diagrams and instructions sent from the Otis development centre in France to the manufacturing unit in China would often be misinterpreted, especially when given to shopfloor employees who lacked sufficient English skills. This was of huge concern due to the safety implications associated with product failure, not to mention the company's reputation. We also show in this chapter how language may act as a counter-structuring agent behind the scenes, supporting or negating the intended purpose of formal arrangements.

The concern for internationalizing firms is that so many of these language effects may not be readily apparent to senior management. The introduction of language standardization can reinforce an overly confident but actually misguided belief that they have dealt with the language problem. In the rest of our book, we shall discuss how pervasive and intrusive language can be as the internationalizing firm seeks to grapple with the managerial challenges of operating in a complex global environment.

REFERENCES

Alavi, M. and D.E. Leidner (2001), 'Knowledge management and knowledge management systems: conceptual foundations and research issues', *MIS Quarterly*, **25** (1), 107–36.

Andersen, H. and E.S. Rasmussen (2004), 'The role of language skills in corporate communication', *Corporate Communications*, **9** (3), 231–42.

Barmeyer, C. and U. Mayrhofer (2008), 'The contribution of intercultural management to the success of international mergers and acquisitions: an analysis of the EADS group', *International Business Review*, **17** (1), 28–38.

Barner-Rasmussen, W. (2003), *Knowledge Sharing in Multinational Corporations: A Social Capital Perspective*, Doctoral Thesis No. 113, Helsinki: Swedish School of Economics and Business Administration.

Barner-Rasmussen, W. and I. Björkman (2007), 'Language fluency, socialization and inter-unit relationships in Chinese and Finnish subsidiaries', *Management and Organization Review*, **3** (1), 105–28.

Birkinshaw, J. and N. Hood (1998), *Multinational Corporate Evolution and Subsidiary Development*, London: Macmillan.

Buckley, P.J., M.J. Carter, J. Clegg and H. Tan (2005), 'Language and social knowledge in foreign-knowledge transfer to China', *International Studies of Management & Organization*, **35** (1), 47–65.

Buckley, P.J., J. Clegg and H. Tan (2003), 'The art of knowledge transfer: secondary and reverse transfer in China's telecommunications manufacturing industry', *Management International Review*, **43** (Special Issue 2), 67–93.

Chen, S., R. Geluykens and R. Choi (2006), 'The importance of language in global teams: a linguistic perspective', *Management International Review*, **46** (6), 679–95.

Chini, T., B. Ambos and K. Wehle (2005), 'The headquarters–subsidiary trench: tracing perception gaps within the multinational corporation', *European Management Journal*, **23** (2), 145–53.

Cohen, W. and D. Levinthal (1990), 'Absorptive capacity: a new perspective on learning and innovation', *Administrative Science Quarterly*, **35** (1), 128–52.

De Meyer, A. (1991), 'Tech talk: how managers are stimulating global R&D communication', *Sloan Management Review*, **32** (3), 49–58.

Dhanaraj, C., M.A. Lyles, K. Steensma and L. Tihanyi (2004), 'Managing tacit and explicit knowledge transfer in IJVs: the role of relational embeddedness and the impact on performance', *Journal of International Business Studies*, **35** (5), 428–43.

Foss, N. and T. Pedersen (2002), 'Sources of subsidiary knowledge and knowledge transfer in MNCs', in S. Lundan (ed.), *Network Knowledge in International*

Business, Cheltenham, UK and Northampton, MA, USA: Edward Elgar, pp. 91–114.

Fredriksson, R. (2005), *Effects of Language Diversity in an MNC*, Master's Thesis, Helsinki: Helsinki School of Economics.

Glaister, K.W., R. Husan and P.J. Buckley (2003), 'Learning to manage international joint ventures', *International Business Review*, **12** (1), 83–109.

Goodall, K. and J. Roberts (2003), 'Only connect: teamwork in the multinational', *Journal of World Business*, **38** (2), 150–64.

Hambrick, D.C., S.C. Davison, S.A. Snell and C.C. Snow (1998), 'When groups consist of multiple nationalities: towards a new understanding of the implications', *Organization Studies*, **19** (2), 181–205.

Hamill, P., A. Liu and R. Wong (2003), *Otis Elevators*, MBA Project Report, Melbourne: Mt Eliza Business School.

Hansen, M.T. (2002), 'Knowledge networks: explaining effective knowledge sharing in multiunit companies', *Organization Science*, **13** (3), 232–48.

Harvey, M. and M.M. Novicevic (2002), 'The co-ordination of strategic initiatives within global organizations: the role of global teams', *International Journal of Human Resource Management*, **13** (4), 666–76.

Hedlund, G. (1994), 'A model of knowledge management and the N-form corporation', *Strategic Management Journal*, **15** (Special Issue 2), 73–90.

Hedlund, G. (1999), 'The multinational corporation as a nearly recomposable system (NRS)', *Management International Review*, **39** (Special Issue 1), 5–44.

Howells, J. and J. Roberts (2000), 'From innovation systems to knowledge systems', *Prometheus*, **18** (1), 17–31.

Janssens, M., J. Lambert and C. Steyaert (2004), 'Developing language strategies for international companies: the contribution of translation studies', *Journal of World Business*, **39** (4), 414–30.

Johannessen, J.-A., J. Olaisen and B. Olsen (2001), 'Mismanagement of tacit knowledge: the importance of tacit knowledge, the danger of information technology, and what to do about it', *International Journal of Information Management*, **21** (1), 3–20.

Kassis Henderson, J. (2005), 'Language diversity in international management teams', *International Studies of Management & Organization*, **35** (1), 66–82.

Kogut, B. and U. Zander (1992), 'Knowledge of the firm, combinative capabilities, and the replication of technology', *Organization Science*, **3** (3), 383–97.

Lahtinen, M. (2000), *Language Skills in Inter-Unit Communication of an Internationalising Company*, Master's Thesis, Helsinki: Helsinki School of Economics.

Lam, A. (1997), 'Embedded firms, embedded knowledge: problems of collaboration and knowledge transfer in global cooperative ventures', *Organization Studies*, **18** (6), 973–96.

Lamberton, D. (1997), 'The knowledge-based economy: a Sisyphus model', *Prometheus*, **15** (1), 73–81.

Macdonald, S. (2004), 'The cost of control: speculation on the impact of management consultants on creativity in the BBC', *Prometheus*, **22** (1), 43–70.

Mahnke, V., T. Pedersen and M. Venzin (2005), 'The impact of knowledge management on MNC subsidiary performance: the role of absorptive capacity', *Management International Review*, **43** (Special Issue 2), 101–19.

Marschan, R. (1996), *New Structural Forms and Inter-Unit Communication in*

Multinationals: The Case of KONE Elevators, Doctoral Thesis No. A-110, Helsinki: Helsinki School of Economics.

Marschan, R., D.E. Welch and L.S. Welch (1996), 'Control in less-hierarchical MNC structures: the role of personal networks and informal communication', *International Business Review*, **5** (2), 137–50.

Marschan, R., D.E. Welch and L.S. Welch (1997), 'Language: the forgotten factor in multinational management', *European Management Journal*, **15** (5), 591–8.

Marschan-Piekkari, R., D.E. Welch and L.S. Welch (1999), 'In the shadow: the impact of language on structure, power and communication in the multinational', *International Business Review*, **8** (4), 421–40.

McEvily, B., V. Peronne and A. Zaheer (2003), 'Trust as an organizing principle', *Organization Science*, **14** (1), 91–103.

Michailova, S. and K. Husted (2003), 'Knowledge-sharing hostility in Russian firms', *California Management Review*, **45** (3), 59–77.

Nahapiet, J. and S. Ghoshal (1998), 'Social capital, intellectual capital, and the organizational advantage', *Academy of Management Review*, **23** (2), 242–66.

Ni, N., L. Riemers and S. Soubiale (2003), *Global Business Strategy, Structure, Communication and Human Resources in a Taiwanese Family-owned Firm*, MBA Project, Melbourne: Mt Eliza Business School.

Nielsen, B.B. and F. Ciabuschi (2003), 'Siemens ShareNet: knowledge management in practice', *Business Strategy Review*, **14** (2), 33–40.

Nonaka, I. and H. Takeuchi (1995), *The Knowledge-Creating Company*, New York: Oxford University Press.

Palo, U. (1997), *Language Skills in Inter-unit Communication of an Internationalising Company: The Case of Outokumpu*, Master's Thesis, Helsinki: Helsinki School of Economics.

Phene, A., A. Madhok and K. Liu (2005), 'Knowledge transfer within the multinational firm', *Management International Review*, **45** (Special Issue 2), 53–74.

Prahalad, C.K. and Y.L. Doz (1987), *The Multinational Mission: Balancing Local Demand and Global Vision*, New York: The Free Press.

Reagans, R. and B. McEvily (2003), 'Network structure and knowledge transfer: the effects of cohesion and range', *Administrative Science Quarterly*, **48** (2), 240–76.

Roberts, J. (2000), 'From know-how to show how? Questioning the role of information and communication technologies in knowledge', *Technology Analysis and Strategic Management*, **12** (4), 429–43.

Schweiger, D.M., T. Atamer and R. Calori (2003), 'Transnational project teams and networks: making the multinational organization more effective', *Journal of World Business*, **38** (2), 127–40.

Simões, V.C., R. Biscaya and P. Nevado (2002), 'Subsidiary decision-making autonomy: competences, integration and local responsiveness', in S. Lundan (ed.), *Network Knowledge in International Business*, Cheltenham UK and Northampton, MA, USA: Edward Elgar, pp. 137–66.

Szulanski, G. (1996), 'Exploring internal stickiness: impediments to the transfer of best practice within the firm', *Strategic Management Journal*, **17** (Special Issue), 27–43.

Taylor, B. (1999), 'Patterns of control within Japanese manufacturing plants in China: doubts about Japanization in China', *Journal of Management Studies*, **36** (6), 853–63.

Tenzer, H., M. Pudelko and A.-W. Harzing (2014), 'The impact of language barriers on trust formation in multinational teams', *Journal of International Business Studies*, **45** (5), 508–35.

Welch, D.E. and L.S. Welch (2008), 'The importance of language in international knowledge transfer', *Management International Review*, **48** (3), 339–60.

Welch, D.E., L.S. Welch and R. Piekkari (2005), 'Speaking in tongues: the importance of language in international management processes', *International Studies of Management & Organization*, **35** (1), 10–27.

Welch, D.E., L.S. Welch and V. Worm (2007), 'The international business traveller: a neglected but strategic resource', *International Journal of Human Resource Management*, **18** (2), 173–83.

Welch, L.S., G.R.G. Benito, P.R. Silseth and T. Karlsen (2002), 'Exploring inward–outward linkages in firms' internationalisation: a knowledge and network perspective', in S. Lundan (ed.), *Network Knowledge in International Business*, Cheltenham, UK and Northampton, MA, USA: Edward Elgar, pp. 216–31.

Young, L.C. and I.F. Wilkinson (1989), 'The role of trust and cooperation in marketing channels: a preliminary study', *European Journal of Marketing*, **23** (2), 109–22.

Zellmer-Bruhn, M.E. (2003), 'Interruptive events and team knowledge acquisition', *Management Science*, **49** (4), 514–28.

5. Language and networks

I'm presently learning Spanish . . . [languages] are very significant with building relationships. I need to actually speak the language in some way. (Comment made by a decision-maker of a small UK firm seeking to expand internationally, in Knowles et al., 2006, 634)

As noted in preceding chapters, networks are an important aspect of international business. Network formation depends on a process of interpersonal interaction based on a meaningful language connection between the parties. Thus language ability is the precursor and basis for meaningful communication and interaction. This chapter examines the role that language plays in network development. We begin with a general discussion of the network concept and distinguish between different types and uses of networks. We introduce the concepts of social capital and human capital, and explore these through a language lens. In so doing, we build the concept of 'language capital'. As shown in Figure 5.1, network development flows from interpersonal interaction based on language, leading to the creation of social, human and language capital. Language shapes social dynamics and affects the quality of connections underpinning interpersonal interaction. Thus language acts as a reconstruction agent: it lubricates key processes that affect relationship development; prevents or supports the building of network connections and linkages between social clusters; and assists in the initiation and continuance of international activities.

As with language in general, the role of language has tended to be overlooked in much of the network literature. However, as our introductory example illustrates, those seeking to expand internationally are all too aware of how language ability plays an important role in accessing key networks and building relationships in the foreign market.

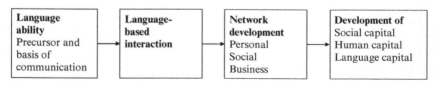

Figure 5.1   Language ability, networks and language capital

NETWORK DEVELOPMENT

Bird (1994) posits that networks are a mechanism for interaction and discourse but also a forum where information can be gathered and disseminated. Networks extend beyond the immediate and obvious connections that individuals and organizations establish. Network literature uses the term 'dyadic' to indicate connections between two parties, but there is general recognition that each party will bring other connections into the exchange relationship, creating a web of both seen and unseen connections that form the network context within which individuals and firms operate (Welch and Welch, 1996). Some connections are particularly strong due to frequent interaction, duration and reciprocity based on trust, and can therefore be readily identified. Other connections may be relatively weak due to infrequent interaction, often unseen or unknown due to immediate contacts being connected to other parties, such as 'a friend of a friend'. This makes it a challenge for anyone to accurately map the full extent of their broader network. And networks are complex webs that evolve in ways that are beyond the control of the individual, or the firm (Marschan et al., 1996).

Personal Networks

Personal networks are an important part of the overall network landscape, as Figure 5.2 suggests. They link internal company processes with those of the external social and business context. Some individuals are more adept at establishing and nurturing personal relationships due to their personality, for example, or through having the requisite language competence.

Personal networks can be separated into two categories: company-based and individual-based, as Figure 5.3 illustrates. Company-based networks comprise contacts made through work-related activities, such as interaction with external clients, government officials, former colleagues and professional bodies. These may be activated to further enable work outcomes for company purposes. In contrast, individual-based networks are the result of social interaction with former school or university colleagues, friends and relatives. These contacts may be activated for personal purposes, such as job seeking. As Figure 5.3 shows, our two categories are not mutually exclusive in terms of how personal networks are developed, activated and maintained. Individuals recognize and maintain personal networks not only for the potential benefit to themselves but also in terms of their performance within business and social contexts. Individuals access their networks in order to gain information and knowledge that they can then use in various ways: to assist in work-related situations; to expand their social connections; and for career-related purposes. These

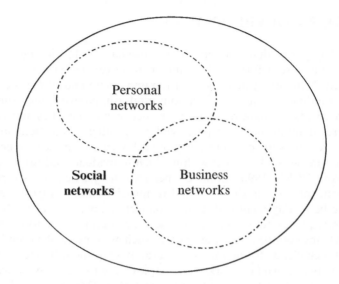

Figure 5.2   Networks as interwoven relationships

connections may have evolved out of the social and business activities on behalf of the company but they tend to develop their own life or 'trajectory' (Hallén, 1992; Marschan et al., 1996). In this regard, network contacts can 'belong' to both company-based and individual-based networks.

People are very conscious of the value of their networks and are prepared to protect them, being very selective in the way in which contacts are activated for organizational purposes (Hallén, 1992). They choose whether, how and when to use their network of contacts, another form of gatekeeping (Collins and Clark, 2003). Trust and shared norms are also considered important in motivating an individual to share their contacts (see, e.g., Young and Wilkinson, 1989; Nahapiet and Ghoshal, 1998; Heumer, 2004). On the other hand, people are often prepared to use their own networks to assist in achieving work outcomes, such as using friends and relatives to assist in translation tasks (see Chapter 2).

Social Networks

Social networks cannot be disconnected from business and personal networks, as depicted in Figure 5.2. It is useful to consider networks as interwoven relationships, encompassing or enfolding these forms. Take for example the local golf club. It is a social setting or venue that facilitates

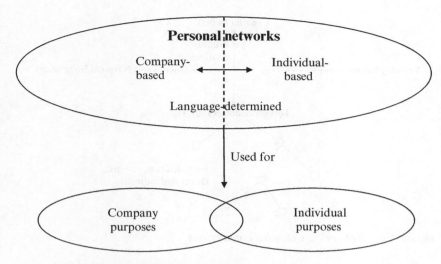

Source: Adapted from Marschan et al. (1996, 143).

Figure 5.3   The many uses of personal networks

interaction. A person may join a golf club for personal pleasure or for business reasons (e.g., entertaining clients or meeting potential business customers) or both – demonstrating the way in which the personal and business may intertwine. These possibilities all occur within the social context of the golf club, generating a set of social ties within which the personal and business elements ebb and flow. In this way, social networks can emanate from and/or respond to business and personal links.

Business Networks

Business networks are connections involving relationships between organizations and business units. Much of the research on business networks has been conducted in the area of industrial marketing and purchasing, looking at the behaviour of buyers and sellers in a business-to-business context. This approach includes an international dimension. While the initial focus was on dyadic interactions, this was later broadened to recognize that 'a single relationship cannot be understood in isolation, but only as part of a complex network of other relationships' (Ford, 2004, 140). The concept of business networks is based on three attributes: actor bonds (connections between actors in a network); activity links (technical, administrative and commercial) that may influence inter-firm

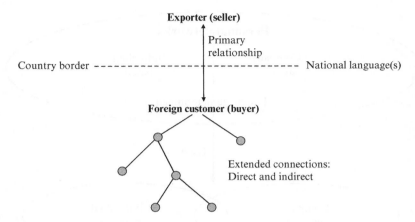

Figure 5.4   Networks: extended connections

connections; and resource ties (such as material and intangibles that result from interaction and may develop relationships that are themselves resource ties). Actor bonds require a shared language if they are to be extended beyond the superficial to become deeper, trusting and perhaps more lasting. Likewise activity links, such as meetings and negotiations between parties, are facilitated by shared language. Translation may be a linking activity. The use of a shared language may also become a resource tie. For example, an exporting firm, because of its foreign-language resources, can communicate directly with its foreign customer in that customer's language. Indeed, one could argue that language underpins all three of these network attributes.

Figure 5.4 illustrates the basic network connections in an exporting situation. The primary relationship is between the exporting company and its foreign customer (see Chapter 7 on the role of intermediaries in this relationship). The foreign customer is in turn embedded in a wider network of relationships – extended connections that may be the result of direct or indirect interactions with other local businesses in that market. As with personal networks, a company may not know the extent of its reach through the extended connections that comprise its business network.

Research has also stressed the dynamic process of network development and relationship building through and beyond the exporting activity itself. This is exemplified in a study of an Australian export grouping scheme involving small firms with operations in Japan. It revealed how one family-owned firm organized for a son to spend a year living with the family of a key actor in the firm's distribution network while simultaneously learning Japanese. This deliberate exercise was directed towards network devel-

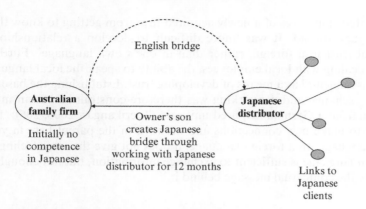

English bridge

Australian family firm

Initially no competence in Japanese

Owner's son creates Japanese bridge through working with Japanese distributor for 12 months

Japanese distributor

Links to Japanese clients

Figure 5.5   Language in network development

opment within the Japanese market, as there was no Japanese language competence within the Australian firm and English had been the initial medium of connection (Welch et al., 1996). Figure 5.5 illustrates how the development of a Japanese language bridge provided an entree into a broader Japanese network that fanned out from the Japanese distributor. This opened up an important market development. Compared to the use of English as a bridge, personal contacts could now be made directly with individuals and firms without the intermediary, which shortened the perceived distance between the two firms.

Within multinational firms, inter-unit information flow and network relations between workers are similarly constrained by 'geographical distances and cultural and language barriers' (Kostova and Roth, 2003, 309). Research into relationships between headquarters and subsidiary units has identified how some units become isolated from the internal knowledge-sharing network due to language problems (see Chapter 4). For example, in their study of Swedish multinationals, Monteiro et al. (2008, 104) use the example of a German subsidiary where 'the German boss was not confident in English, so he never participated in the informal discussion that led to knowledge sharing. The solution was simply to put a proficient English-speaker in place as the deputy to the German boss.' As Marschan's (1996) KONE study showed, facility in English did not extend very far in some of its subsidiaries.

Cross-border mergers and acquisitions (M&As) are another arena where language effects inhibit or facilitate integration and the development of networks. For example, Teerikangas (2006, 204), in her study of French, German, Danish, UK and American cross-border acquisitions undertaken by Finnish multinationals, found that language barriers prevented employees of a newly acquired firm from getting to know their colleagues abroad. It was 'more difficult to develop a relationship of mutual trust in a foreign, rather than in one's own language'. Further, when dealing with local employees, the ability to speak the local language was instrumental as a means of developing trust. Establishing the base for social exchange and networking was therefore constrained. As an interviewee from a German acquired unit said (Teerikangas, 2006, 206): 'It is easier to make new connections and network in the parent firm in your own language. In a foreign language, it does not give the same feeling. A foreign language is sufficient to exchange information, but not enough to convey the contextual message behind it.'

LANGUAGE AND SOCIAL CLUSTERS

The impact of language on network development is further accentuated by the role it plays in the formation and operation of social clusters, a feature of social systems and network evolution. Language assists in forming social ties, and therein acceptance, in a social cluster. Language can be viewed as a drawbridge whereby actors in a social cluster choose to lower it to include those who share the language. Language codes have long been used in secret societies to exclude outsiders (the drawbridge raised to firmly exclude them). Thus language deficiency may keep people apart, limit their access to social networks, or lock them into a social cluster. An example is the way in which migrant women may be confined to an ethnic-based circle of relatives and friends due to a lack of the requisite local language, thus isolating them from the broader community.

A related aspect is the similarity factor that underpins social networks (Mäkelä et al., 2007). A connection is more likely to occur between similar rather than dissimilar people, so-called homophily: the 'tendency to associate with people "like" yourself' (Watts, 1999, 13). The concept of homophily has received extensive support in work within the social networks area. Its central idea, as argued by McPherson et al. (2001), is that interpersonal similarity breeds connection, and language is a component of similarity between individuals.

Individuals as Language Bridges between Social Clusters

An argument within social network theory is that 'information regarding new ideas and opportunities disseminates through bridge ties that link people in separate social clusters' (Ellis and Pecotich, 2001, 120). Individuals may act as bridge-builders between social clusters. For instance, an Australian manager in KONE's Hong Kong subsidiary commented: 'They [at headquarters] sent a guy ... as a technical director, a Finn ... He helped me to build an informal communication network within the organisation.' Goodall and Roberts (2003) found that expatriates competent in the common corporate language (CCL) formed an expatriate network – a social cluster that excluded local employees who lacked such language competence. At the same time, expatriates who lacked competence in the host country's language were restricted in their access to a variety of local social/business networks. Expatriates and locals that had relevant language competence (both company and local) were key bridge-builders. Naturally, there is no certainty about whether such individuals are prepared to act as bridges, to play a boundary spanning or gatekeeping role.

Figure 5.6 illustrates two social clusters with different languages, for example a Portuguese social cluster, and a Danish social cluster. Person B is the CEO of a small Portuguese winery and seeks to enter the Danish market. Person A has been identified as a possible contact in a Danish importing firm. Neither speaks each other's language but both are able to function in English, which becomes the language 'bridge'. Over time, this shared language enables the development of connections and interactions between the clusters. Others in the Danish social cluster associated with the importing firm may hear about opportunities in the Portuguese market through A's contact with B. Likewise, in the Portuguese social cluster, Person B can become the language bridge for other Portuguese firms desirous of entering the Danish market, using B's connections in the Danish social cluster.

Beyond that initial connection, however, it is unclear how further

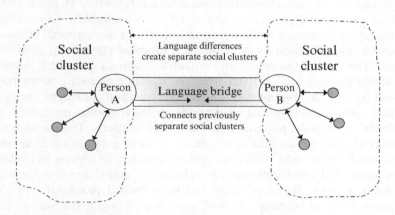

Figure 5.6   Language creates and bridges social clusters

connections might unfold, between whom and even what language will be employed. Language ability, then, is a necessary but not a sufficient condition for inclusion in a social cluster or to act as a bridge between clusters. Language bridges can be built from either side. They do not necessarily require dual language facility on both sides, but one party has to be able to cross the language bridge.

Little is known about the dynamics generated by language processes within social clusters once language has acted as a bridging mechanism between individuals from different social clusters. Motivation is an important aspect of this, along with common experiences. Through what Portes (1998) terms 'shared destiny', in social interactions within the cluster, Person A (in Figure 5.6) may bring to bear pressure on others to learn the bridging language. Accompanying this, from a business point of view, may be a demonstration effect. If the bridging activity has led to the opening or potential opening of new business in another country, there may be direct organizational pressure for others to develop requisite language competence in order to further the business opportunity. The end result will be various modifications and reshaping of the connections within each cluster as well as between the clusters.

Social Capital

There are various definitions of the concept of social capital, as the following samples indicate: the sum of an individual's personal networks (Belliveau et al., 1996); the private good of an individual or group (Burt, 1992; Lin, 2001; Kostova and Roth, 2003); a process 'by which social actors create and mobilize their network connections within and between organizations to gain access other social actors' resources' (Knoke, 1999, 18); or a public, collective asset of a social entity available to all members of the group (Coleman, 1988; Fukuyama, 2001). In international business research, the definition by Nahapiet and Ghoshal (1998, 243) is widely used: 'The sum of the actual and potential resources embedded within, available through, and derived from the network of relationships possessed by an individual or social unit.' The common consensus, though, is that social capital formation depends on interpersonal interaction in order to develop the required network of relationships. The research on industrial networks and the development of the concept of social capital have much in common. There are similar objectives in seeking to explain how social and organizational networks evolve and shape international business activity. However, there has been limited recognition of the important role of language. In both schools of thought, the 'sum of the parts' has been the focus. Social network theory stresses the collective:

the organization. For example, Nahapiet and Ghoshal (1998) are concerned with how social capital contributes to organizational competitive advantage. Industrial network theory has tended to emphasize the firm, rather than individual actors – that is, considering business rather than individual networks (see, e.g., Håkansson, 1986; Ford, 2004).

In their review of social capital literature, Adler and Kwon (2002) identify two research branches, bridging (structural connectedness) and bonding (relational closeness). It is worth taking a brief look at these two, using Adler and Kwon's review as a starting point.

Bridging

This branch of research concentrates on the formal structure of a network within which the network actor is located. Network mapping, or sociograms, are used to show patterns of interconnectedness – who is connected to whom. Of interest is whether the network is closed or open (that is, the extent to which actors' contacts are themselves connected – see Coleman, 1988), and the role of trust in determining the strength of the social capital benefits that accrue to network members from this connectivity. Structuralists also consider disconnections between networks, referred to as structural holes. For example, Burt (1997, 340–41) explains that disconnected people 'stand on the opposite sides of a hole in a social structure' and that the hole acts as a buffer 'like an insulator in an electric circuit'. Information may circulate among the various members in a particular network to the extent that sources become redundant. However, accessing another network has additive rather than redundant effects, allowing new information to cross the hole. Our concept of language nodes explained in Chapter 3 is an example of how individuals act as bridge-builders, gleaning new information through their networks, creating links between the various parts of the internationalizing firm and its diverse external stakeholders. We return to this aspect in a later section of this chapter.

Bonding

The emphasis in this stream of research focuses on the relationship – such as the strength of the network relationship, its nature (friendship versus business) and the use of networks for different purposes. Granovetter (1973, 1361) is associated with work on relationship strength through his investigation into the use of personal contacts or networks in job seeking. He made the observation that people tended to cluster into close-knit networks; that is, they formed what he termed strong ties. The strength of an interpersonal tie is defined as 'a combination of the amount of time, the emotional intensity, the intimacy (mutual confiding), and the reciprocal services which characterize the tie'. Strong relationships are regarded as assisting the transfer of complex knowledge, as the more frequent the interaction, or the more relational parties are emotionally attached, the more likely information and knowledge is shared (Reagans and McEvily, 2003). Weak but more extensive relationships, however, can assist in providing non-redundant information (Bartol and Zhang, 2007).

The ability to develop strong relationships, and ultimately social capital, is of course language-dependent. Indeed, it is difficult to imagine strong relationships evolving when there is no shared language between the parties involved. Further, networks research has shown the link between the strength of a relationship and trust between network parties. A shared language is thus critical to relationship evolution and the development of trust within the internationalizing firm. A study of 310 inter-unit relationships within Chinese and Finnish subsidiaries revealed that 'language fluency related significantly with shared vision and perceived trustworthiness' (Barner-Rasmussen and Björkman, 2007, 105). This interaction is shown in Figure 5.7. A basic vocabulary or the use of a translator will contribute to relationship development only to a limited extent. The ability to interact in a meaningful way will vary according to the level of shared language fluency between the parties, as Figure 5.7 illustrates. Even with low levels of fluency, relationships may be built, but again the degree to which these will produce a level of trust that facilitates a deeper exchange of information is limited. With situations involving more complicated or confidential information and knowledge, higher levels of fluency will normally be required. It is hard to build a strong, trusting relationship via language intermediaries such as translators.

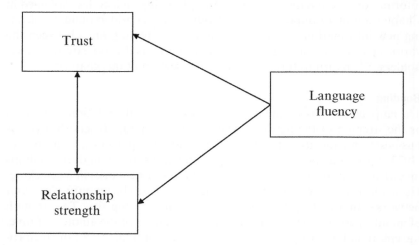

Figure 5.7   Language fluency and development of relationships

One of the more influential articles in the international context straddles both branches of social capital. Nahapiet and Ghoshal (1998, 244) look at both the structure of network relationships and their content through three categories: structural (the configuration of linkages between people or units); relational (the kind of personal relationships people develop with each other through interaction over time); and cognitive (shared representation, interpretations and systems of meaning). The cognitive dimension includes aspects such as shared codes and language and shared narratives. In this work, shared language enhances access to people and information, and the development of knowledge and thereby social capital. Our analysis suggests that language affects all components of social capital, that is, the structural, relational and cognitive, as well as the interaction between these three dimensions. However, there is little examination of how shared language affects interaction among and within the three dimensions. Likewise, there is scant attention to how shared language shifts from the individual to the collective social domain, and vice versa. There is, however, some recognition that the motivation to develop social capital and then share it as a public or organizational good rests with the individual (Adler and Kwon, 2002).

Human Capital

It is important to distinguish between social capital and human capital – two concepts that are somewhat intertwined. Burt (1997, 339) makes this clear when he comments that 'social capital is a quality created *between* people, whereas human capital is a quality *of* individuals [our emphasis]'. Human capital is commonly defined as an individual's set of knowledge, skills and abilities acquired through education and experience. The important aspect here is that organizations do not own human capital: it 'walks out the door' each night (Youndt et al., 2004). However, through the employment process, an organization creates its human capital pool. Further, activities such as company-based training influence the quality of this resource as well as being a mechanism to retain desired employees (see Chapter 6). In this sense, organizational human capital is generally considered as the combined sum of its individuals' human capital (Wright et al., 2001). The dilemma is that individuals own their human capital. They decide whether to invest in their human capital based on perceived as well as actual costs and benefits. For instance, to make the time and effort required to learn a language may be weighed against likely outcomes, such as promotion with monetary reward. Like companies, people seek a return on their investment and will protect and trade their human capital for personal gain. To use terms from economics, organizations only rent their

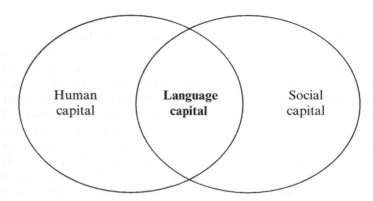

Figure 5.8   The concept of language capital

human capital and individuals can be very adept in privatizing the gains in the interest of self-advancement while socializing the costs in terms of benefiting from societal-provided education, company-provided training and the like.

From our perspective, language ability is an intrinsic part of human capital, and it is also difficult to separate it from an individual's social capital. It is an active agent in the interaction process between human and social capital – see Figure 5.8. We use the term 'language capital' to signify how language can be regarded as a unique resource that increases an individual's stock of human capital. Organizational language capital may be seen as the pool of language capability upon which the organization can draw. Of course, language capital is not confined to individuals, in that part of organizational language capital is codified in its various procedures and systems, such as corporate specific jargon and machine translation programs.

Given that language capital is interwoven with human capital, individuals may decide whether to indicate language fluency on recruitment or redeployment; whether to attend language classes in order to develop their language capital; or to actively employ their language capital for the benefit of the employing organization. Language ability also delivers the potential for wider interpersonal interaction to build social capital. However, one should not automatically assume that language ability necessarily translates into willingness to use this language at the workplace. People can be quite instrumental, actively 'structuring their social networks to achieve their goals' (Ibarra, 1995, 677). The resultant tacit and explicit knowledge gained through networking builds their stock of human capital (Luthans and Youssef, 2004).

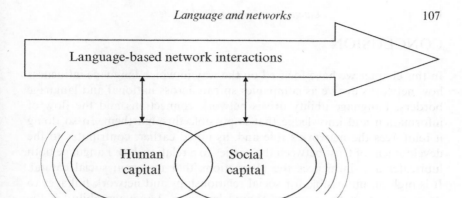

Figure 5.9   Language and the development of human and social capital

The active, continuing role of language in social and human capital development is further illustrated in Figure 5.9. Both human and social capital are constantly changing over time as learning occurs. Language acquisition allows access to other actors in the network, or entry into other networks, thus expanding social capital. Similarly, network interactions may facilitate human capital development through the encouragement to become more fluent in the requisite language, facilitating the deepening of social relationships and hence trust. The double-headed arrows in Figure 5.9 depict this dynamic process. The more language-fluent an individual becomes through interaction with other network actors, the more likely human and social capital will increase. This contributes to the incentive to at least maintain language fluency and may be the catalyst to learn additional languages, thus adding to language capital.

A study of language issues for Finnish firms operating in Russia (Bloigu, 2008) highlights the importance of interpersonal relations in conducting business with Russian counterparts, as well as the overwhelming need for that business to be conducted in the Russian language. This requirement created pressure on Finnish firms to either provide language training for Finnish employees or to hire Russians and, where necessary, provide them with English or Finnish lessons. This effectively added to Finnish firms' stocks of language capital. To the extent that this was successful, it enabled Finnish firms to build social capital through enhanced engagement within the Russian business community, as Figure 5.9 suggests.

The above discussion has highlighted how language affects the process of network development and maintenance: acting as a precursor to international connections; a bridge between social clusters; and the basis of continuing interaction. Thus language affects the shape, structure and content of social, business and personal networks.

CONCLUSION

In this chapter we have focused on the way in which language influences how networks evolve as companies spread across national and language borders. Language ability drives network connections and the flow of information and knowledge that is possible through them. In so doing it reinforces the network's role and, as noted earlier, contributes to the development of trust between the parties to a relationship. Language both lubricates and influences the interactions that underpin social capital. It is nigh on impossible for social relationships and network linkages to develop without the requisite shared language. Language ability is the precursor: it shapes international business interactions and is the basis for the unfolding connections. It not only opens the door to the development of social capital, but exerts a continuing influence on the direction and character of unfolding relations.

Language frames the nature of contact between individuals, regardless of whether the context is the internal work situation within an internationalizing firm or with external parties, such as customers/clients and government agencies or in non-business social situations. The ensuing networks are used as communication channels and thus influence the movement of information and knowledge in international business exchanges, a critical part of company viability. For instance, Goodall and Roberts (2003, 162) found that internal language-based expatriate networks enabled swift and efficient responses between the Chinese and Colombian units of a European oil company: 'Local staff don't have the right languages [English and corporate speak] . . . It is much easier, quicker, and productive therefore, to talk to another expatriate'. Access to network-based information is not always constrained to direct work-related issues. Farh et al. (2010) posit that social networks may be tapped to assist in expatriate cultural adjustment, though there is only fleeting reference to how the lack of language competence may constrain access to local networks, and to broader organizational networks.

The general neglect in the international business and management literature of the role of language in the development of social capital, human capital and networks is surprising. After all, in the international context, in many situations, language is the supreme arbiter of the nature, quality and dynamics of network development that form social capital. In general, though, the concentration on connections between organizations or business units has meant that people, the heart of social networks, have tended to be downplayed, particularly in terms of basic individual capabilities such as language competence.

REFERENCES

Adler, P.S. and S.-W. Kwon (2002), 'Social capital: prospects for a new concept', *Academy of Management Review*, **27** (1), 17–40.

Barner-Rasmussen, W. and I. Björkman (2007), 'Language fluency, socialization and inter-unit relationships in Chinese and Finnish subsidiaries', *Management and Organization Review*, **3** (1), 105–28.

Bartol, K.M. and X. Zhang (2007), 'Networks and leadership development: building linkages for capacity acquisition and capital accrual', *Human Resource Management Review*, **17** (4), 388–401.

Belliveau, M.A., C.A. O'Reilly III and J.B. Wade (1996), 'Social capital at the top: effects of social similarity and status on CEO compensation', *Academy of Management Journal*, **39** (6), 1568–93.

Bird, A. (1994), 'Careers as repositories of knowledge: a new perspective on boundaryless careers', *Journal of Organizational Behavior*, **15** (4), 325–44.

Bloigu, K. (2008), *Russian or English? Examining the Role and Importance of the Russian Language in the Russian Business of Finnish Companies*, Master's Thesis, Helsinki: Helsinki School of Economics.

Burt, R.S. (1992), *Structural Holes: The Social Structure of Competition*, Cambridge, MA: Harvard University Press.

Burt, R.S. (1997), 'The contingent value of social capital', *Administrative Science Quarterly*, **42** (2), 339–65.

Coleman, J.S. (1988), 'Social capital in the creation of human capital', *American Journal of Sociology*, **94** (Supplement), S95–S120.

Collins, C.J. and K.D. Clark (2003), 'Strategic human resource practices, top management team social networks, and firm performance: the role of human resource practices in creating organizational competitive advantage', *Academy of Management Journal*, **46** (6), 740–51.

Ellis, P. and A. Pecotich (2001), 'Social factors influencing export initiation in small and medium-sized enterprises', *Journal of Marketing Research*, **38** (1), 119–30.

Farh, C.I.C., K.M. Bartol, D.L. Shapiro and J. Shin (2010), 'Networking abroad: a process model of how expatriates form support ties to facilitate adjustment', *Academy of Management Review*, **35** (3), 434–54.

Ford, D. (2004), 'The IMP Group and international marketing', *International Marketing Review*, **21** (2), 139–41.

Fukuyama, F. (2001), 'Social capital, civil society and development', *Third World Quarterly*, **22** (1), 7–20.

Goodall, K. and J. Roberts (2003), 'Only connect: teamwork in the multinational', *Journal of World Business*, **38** (2), 150–64.

Granovetter, M.S. (1973), 'The strength of weak ties', *American Journal of Sociology*, **78** (6), 1360–80.

Hallén, L. (1992), 'Infrastructural networks in international business', in M. Forsgren and J. Johanson (eds), *Managing Networks in International Business*, Philadelphia, PA: Gordon and Breach, pp. 77–92.

Heumer, L. (2004), 'Activating trust: the redefinition of roles and relationships in an international construction project', *International Marketing Review*, **21** (2), 187–201.

Håkansson, H. (1986), 'The Swedish approach to Europe', in P.W. Turnbull and

J.-P. Valla (eds), *Strategies for International Industrial Marketing*, London: Croom Helm, pp. 127–64.

Ibarra, H. (1995), 'Race, opportunity, and diversity of social circles in managerial networks', *Academy of Management Journal*, **38** (3), 673–703.

Knoke, D. (1999), 'Organizational networks and corporate social capital', in R.Th.A.J. Leenders and S.M. Gabbay (eds), *Corporate Social Capital and Liability*, Boston, MA: Kluwer, pp. 17–42.

Knowles, D., T. Mughan and L. Lloyd-Reason (2006), 'Foreign language use among decision-makers of successfully internationalized SMEs', *Journal of Small Business and Enterprise Development*, **13** (4), 620–41.

Kostova, T. and K. Roth (2003), 'Social capital in multinational corporations and a micro–macro model of its formation', *Academy of Management Review*, **28** (2), 297–317.

Lin, N. (2001), *Social Capital: A Theory of Social Structure and Action*, Cambridge: Cambridge University Press.

Luthans, F. and C.M. Youssef (2004), 'Human, social and now positive psychological capital management: investing in people for competitive advantage', *Organizational Dynamics*, **33** (2), 143–60.

Marschan, R. (1996), *New Structural Forms and Inter-Unit Communication in Multinationals: The Case of KONE Elevators*, Doctoral Thesis A-110, Helsinki: Helsinki School of Economics.

Marschan, R., D.E. Welch and L.S. Welch (1996), 'Control in less-hierarchical MNC structures: the role of personal networks and informal communication', *International Business Review*, **5** (2), 137–50.

McPherson, J.M., L. Smith-Lovin and J.M. Cook (2001), 'Birds of a feather: homophily in social networks', *Annual Review of Sociology*, **27**, 415–44.

Monteiro, F., N. Arvidsson and J. Birkinshaw (2008), 'Knowledge flows within multinational corporations: explaining subsidiary isolation and its performance implications', *Organization Science*, **19** (1), 90–107.

Mäkelä, K., H. Kalla and R. Piekkari (2007), 'Interpersonal similarity as a driver of knowledge sharing in multinational corporations', *International Business Review*, **16** (1), 1–22.

Nahapiet, J. and S. Ghoshal (1998), 'Social capital, intellectual capital, and the organizational advantage', *Academy of Management Review*, **23** (2), 242–66.

Portes, A. (1998), 'Social capital: its origins and applications in modern sociology', *Annual Review of Sociology*, **24**, 1–24.

Reagans, R. and B. McEvily (2003), 'Network structure and knowledge transfer: the effects of cohesion and range', *Administrative Science Quarterly*, **48** (2), 240–76.

Teerikangas, S. (2006), *Silent Forces in Cross-border Acquisitions: An Integrative Perspective on Post-acquisition Integration*, Doctoral Thesis Series 2006/1, Helsinki: Helsinki University of Technology.

Watts, D.J. (1999), 'Networks, dynamics, and the small-world phenomenon', *American Journal of Sociology*, **105** (2), 493–527.

Welch, D.E. and L.S. Welch (1996), 'The internationalization process and networks: a strategic management perspective', *Journal of International Marketing*, **4** (3), 11–28.

Welch, D.E., L.S. Welch, I.F. Wilkinson and L.C. Young (1996), 'Network analysis of a new export grouping scheme: the role of economic and non-economic relations', *International Journal of Research in Marketing*, **13** (5), 463–77.

Wright, P.M., B.B. Dunford and S.A. Snell (2001), 'Human resources and the resource based view of the firm', *Journal of Management*, **27** (6), 701–21.
Youndt, M.A., M. Subramaniam and S.A. Snell (2004), 'Intellectual capital profiles: an examination of investments and returns', *Journal of Management Studies*, **41** (2), 335–61.
Young, L.C. and I.F. Wilkinson (1989), 'The role of trust and cooperation in marketing channels: a preliminary study', *European Journal of Marketing*, **23** (2), 109–22.

6.　Language and human resource management

This chapter is concerned with the human resource management (HRM) aspects of language within the internationalizing firm. For readers less familiar with HRM, the HR department is the functional area usually delegated responsibility for managing the activities relating to employees – what used to be called personnel management. Starting in the USA in the early 1980s, the term 'human resource management' gradually replaced 'personnel' as the HR profession sought a more strategic role, arguing that people management should be regarded as an integral part of organizational decision-making. The use of the term human resource management has now become almost universal.

Traditionally, the HR function is concerned with activities such as recruitment, selection, training and career pathing, health and safety; and ensuring that the firm adheres to legal obligations pertaining to employment (what some HR authors refer to as the policing role; see, for example, Ulrich, 1997). Often, HR managers handle the retrenchment of employees due to managerial actions such as plant closure, or as a result of a merger/acquisition. In addition, the HR department may be involved in developing a code of ethical conduct as part of the firm's approach to corporate social responsibility to all its stakeholders.

An aspect worth noting is HR's low status – as a profession and as an organizational functional area. Caldwell (2008, 277) cites many reasons for this. By its very nature, managing human resources crosses functional boundaries. It is an activity not confined to the HR department. Because others in the firm are also involved in people management, HR expertise is seen as substitutable. This was exemplified in the 1990s when it was popular in Western multinationals to devolve responsibility for much of what had been the domain of the HR department to line management, who had their own ideas of how to manage their employees (Farndale and Brewster, 2005). Several of what could be seen as key HR activities (such as recruitment and payroll) are routinely outsourced to external providers. Caldwell (2008, 277) considers that such a blurring of responsibility has led to 'unclear accountabilities and performance measures, and invariably problematic dependence on line managers for delivery' of HR activities.

Those in the HR department may be held accountable, or assigned blame, for negative outcomes, such as a business unit's high employee turnover due to poor line management, whereas 'line managers who invest in projects with a low return on investment (a financial measure) do not get to blame finance for their poor decisions' (Lewis and Heckman, 2006, 152). Strauss (2001) argues that, compared to other functional areas, HR is more susceptible to the whims of managerial fads. Indicative of its overall low standing is the fact that there has been limited research into the effects of the firm's international growth on the HR function (Stiles, 2012) and people management more generally. Taken together, these various aspects reduce the capacity of those within the HR department to have a strong voice.

Early work in international business indicated that the two functions most likely to be localized in foreign operations were marketing (see Chapter 7) and HRM due to a perceived need for local responsiveness and sensitivity. HR policies tend to be localized as firms are required to comply with government and legal dictates related to employment contracts, hiring and firing, occupational health and safety requirements, training, and performance evaluation procedures. There are also regional aspects such as the European Union Directives that affect how HR is conducted. Localization is also a major driver in approaches to staffing foreign units and it is common to see locals (that is, host country nationals) employed in the HR department of the various subsidiaries. For example, in a study of Finnish companies operating in Russia, respondents stressed the importance of having locals as HR managers. Language skills were a major factor in this decision (Bloigu, 2008).

However, as we discussed in Chapters 3 and 4, the internationalizing firm requires a degree of standardization to facilitate the transfer of work procedures and practices for consistency of output, and to assist in staff deployment around its various departments and subsidiary units. How this duality is resolved, of course, is influenced by its home country's approach to people management and the degree to which it is constrained in integrating policies and procedures by national requirements in each of its foreign markets.[1] There is emerging evidence, though, that national differences are becoming less pronounced due to the influence of management education (see, for example, executive MBA courses, Tietze, 2004) and cross-border employee training programmes. The transfer of HR 'best practices' by global organizations to their local units, alliance partners, local suppliers and contractors also further universalizes approaches to people management. Competition for skilled employees is a driver here. It is against this backdrop that we begin our discussion of how HRM is influenced by and influences language.

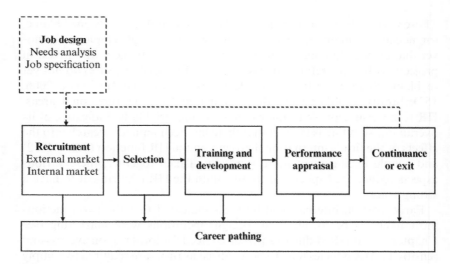

Figure 6.1   The employment process

THE EMPLOYMENT PROCESS AND LANGUAGE

Our starting point is the typical employment process that a company may follow when building and maintaining its pool of human capital.[2] As shown in Figure 6.1, this process involves several stages all aimed at attracting, utilizing and retaining suitably skilled employees so that the firm has the right people in the right place at the right time. It should also be recognized that, while the employment process is somewhat universal, how it is implemented will vary across cultures, industry sectors and companies.

Job Design

We use a dotted box in Figure 6.1 to indicate that aspects related to job design are behind the scene, a back-office activity. It is therefore somewhat opaque as for most new hires the interface with a firm begins with the recruitment process. Job design involves detailing the requirements of the position as well as the characteristics and skills of the potential incumbent. The needs analysis step of job design is an important part of forecasting future requirements, linking the employment process to intended strategic changes, succession planning and employee development. It can also be a formal justification as to why a new hire is warranted.

The purpose of a job description is to specify work duties and responsibilities of the position, the compensation level and related terms and conditions of employment. For example, in Fazer Group, a leading bakery and confectionary company in the Baltic region, individuals recruited to international roles, particularly at senior management levels, need to be able to understand, speak and produce text in English. These requirements are stipulated in Fazer's language policy. A job description forms the basis of the recruitment and selection process, as well as being used later for performance assessment in some cases. People may fall back on the job description to explain work behaviour. As we note in Chapter 2, employees could justify why requests for translation were rejected on the grounds that they were not part of their job description. This stage of the employment process may be mandated by company policy, with appropriate procedural input from HR to ensure that the internationalizing firm complies with local laws pertaining to aspects such as minimum wage and employment conditions. In some instances, the job description may be written in the common corporate language (CCL). The Swedish bank, Handelsbanken, for example, requires that all job descriptions be written in Swedish, its corporate language (Muukari, 2008).

Underscoring the opaque nature of this step in the process is the fact that the HR department is often reduced to an advisory role. The decision to hire typically falls within the domain of senior and line management. As we have already discussed, individual line managers in the various units may intervene and dilute or even ignore HR policy directives regarding language (see Chapter 3). They may not include relevant language skills in the specification of a particular job, sometimes contrary to company procedures and/or policies.

Recruitment

Searching for and attracting potential candidates is the major task of the recruitment process. As indicated in Figure 6.1, firms can seek potential employees from the external market, competing with other firms for the desired candidates. This approach to recruitment is referred to as 'buying in'. There is an expectation that the relevant employment market will provide the required candidates, and access to a suitable pool of employees can be a factor in top management decisions concerning where to locate a foreign subsidiary. Buying in is seen as a cost saving strategy that does not appear to be related to firm size. For instance, Crick's (1999) study of UK exporting firms reported no statistical difference between the various-sized firms surveyed in terms of their intent to externally recruit new employees with language skills. The ELAN (CILT, 2006, 28) study found that 22 per cent of surveyed European firms were recruiting native speakers with foreign-language skills. Comments from respondents include: 'We pay attention to language skills in personnel selection'; 'We must take language skills into consideration all the time. It is important in the recruitment process.' A follow-up study of 40 EU firms that were included in the ELAN study confirms the continued stress on foreign-language skills when recruiting staff. While competence in English was the primary skill, successful hires had to also have competence in at least one other language (Hagen, 2011).

Alternatively, as Figure 6.1 shows, an organization may take a build approach, using its internal job market (that is, drawing from its exist-ing employees). This is often linked to career progression, management development, or as a way of retaining key employees. Of course, any search can cast a wide net, attempting to attract both internal and external prospects – that is, simultaneously using buying in and building options.[3]

Internal job advertisements nowadays tend to be posted on intranet sites. Our early work in KONE identified the posting of internal vacancies in the CCL rather than the local subsidiary language as an impediment to those in subsidiary units not fluent in the CCL (Marschan-Piekkari et al., 1999). Such a policy may have inadvertently excluded potential candidates. We take up this point later when discussing training and development and career pathing. The language competence requirement can be stipulated in the relevant job advertisement. Muukari (2008) analysed the internal job advertisements in Handelsbanken and provides many examples of how language was included. Words such as a 'must', a 'plus' and an 'advantage' were used. A study by Peel and Eckart (1997, 40) of Welsh exporting firms found a difference between small and large firms. Larger firms in their sample placed a higher proportion of job advertisements stipulating 'that foreign language skills were required' than did their smaller counterparts.

When dealing with the external market, the recruitment stage is often the first connection potential employees have with an organization. How it handles the search and hiring process can affect its reputation and therefore its ability to attract the desired candidates in the present as well as in the future. While it might not be widely acknowledged, recruitment is linked to corporate branding as potential employers. Job searching is a two-way process: organizations seek appropriate candidates, and indi-viduals look for employment that matches their aspirations and skills. The new generation of employees, generation Y and Z, has been characterized as hard to please when it comes to selecting the ideal employer (Tapscott, 2009; Tienari and Piekkari, 2011).

Stipulating a foreign language as a requirement can have a signal-ling effect. It indicates that the position will entail, at some point if not immediately, globally oriented work, even an international assignment.

This may be a selling point for some potential candidates. The German multinational, Siemens, though its corporate language is English, is able to attract bilingual candidates who are also fluent in German (Fredriksson, 2005). Similarly, Sørensen (2005), in his preface, cites a Danish managing director explaining that having English as the corporate language signalled 'it is an international corporation capable of carrying out global activities'. The signalling effect of language requirements extends to a broader group of stakeholders, as illustrated by the results of a Finnish study of SMEs. Some participants reported that stressing language requirements when recruiting in the foreign market sent an important signal to external clients, suppliers and customers as well as to the local job market (Pohjanen-Bernardi and Talja, 2011).

Acquiring a requisite level of fluency in any foreign language requires considerable time, cost and effort. Those with requisite language capabilities are likely to be attracted to situations that would allow a return on that investment. Indeed, in her study of the Swedish bank, Handelsbanken, Muukari (2008) reports that, for some interviewees, the attraction was the opportunity to work where their language skills would be appreciated. In her multiple case study of Austrian and Danish multinationals, Bellak (2014) found a similar reaction among Danish and Austrian interviewees. Koho's (2007) study of the role of language skills in the recruitment of university graduates in the Finnish job market shows that there is a wide gulf between what is communicated at the recruitment stage and what is the real use and benefit of language skills. Koho interviewed HR professionals and key individuals who were responsible for recruitment in five large industrial companies and two consultancies based in Finland. Although a broad range of language skills is appreciated and valued, in practice only English skills are necessary in order to thrive in these multinational corporations. The benefit of the mastery of other languages such as French, Spanish and German was considered as relatively minor. Koho reports that only those working in close contact with foreign customers found it useful to be able to communicate in the customer language. Of course, foreign language skills may be a way of differentiating oneself from other candidates in a tight labour market, even if the internationalizing firm does not specifically stress this in the recruitment process.

Apart from attracting external candidates, emphasizing language requirements as part of recruitment also can have a signalling effect within the internal job market. For example, based on their study of English-language proficiency in Japanese companies, Yamao and Sekiguchi (2014) suggest that emphasizing foreign languages during recruitment and promotion signals the globalization intent of the company and can act as a way to enhance employee commitment to its globalization goals.

Likewise, the stress on languages was considered justified by interviewees in Lahtinen's (2000) study of the Finnish multinational, Wärtsilä, and its Italian subsidiary. Those working in the Italian design and service departments were expected to be in contact with co-workers in other subsidiary units and therefore English (the corporate language) was not a 'must' but rather a 'standard' requirement. Finnish expatriates in this study debated as to whether they should only speak English at work in order to help Italian co-workers to improve their English language skills and so have an enhanced opportunity for other positions within Wärtsilä.

Various media are involved in advertising job vacancies, but it is well recognized that a powerful recruiting agent is word of mouth. Regardless of the medium used, the stress on language can have a downside. A person may not apply for a position due to a perceived lack of language competence and hence deselect him/herself. To overcome this, during recruitment, the job advertisement can indicate language fluency as a 'desired' rather than 'requisite' skill, with the intention to attract candidates who may see the position as a chance to improve their language fluency, or provide some leeway for the organization to hire suitably skilled employees who are willing to learn the requisite language or improve their level of fluency, thus enlarging the pool of potential candidates. The challenge is to balance language requirements with technical skills, competence and relevant work experience so that job-related performance needs are met. As Sulonen (2011) found in her Quebec study, language needs were position-dependent: subsidiary managerial positions and front-line staff who were expected to interact with customers were examples where bilingual competencies were considered essential for job performance.

The recruitment process is resource intensive. If the firm does not localize the HR function, outsourcing may assist in ensuring compliance with local employment laws and hiring customs. External service providers such as recruitment agencies and headhunting firms can handle the recruitment process, and supposedly free up HR professionals' time so that they can attend to more strategic issues. In reality, the time taken to select the suitable external provider of such services and establish a working relationship may negate any time savings. Outsourcing of recruitment is often seen as a direct cost-saving strategy but may come at the expense of employing the most appropriately qualified person for the position. That is, placing what is a critical activity in the hands of external agents may be a false economy (Heikkonen, 2012). Moreover, successful outsourcing requires monitoring to ensure that the search process is adequately handled and that candidates are screened appropriately. The HR department may assume this monitoring role, again negating cost savings.

Selection

As Figure 6.1 shows, recruitment is followed by selection, which involves gathering the data to assist in making hiring decisions. The job specification usually is the guide to matching the person to the job. The common practice is to perform an initial screening process to compile a short-list of potential candidates. These individuals may be interviewed by the employing manager, or by a specially convened committee with limited if any involvement of HR staff.

Employer branding is a factor. How the process is conducted can influence acceptance decisions by those being offered the job, as well as having a negative impact on the company image if notification of unsuccessful applicants is handled badly. Intangible aspects such as loss of managerial control, company reputation and the nature of the specific position need to be weighed against cost savings. For these reasons, companies are less likely to leave the selection process and final decision in the hands of an external service provider.

Accepting a candidate who appears to have the required attributes and skills, but who later fails to meet expectations, is referred to as a false positive selection decision. This can include selecting a person on the grounds of 'organization cultural fit' (looking for malleable clones) rather than on job-related criteria. Conversely, rejecting a candidate who would have actually performed well is a false negative selection decision. In other words, selection is an imprecise activity, with a subjective bias despite objective intentions.[4] Of course, the process is culturally bound with distinct national variations. For managers in multinationals, behavioural variations during interviews, for example, may complicate the hiring decision when dealing with foreign applicants.

If language capability is a required attribute, interviews may be conducted in the relevant language as a way of gauging fluency. Koho's (2007) study of six Finnish-based companies referred to above found that recruiters would always test the applicant's skills in English during the job interview – English being the CCL of the study's participants. On the surface, this seems an obvious tactic. However, in Koho's study, the gauging of language fluency concerned only oral skills, with other tests seldom used. Peltokorpi (2007) found that Japanese employees tend to be more competent in written than in spoken English. In such a case, the potential for a false negative selection decision may be increased as a result of judging only by verbal fluency. Moreover, the value of language testing during the selection interview depends on the interviewer or tester being sufficiently competent in the requisite language to make an accurate assessment. Also, there is a risk that the recruiter pays more attention to pronunciation and accent, for example, rather than vocabulary and the contents of communication. Inherent in the selection process is what is referred to as the self-referencing problem; in this case judging applicants on the basis of how one was taught to speak, which becomes the benchmark. Another danger is that a focus on language skills may come at the expense of other job-related requirements (such as specific technical competence).

Another consideration is that generally the selection decision rests with the line manager, who may not consider the broader language aspect, particularly if the manager is not language sensitive, or has particularly high expectations. Lehtovaara (2009) reports such a case in her study of language issues in the UK charity, Oxfam, which has four official corporate languages: English, Spanish, French and Portuguese, though English is dominant. A local country director rejected a candidate who was fluent in English and French but only average in Spanish, on the grounds that a very high degree of fluency in Spanish was necessary due to the position being located in the Spanish-speaking region of Oxfam. The likelihood that the candidate would improve when working in a Spanish-speaking environment was not considered.

While language fluency may give a prospective candidate an edge over other applicants, in general, technical and professional skills tend to be given more weighting. This is exemplified by the comment of a manager of a UK company who reflected on the drawbacks of prioritizing language ability when selecting staff: 'They are linguists first and sales people second and it doesn't always work out very well. If you get people with both, these are top-grade people, and you pay an awful lot of money' (MacDonald and Cook, 1998, 222). A different perspective is provided by a Finnish HR manager: 'We do not have any position in this company in which we would reject a good candidate with professional competence because his/her foreign language skills do not meet our expectations', but then adds: 'of course we expect that the applicant is willing to learn the needed language' (Muukari, 2008, 85). In other words, emphasis is placed on attitude, with the applicant indicating preparedness to make a sizeable personal investment in language acquisition should they be successful.

Selecting staff for international assignments has been the subject of much research, with a consistent result indicating that job ability and technical skills are the predominant criteria. Language skills, in terms of the foreign location involved, are often treated as 'desirable' rather than essential, or not given much weighting in the initial selection process. Nonetheless, HR managers are aware of the impact of language on successful assignment outcomes, as data from a 2012 report produced by the consulting firm Global Mobility indicated. Thirty-five per cent of surveyed multinationals listed language difficulties as a factor that makes a particular assignment destination challenging. In their review of the extant expatriate selection literature, Caligiuri and Tarique (2012, 325) discuss the link between relevant foreign language skills and cross-cultural adjustment. They conclude that 'at a minimum, in most circumstances an attempt should be made to find a qualified candidate with language skills – while for some positions the language skills may be more critical than with others'. However, they assume that there are sufficient candidates with the required managerial and/or technical skills, combined with the relevant language fluency, from which to draw. Reality often does not match the ideal when it comes to selection, and the exclusion of HR staff from the decision-making process may help explain why this is a persistent finding.

Once the selection decision has been made, the HR department tends to play a more active role. Apart from the administrative aspects related to employment (such as recording relevant personal data, filling in salary and taxation forms, and a health check), there may be an official orientation (induction) into the workings of the particular receiving section, and the company as a whole. At this stage, details of language skills may be recorded. Golla, a Finnish producer of bags and accessories for mobile devices, is a good example. Established in 1994, by 2011 the company employed about 75 people. Of these, 30 were employed at headquarters. They spoke the ten different languages that covered Golla's key foreign markets. One of the founding managers and Golla's managing director in 2010 commented in an interview that he pretty much knew by heart everybody's language skills. However, with the recruitment of a HR manager, Golla now has a record of the language skills of its staff on its intranet site. When interviewed, the HR manager emphasized that only those languages the employee is willing and able to use in professional situations are listed. The written record provides a good overview of Golla's language resources and where they are located, and assists in utilizing these resources (Pohjanen-Bernardi and Talja, 2011).

Technological advances have altered some of the administrative activities that had been within the domain of the HR department. E-enabled (electronic) intranet systems are becoming commonplace and individuals can access and maintain their own records, for example. These systems use intranet and web-based technologies to facilitate interaction related to HR information between various groups of employees across organizational, managerial, functional and unit boundaries. However, usage of such a system can be language-dependent. This emerged from a study by Heikkilä and Smale (2011), who investigated the acceptance and use of e-HRM systems in subsidiaries of two European multinationals. The e-HRM systems in the case companies operated in the corporate language, English. The 18 HR managers interviewed reported that access to the e-HRM system required English skills, thus restricting its reach due to lack of language competence. The authors found that English as a corporate language had unintended consequences, as not all users could operate in English, so access to the computerized e-HRM system was effectively denied. Interviewees in this study with poor English skills, such as older and blue-collar employees and payroll administrators, required extensive language support from the HR department. Consequently, the aims of the new e-HRM system to streamline the process and save costs were undermined by the language requirement. HR professionals spent more time assisting employees than was originally intended. An interesting finding was that, since local jobs requiring local language skills were also advertised on the e-HRM system, HR professionals ended up receiving a large number of English resumes from applicants who were not suitable for these positions.

The above discussion centres on the 'buy in' or 'build' options. However, entering into an international joint venture or a merger or acquisition produces an inherited workforce. As we shall explore later, managing the integration process will pose different language aspects related to retention, promotion and development. To that extent, one could argue that the employment process begins with (re)training and development, the topic of the next section.

Training and Development

There are several issues related to the provision of training and the influence of language. These include: who provides, who attends, the location, the language of instruction, the combination of language and general training, and information dissemination.

Training aims to provide the individual with the appropriate skills to perform the job as expected. As Figure 6.1 shows, it is an activity that can occur at any stage once the person has been selected, and takes many forms. Perhaps the most common form of training occurs on the job. It is an obvious way for companies to ensure that their employees have the required skills and that these skills are maintained. Development, in turn, is more future-oriented, aimed at providing additional knowledge and skills that will allow the individual to advance, usually up the managerial ladder. Language competence may be a deciding factor in selecting graduates for such attention. The international bank, Standard Chartered, for example, 'seeks out bilinguals for its international graduate training scheme' (*The Financial Times*, 2013). Generally speaking, lower-level positions do not provide the same development opportunities as middle and upper management positions, so training is confined to skills required for adequate job performance. Those hired to work on a factory production line, or at the service counter in a fast-food outlet, may receive on-the-job training to ensure that they initially have and maintain relevant skills. Training is also linked to matching organizational requirements as situations change. Organizational restructuring or the merger process can lead to redeployment necessitating retraining (or reskilling) for those involved. The study of Nordea found that the adoption of Swedish as the new corporate language caused an increased demand for Swedish-language classes (Piekkari et al., 2005).

Job rotation may be used as part of training. A typical example is that of graduates who may spend a set period of time in various departments. It provides the individual with a broad company perspective before being deployed to a specific department or job role, and can have a language component. For example, the Finnish forestry company UPM-Kymmene has used a rotation system as part of its development plan, recognizing that movement around various units assists employees to improve or acquire language skills as well as technical, managerial and company knowledge (Nousiainen, 2011). International assignments are a form of job rotation when used for competence and management development. There is a vast body of literature pertaining to the management of international staff transfers, particularly that of expatriates who form the primary group within this category (see, for example, Stahl et al., 2012, for a comprehensive review). The duration of assignments varies from short-term (generally three to six months) through to a full expatriate posting of three years or more. The length of international deployment is job-determined: some short-term assignments may be linked to managerial training; others will be to fill a specific job role that is matched with existing technical competence. As with the length and type of assignment, language demands will be dependent on what the specific role involves, and of course the motivation of the individual. As mentioned earlier, studies indicate that at least a degree of competence in the host language can assist with cultural adaptation and work performance (see, for example, Selmer, 2006).

While it is not generally recognized, expatriates have a training role in terms of knowledge and skills transfer to local employees and some competence in the host language facilitates this transfer process. This aspect emerged in the case of KONE. The then training officer in KONE's headquarters admitted that the company moved overseas technically competent engineers with poor language skills (Marschan-Piekkari et al., 1999, 385):

> The difficulty in sending such persons abroad is that technical knowledge is not necessarily transferred in an efficient way. If the technical person concentrates

too much on the project itself, stays for a fairly short time and does not interact with local staff, the competence level of local personnel does not increase . . . We have to require language skills.

It is revealing that such a fundamental aspect of knowledge transfer can be ignored.

Global HR managers can be active in influencing the development of training programmes, evaluating external service providers, and in the dissemination of forthcoming programme offerings and their availability. As mentioned earlier, company information regarding employee matters such as training and development opportunities, internal job vacancies and promotions are disseminated in the CCL via in-house newsletters and intranet bulletins.

Another issue is the location of company training programmes. There are, broadly speaking, three possibilities – global training centres, regional training centres and local subsidiary training – and, with large multinationals like Siemens, combinations of these. The location of training can be influenced by factors such as managerial level (top management, for example, are most likely to attend centralized global programmes) and the purpose of the training (technical versus language-only). The advantages of global training centres, from the MNC's perspective, are obviously economies of scale providing cost savings, and the assurance that the appropriate knowledge and skills are covered in a standardized way, enhancing transfer to all units in a timely fashion. For the individual, though, attendance at such programmes is corporate language dependent. Expatriates tend to have fluency in the corporate language, but it is a barrier for those in subsidiary units who lack the requisite language competence. An illustration from our own teaching experience is that of a Norwegian fishmeal producer, EWOS, that held a management training session in a neutral location, London. In attendance were the purchasing managers from its various country subsidiaries (Scotland, Canada, Ireland, Chile and Norway). The language of instruction was English, the corporate language. This posed a challenge for one participant – a Chilean – whose fluency was sufficient to follow the content, but sessions were dominated by native English speakers, and Norwegians who were highly competent in English. This tended to inhibit his input. In the informal and social settings accompanying the training, the Chilean was also constrained.

The regional approach to training could be seen as a compromise – a mid-way point between local and global training. This organizational response reflects the rationale provided in the general international business literature on the role of a regional centre (Piekkari et al., 2010). At the time of the KONE study, for example, subsidiary managers in the

German and Austrian subsidiaries realized that a lack of English language fluency was a barrier to their employees. English was the language of instruction at KONE global training programmes. Their solution was to combine to provide the necessary management and technical training to both subsidiaries' staff in the German language. Likewise, the Spanish and Italian units found that they could provide more training to their employees by sharing budgets and offering programmes in a shared location using Spanish or Italian. Thus the regional solution came at the expense of the individuals attending, who were effectively not encouraged to learn the corporate language that would enable them to participate at the global level, with the social network and other benefits that would have ensued. Social network development remained at the regional level. It should be noted that it was not always driven by budgetary concerns, but as a response to a shortage of suitably fluent locals who would have been capable of attending the global training centre. The need for important technical training was the driver in regional training attendance. Another regional approach is that taken by an Australian international project firm.[5] As most of its project work was in the South-Asian region, it established a regional centre in Indonesia, with a sizeable contingent of HR professionals assigned to provide expatriates, third-country nationals and local employees with technical training, problem-solving and safety procedures related to specific project work. Cross-cultural aspects were an important part due to the team-based, multicultural nature of project work. The language of instruction was English when pairing expatriates with locals in training sessions.

The Finnish multinational, UPM-Kymmene, takes a local approach (Nousiainen, 2011). Subsidiary units hold training sessions in the relevant local language. The exception was the use of English (its corporate language) when participants did not have a common mother tongue. English became the bridge to facilitate training, what Sørensen (2005) terms an intermediary language, or what some of our linguistic colleagues would term 'vehicular language'. This is not a fail-safe solution, though, as a participant in another study recounted. The after-sales training programme was conducted in English. 'Those who did not understand [all that was said] almost fell asleep' (Pohjanen-Bernardi and Talja, 2011, 56).

Training may be localized but the corporate language can still be the language of instruction. For instance, a study of Chinese subsidiaries found that management training programmes conducted at local centres were conducted in English. Employees who were proficient in English were given priority in participating in training programmes and in turn had more opportunities for promotion (Lu, 2014). Combining competence and management training with language requirements underscores the importance of the corporate language, sending a clear signal to those employees who seek a corporate, including international, career path.

Language Training

There is a range of options in terms of language-training provision. Bellak's (2014) study of Danish and Austrian MNCs, for instance, found that the case companies all provided language classes in English, their official corporate language; the Danish MNCs made these available to all levels of employees. In addition, these MNCs bought in language competence through recruitment practices.

In-house language-training options are generally seen as beyond the means of the typical SME, and the ELAN study provides supporting evidence. Smaller companies provided less training than the larger companies (49 per cent compared to 86 per cent) and preferred to buy in language competence (CILT, 2006). As we noted with recruitment, cost considerations often lead companies to use external language training providers, with employees subsidized to attend. Such programmes are aimed at existing employees rather than new hires who already have the required language fluency.

A study of UK-based exporting firms (mainly SMEs) found that of the 250 respondents surveyed, only 20 reported language training for staff at any level (MacDonald and Cook, 1998). Those who provided training did so mainly for sales staff who travelled abroad, and for management. There was a mixture of language approaches: in-house training, external courses, and using language tapes in the car or at home. Although the type of language training was not investigated, a study of Welsh SMEs reported similar findings with regard to the provision of language training. A higher proportion of larger SMEs provided language training, or indicated that they were intending to do so, than did the smaller SMEs in the sample (Peel and Eckart, 1997).

Another interesting finding from the ELAN study mentioned above was the difference between offering language training and its take-up. In total, while 49 per cent indicated they offered language training, only 35 per cent reported that they had actually trained staff in one or more languages during the previous three years. There were country differences. Companies in the Czech Republic reported more training (79 per cent) compared to the UK (10 per cent) and Greece (5 per cent). While language training may be a considerable investment for the company, employees often face conflicting priorities affecting their motivation and possibilities of studying languages for the job.

In Koho's (2007) study of Finnish university graduates, the recruiters interviewed pointed to the fact that while language training in several languages was available at company expense, very few were actually called upon to use foreign languages other than English in their normal daily work. One has to ask why Finnish firms would be so generous. Koho (2007) could not provide an answer, but speculated that it may be a way of motivating employees or generating loyalty. However, there is an inherent danger of raising expectations about the use of language skills in the companies concerned. For example, MacDonald and Cook (1998) refer to the case of one employee who left the firm because she was not using her language skills.

Who attends language training programmes, though, is generally the domain of the line or subsidiary manager. Marschan-Piekkari et al. (1999) found that, despite being allocated a budget to provide their staff with language training, some KONE subsidiary managers did not alert their employees to the opportunity to attend company-sponsored language classes. In the Finnish unit of Handelsbanken, it was left to the supervisor to decide who could attend company-provided language training and evaluate its outcomes. Handelsbanken's HR policy defined the language training possibilities of the unit (Muukari, 2008).

Experienced companies with active HR departments tend to encourage those accepting an international assignment to attend cultural awareness training programmes before relocation and, as part of this preparation, language classes may be involved. In a study of expatriates from Singapore, Japan, Korea, Germany and the USA, respondents rated host-language training as more important than other forms of pre-departure training (Osman-Gani, 2000). A strong weighting on language training (61 per cent) was reported by *Forbes Insights* in a 2011 magazine survey of 100 US executives from large corporations. Respondents reported that bilingual employees were considered to be more effective. One of the barriers to provision of language training generally reported in such surveys is time constraint, as individuals may be given insufficient notice before departure, thus precluding attendance at such training, or support and time once in the host country. Of course, it is also dependent on whether or not there is access to appropriate classes. As Peltokorpi (2007) points out, access to Japanese-language training for Nordic expatriates was limited due to a scarcity of local providers.

A different situation was reported by Fredriksson (2005). She found that Siemens employees transferred into the Finnish operation were not provided with classes in the local host language (Finnish) but those transferred into the German operations were given German-language instruction. This signalled the importance of German, even though English was Siemens' corporate language. Of course, expatriates can initiate language training in the host country when they realize that some knowledge of the local language would assist their performance. As Charles and Marschan-Piekkari (2002) argue, language training is too important to be left to the subsidiary manager to decide. It should be a corporate-level function to ensure that employees in all units are provided with similar opportunities, and the focus should be broader than the provision of corporate language training to allow the development of a portfolio of language skills on which the organization can draw.

As we saw in the Handelsbanken case, the emphasis on language in the recruitment stage and its reinforcement through company internal communication sends a specific signal to employees that they should invest in language capital (see Chapter 5). Taking advantage of the provision of company-funded language lessons can provide access to enhanced training options, international assignments and career progression. The HR manager of a Finnish-owned subsidiary in China commented: 'Departments should identify potential talents according to certain criteria. If they have good English skills we will send them to the global leadership program' (Lu, 2014, 189). Thus language fluency provides the individual with the means to develop a more extensive social network that can lead to a wider range of promotional opportunities and other career advantages (Mäkelä et al., 2010).

The issue of language training may be job-specific. For example, the street sweepers at Disney's theme parks in the USA and France are considered as a critical resource in enhancing the Disney experience – perhaps providing more value to Disney than its higher-profile Disney characters. Street sweepers are often the point of contact when park visitors require information. How the street sweepers respond to varying and unanticipated requests and circumstances in a friendly manner affects visitors' perceptions. Boudreau and Ramstad (2007) argue that investments in the sweepers' ability to communicate and provide accurate answers are pivotal in generating value.

Language training also may be a response to a specific foreign-market need or situation confronting the internationalizing firm. An interesting example comes from a Danish study of international outsourcing. The case firm, SimCorp, a Danish multinational with English as its corporate language, used outsourcing in its Ukrainian operations. Two local providers were used to develop software. SimCorp insisted that those working in the development teams in these local providers had to be fluent in English due to the interaction with SimCorp counterparts. This job requirement motivated locals to invest time in improving their English. One local provider offered courses at its own expense to those of its Ukrainian employees identified by SimCorp as having the required technical expertise, but who 'lacked English communication skills' (Benito et al., 2013, 219). Apart from the obvious career benefits for the individuals involved, such language training helped in the Ukrainian software development activity, thus benefiting SimCorp.

Another example of external language training comes from Indian employees working for call centres. They are trained to speak English with accents and idioms so that US, UK and Australian customers are often unaware that their 'local' call has been diverted to a call centre in India. Such training is provided by the contracted call centre. Opportunities to work for the multinationals that contract work to call centres are virtually nonexistent (see, for example, Mirchandani, 2012). Thus type and level of a job within a particular organization are determining factors when it comes to provision of language-training opportunities that may lead to career development. As shown in Figure 6.1, training and development are linked to career pathing, which we discuss later.

Performance Appraisal

We include performance appraisal as part of the employment process in Figure 6.1 as it has a bearing on whether the individual remains employed, promoted, or provided with additional training and development. Systematic assessment of employee performance is a common aspect of modern organizational life. Sometimes referred to as evaluation or assessment, performance appraisal varies according to company policies, national or cultural differences, and level of position involved. In general, it involves at least annual performance reviews between employee and the relevant line manager where individual performance is discussed with the objective of measuring (albeit subjectively) accomplishments against agreed-on expectations. In our discussion below we approach language from two perspectives: the language used in conducting performance appraisal interviews; and language competence as a factor to be considered when evaluating employees' performance and promotion opportunities.

In her study of Finnish-owned subsidiaries in China, Lu (2014, 189) examined localization of HRM practices. Her findings suggest that local employees whose English was not sufficiently proficient were excluded from higher management positions in the Chinese subsidiary. As a HR manager described:

> Many engineers here have good technical competence but their English is not so good. When the promotion opportunity comes we cannot give them the position if they do not understand English, because we often need to contact the

HQs and our customers who are international companies. We cannot allocate an interpreter for them [the engineers].

Based on his Japanese study, Peltokorpi (2007) suggests that local staff can be encouraged to learn or improve requisite language skills by including language facility as part of expected performance in appraisal sessions. This was the case for some of the Finnish SME companies such as Golla in the study by Pohjanen-Bernardi and Talja (2011), where language skills are considered in yearly performance assessments. However, Koho's (2007) findings on the Finnish recruitment of recent university graduates suggest that in the seven multinational corporations she studied, language skills almost never affected the employees' level of salary.

It can be a contentious issue in the multinational setting if MNCs attempt to standardize performance appraisal through a global system in order to facilitate employee deployment. Such standardization can be applied to include the use of the corporate language. For instance, in some Finnish subsidiaries operating in China, subsidiary managers were required to ensure that the appraisal discussion be conducted in the corporate language – English – and the relevant performance appraisal forms filled out in English (Lu, 2014). However, this was not always followed in practice.

Based on their interview study of Japanese-owned subsidiaries in Germany, Lincoln et al. (1995) suggest that relationships between expatriate supervisors and employees were likely to be negatively affected if subordinates possessed a significant linguistic advantage. The study found that Japanese managers were reluctant to conduct direct appraisals of their German subordinates in English, the corporate language commonly used among Japanese subsidiaries in Germany. The German subordinates tended to enjoy a relaxed facility with English that few of their Japanese managers shared. This is another example of how language facility can alter the power relationship within the work setting.

In extreme situations, supervisors may end up carrying out performance appraisals of employees with whom they do not have a shared language. Piekkari et al. (2005) describe a situation that emerged in a Nordic financial institution where a Swedish manager responsible for a Finnish-speaking unit found himself conducting appraisal interviews through an interpreter. At that time, investments made by the Nordic financial institution in language training had not yet materialized. Consequently, these otherwise capable and useful employees appeared unintelligent in their encounters with the Swedes. They often remained silent in situations where normally they would have actively participated. Their professional competence was hidden behind the language barrier and they seemed to be underperforming (Piekkari et al., 2005). Such experiences are likely to impede career advancement with the current employer and lead to careful consideration of external career opportunities, which we discuss in the next section.

Apart from the intention to assess individual performance, appraisal can be seen as part of the organization's overall performance management system. It can be used as a managerial tool. For example, data can be used to determine the employment consequences resulting from mergers or internal restructuring. However, this assumes that organizations collate performance data into accessible systems, and that the data provide an accurate picture of the organization's human capital pool. An early example comes from Fixman's (1990) study of nine US firms. She reported that it was difficult to find any companies that included foreign-language skills in their employees' performance reviews.

Continuance or Exit

The final stage of the employment process depicted in Figure 6.1 refers to its duration. In the latter part of the twentieth century, in Western, particularly Anglo-American, companies, there was a lessening of what has been termed jobs for life. From a management perspective, being able to shape the workforce according to economic and market demands was a major benefit. However, this resulted in reduced company loyalty as employees started to manage their careers themselves, which encouraged inter-company mobility. The changing nature of the employment contract that has resulted in 'loyalty to self' rather than 'loyalty to the employing company' has produced a competitive job market – what has been popularized as the 'war on talent' (Collings and Mellahi, 2009). This applies to management and functional areas, where needed skills are in short supply locally and globally.

We made the point earlier that language skills are part of an individual's stock of human capital. As the multinational does not own an individual's human capital, employee retention becomes an issue. A key motivation behind HR practices is to ensure that what walks out the door at night returns the next day – or at least those individuals that are considered a valuable resource. MacDonald and Cook (1998, 223) provide an example of an employee who left because her language skills were not being used. The interviewee commented: 'She had good language skills when she joined, which is why we recruited her . . . [but over time] she used her languages less and less.'

Alongside this consideration is the desire to maximize the return on investment made in human capital through job-related activities, of which training and development are a considerable part. The dilemma for an international firm is that training increases the individual's stock of human capital, which employees can use for their own purposes – what economists call privatizing gains while socializing costs. Thus, if an individual has invested considerable time and effort in language acquisition (even if the training was provided by the firm) and then finds it is not being used, the person may decide to seek employment elsewhere.

Poaching of suitably trained employees, including those on the factory floor, by local or foreign competitors is a genuine concern, as these companies can reap the gains at the other company's expense (Peltokorpi and Vaara, 2012). Another concern is the paradox referred to as the expense of cheap labour. Multinationals will move operations to countries where the cost of labour is relatively low, but then incur costs associated with educating and training employees, eventually increasing the cost of labour in that particular country. Hence the link between provision of necessary company training and employee retention is of managerial concern (Bellak, 2014).

Klitmøller and Bjerregaard (2013) conducted an ethnographic case study of a Danish subsidiary, a *maquiladora*, located in a special economic zone in Mexico. Subsidiary management had decided to remove the English classes offered to employees during work hours in response to headquarters' productivity programme that regarded them as redundant and a 'waste'. The Mexican white-collar workers were of a different opinion and heavily criticized this decision because they considered English as a necessity to reach their personal long-term career goals. In Mexico the local competition for educated employees is strong, as a white-collar worker commented (Klitmøller and Bjerregaard, 2013, 121):

> If you want a good future and a good career you have to learn English. The salaries here in DanCan Mexico [the company anonymized] are not the best, but I do not care about that. What I care about is getting experience and skills. So I can survive as long as they have English classes. It's an investment in the future. So now that they have removed them, I do not want to work here anymore.

Thus the removal of the English classes triggered the employee's intention to leave the company. Lu's (2014, 189) study of HRM practices in foreign-owned subsidiaries provides further evidence of the value placed on language competence for career development. One of the HR managers even advised the children of his relatives as follows: 'If you want to work in a foreign company, the shortcut to success is to have good English. Even if you are not very competent technically you will have more opportunities than others if your English is good.'

Clearly, then, investing in human capital can work as a factor in employee motivation to stay. An interesting outcome of teaching an MBA programme in China in 2002 was the emphasis class participants placed on the value of working in the Chinese subsidiaries of Western multinationals. Aside from monetary aspects, development opportunities were listed as important. Language was a part of that, as our Chinese participants volunteered that having to operate in a foreign language was one of the advantages of working for a Western multinational. A majority of the class participants were being subsidized by their respective foreign employers to attend the MBA programme, which was being offered in English. At the time, some companies, such as the Swedish–Swiss multinational ABB, offered Chinese employees English-language training. ABB paid the full cost of lessons for those at the managerial level and 70 per cent of the cost for all other employees. This was reinforced by encouraging employees to speak English during management meetings and have English-only days. It would seem from comments made in the MBA class that attachment to the subsidiary was linked to employee career aspirations being matched with company opportunities – foreign companies were endeavouring to ensure that these individuals contributed to subsidiary performance, at least long enough for there to be a satisfactory return on investment in their pool of human capital. Based on her study of Finnish multinationals operating in Russia, Bloigu (2008) suggests that hiring employees who are willing to learn languages may have increased commitment to stay, at least long enough for the companies to recoup the cost of language training. The term normative commitment is used to describe the attitudes of employees who feel obliged to remain with their employer: that is, stay because the company has provided opportunities such as language training and therefore deserves some reciprocal loyalty (see, for example, Allen and Meyer, 1990, for a discussion of the concept of organizational commitment).

Exit

The relevant literature refers to involuntary and voluntary redundancy to explain how exit occurs. Involuntary redundancy is when the organization dismisses the employee, usually on the grounds of non-performance or violation of acceptable behaviour. Of course, involuntary redundancy includes instances of retrenchment as a consequence of managerial decisions (also referred to as job shedding, downsizing or outplacement).

Voluntary redundancy refers to a person resigning or taking retirement. This can be due to the decision to take a position with another company (that is, career mobility) or, in cases of organizational job shedding, taking a redundancy or early retirement package. A stress on language competence may influence continuance decisions. Individuals without the requisite skills, or where advancement is perceived to be too language-dependent, may seek opportunities in more domestically oriented companies. Alternatively, employees may be poached or headhunted by competitors on the grounds of their language skills in conjunction with requisite skills and experience. Exit interviews may be conducted, usually by the HR department, as a way of finding out causes for voluntary redundancy as part of a feedback process to assist in better HR planning and improvement of HR practices.

The study by Piekkari et al. (2005) of the language consequences of the Nordic bank created from the merger of a Finnish and Swedish bank highlighted the effect on staff retention. Interviews with Finnish employees who had left the bank during the turmoil of the merger confirmed that the imposition of a new corporate language, Swedish, was one of the reasons that had influenced their decision to change employers.

Research on language use and its consequences has been conducted in firms located in Japan because language is a particularly salient identity marker in this context (SanAntonio, 1987). For example, Peltokorpi and Vaara (2012) conducted a qualitative study of language policies and practices in 101 foreign-owned subsidiaries in Japan. The majority of the foreign-owned subsidiaries they studied had English as the CCL. They interviewed parent-country nationals (that is, expatriates), local Japanese managers and employees as well as consultants. Most of the expatriates worked as subsidiary presidents, while a much smaller number of Japanese interviewees had this position. Peltokorpi and Vaara (2012, 828, 819) found that 'bilingual HCN [host-country national] talent, who mastered both English and Japanese, can also readily improve their salaries, organizational rank, and company status by calculated moves in foreign subsidiaries in Japan'. Their findings suggest that, unlike the usually low voluntary turnover in domestic companies, language-competent Japanese had low organizational attachment and frequently 'job-hopped' using their language-based career capital as 'free agents' on the job market. Also, the study indicated that English as a corporate language created a divide between senior and junior Japanese managers. While the older managers had a higher status in the organizational hierarchy based on seniority, they did not possess the relevant language facility. 'That is why they have quit the company', as a Japanese manager explained; 'they were not able to advance in the company'. When junior Japanese managers were promoted based on their superior language skills, it caused perceptions of unfairness. In 18 subsidiaries such promotions resulted in voluntary turnover. Overall, Japanese staff with insufficient proficiency in the corporate language were the least attached to their organizations, thus showing the highest levels of turnover intent.

Turnover is also recognized as a problem among those returning from longer-term international assignments. A consistent finding of the relevant studies is that lack of ability to utilize new knowledge gained from the international experience is a motive for exiting (see, for example, Lazarova and Cerdin, 2007). Language skills can readily become rusty if not continually used, so movement to another organization that would provide the opportunities to use the language or languages may be a reason to change employers.

Decisions related to continuance or exit can be influenced by another aspect of employment – career pathing – to which we now turn.

CAREER PATHING

In the following we discuss how language skills may steer, shape and redirect individuals' career paths. Of course, the reverse effect often happens – that is, a particular career path may influence the development of language skills. As we found in the original KONE study, there were examples of individuals being sent as expatriates to foreign units where they initiated the acquisition of the relevant language in order to enhance their job performance, which in turn furthered their careers.

The concept of career pathing captures the relationship between the individual and his or her work over time. As Figure 6.1 shows, career pathing cuts across the entire employment process, from recruitment to continuance or exit. Arthur and Rousseau (1996, 8) define careers as 'the evolving sequence of a person's work experiences over time'. Contemporary scholars tend to define careers more broadly 'as an individual's work-related and other relevant experiences, both inside and outside of organizations that form a unique pattern over the individual's life span' (Sullivan and Baruch, 2009, 1543). Since the late 1990s, scholars have become increasingly interested in careers and career mobility (for example, Ng et al., 2007; Sullivan and Baruch, 2009), which refers to job change, organizational change or occupational shift.

Career mobility re-emerged as an issue in the international literature due to interest in what was termed the boundaryless career (see, for example, Arthur and Rousseau, 1996; Sullivan and Baruch, 2009). Literally speaking, the boundaryless career means unlimited career paths (Inkson, 2006), but in practice the concept seems to refer to the crossing of career boundaries within and around organizations (Inkson et al., 2012). These include occupational, organizational, hierarchical, cultural and geographical boundaries.

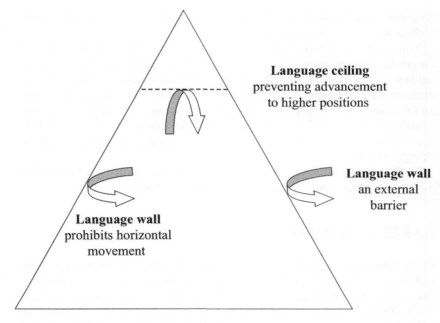

Figure 6.2   Language ceiling and walls

Language and Careers

Despite the resurgence of interest in international careers, language as
a career-boundary or career-path influencer has received limited attention. To a certain extent, we can draw a parallel with the so-called glass
ceiling: the invisible barrier that prevents women's career progression to
top positions in organizations. The invisible barrier we stress by looking
at careers through a language lens has led us to coin the terms *language
ceiling* and *language wall*. These are depicted in Figure 6.2. The invisible
language ceiling slows down or even prevents those who have limited skills
in the corporate language from pursuing vertical career opportunities. In
a similar vein, individuals – male or female – may hit a language wall when
trying to engage in horizontal career moves, such as moving to a different
functional area, or taking an international assignment. Those wishing to
join a particular firm could hit the language wall – not being hired due to
a lack of language skills. While we see our terms as androgynous, from a
gender perspective, one could use the term *double glazing* to indicate that
women may be faced with both language and gender-induced barriers.
    Research on Japanese-owned subsidiaries in different parts of the

world (Lincoln et al., 1995; Wright et al., 2001; Yoshihara, 2001) and foreign-owned subsidiaries in Japan (Peltokorpi and Vaara, 2012) supports our concept of the language ceiling. A further example is provided by SanAntonio's (1987, 196) ethnographic study of an American high-tech computer company in Japan that had a policy of requiring English to be used in all overseas offices. When opportunities arose for promotion, American managers would often recommend English-fluent Japanese employees because they were judged 'to be intelligent, ambitious, and interested', rather than those who lacked the language facility. Likewise, Peltokorpi and Vaara (2012, 815, 823) found that English-language skills were a prerequisite for the promotion of Japanese employees. An expatriate who held the position of subsidiary president commented: 'If they [local Japanese employees] don't speak English, they cannot be promoted to higher levels.' Another subsidiary president also reasoned: 'No matter how good you are in marketing or another function, you need to speak English. All correspondence is in English. And our language competencies here are so poor. Even though I have intelligent employees, I cannot promote them.' Thus, due to limited language skills, key individuals were prevented from advancing in their careers.

In their study on European and US corporations Neeley et al. (2012, 238) quote an interviewee who rhetorically asked: 'What's going to happen to my career if I don't master the English that's considered to be so important that [our] executives are imposing it in meetings? What's my future?' In a different study, Neeley (2013, 487–8) examined a French high-tech company that mandated English as a CCL. She reports similar career concerns among her French-speaking informants who were employed by a French high-tech company that had adopted a strict English-only policy. They were worried about 'having reached a [language] ceiling within the organization'. As one participant commented, 'I worry that my English [will] be compared to better speakers, and they will get promoted and I won't.' Although previous research does not distinguish between female and male employees' attitudes towards self-evaluated language skills, there may be gender-based differences with respect to applications for promotion. Taken together, these studies suggest that the imposition of a mandated language steers and shapes vertical career progression in important ways.

Alongside the glass-ceiling effect that limits vertical career mobility, individuals may also hit the language wall when engaging in horizontal career moves within a multinational, such as for international assignments. This was a factor for participants in Neeley's (2013) study mentioned above. The following quote was offered by a French manager who perceived himself as a low-fluency English speaker and expressed concerns about his career (Neeley, 2013, 488):

> It's embarrassing when [Frencho, the case company] says, 'We want to go international' . . . I am out of the game because I don't have language skills . . . There will be more reorganizations and all the international jobs are going to be given to people . . . who can show that they can master both English and French, and I don't have these skills.

The above quotation suggests that the inability to undertake international assignments due to a language deficiency may create two classes of employees. As we explore later in this chapter, in the long run, limited language competence may lead to a situation where the individual is locked into his or her current position with only domestic responsibilities.

Career decisions revealed in the Piekkari et al. (2005) study referred to above provide an example of moves to retreat inside a language wall. Some Finnish-speaking employees initiated horizontal career moves to avoid having to operate in the imposed Swedish corporate language and therefore 'escaped' to Finnish- or English-speaking units. Horizontal career moves may also be perceived as a downward shift along the career ladder if the new unit or department has a lower status within the organization than the original one.

The experience within Golla, the Finnish producer of bags and accessories for mobile devices, further illustrates how a language wall may arise. One of Golla's core competences is its colourful and original product design. While the corporate language is English, Golla's design team uses Finnish as its working language. The managing director justifies the language choice by saying that sometimes it is difficult to explain things even in your mother tongue, let alone in broken English. He explains that the design team made an attempt to use English when a foreign trainee joined the team for a limited period of time but it did not work out and the team reverted to Finnish.

A variation of the language wall is where an individual is effectively trapped due to language fluency, rather than its lack. For example, a China expert who possesses mastery of Mandarin may be offered only China-specific jobs. Such situations may have a stagnating effect on his or her long-term career development – that is, a career impeded by a *language trap*. Of course, individuals will vary in their responses to language-determined effects on their careers. These will range from language acquisition through to exiting the organization. We explore these options in the following section.

Language-driven Career Paths

Figure 6.3 integrates the previous discussion on selection, training and development at the personal level. We take three hypothetical cases to demonstrate the linkage between recruitment, selection and training

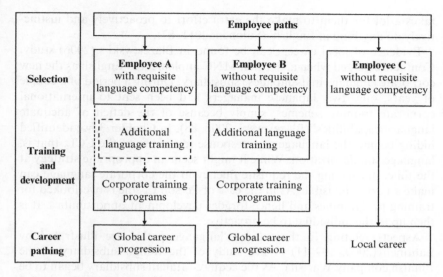

Figure 6.3   Individual employee paths shaped by language

from a language-competence perspective. Person A has fluency in the requisite language on recruitment and this competence enables Person A to be available for job rotation and promotion, and attendance at corporate training programmes (shown as a dashed arrow linking Employee A to the corporate training box in Figure 6.3). The dashed line to language training indicates that the requisite language on hiring may have been the corporate language, but an assignment to a foreign unit may require additional language skills, and such training may or may not be provided (indicated by the use of a dashed line around the additional training box).

Person B is assumed not to have requisite language skills on selection. This may be because the need for a CCL was not stressed at the time or that language skills were not a formal prerequisite. However, due to work demands or individual aspirations, Person B avails him/herself of company-provided language training that opens up opportunities to attend corporate training programmes held in the corporate language. This hypothetical situation assumes that the requisite language is the corporate language. Person C, however, is content to stay local in terms of language. The Quebec study referred to earlier provides a good example. The law in this Canadian province makes French the primary workplace language to the detriment of English, so there was little incentive to invest in improving English-language fluency. One company top manager in the study referred to this as being 'cocooned': 'they speak only French and it takes a lot for them to make the extra effort to proactively and instinctively do anything in English' (Sulonen, 2011, 87).

Evidence of local careers can be found in Blazejewski's (2006) study. Conflicts emerged when a German MNC implemented English as the new corporate language in its Japanese subsidiary. During a period of a couple of years, only two Japanese managers had been sent to international corporate training schemes 'simply because of the deficit of adequate language capabilities' (Blazejewski, 2006, 88). In Chapter 3, we identified hiding behind the language as a response to the use of the CCL, that is, language standardization. While it might seem an appropriate strategy at the time, not having the requisite fluency in the corporate language can make a person invisible. As in the case of Person C, s/he is overlooked for training programmes and hence forgoes development opportunities. It is then up to the individual to be proactive.

Aspects relating to these three 'language paths' are illustrated by Lahtinen (2000, 109–11) in her study of the Italian subsidiary of the Finnish company Wärtsilä. As the acquired Italian subsidiary began to be integrated into the global corporate family, English demands intensified due to an increased presence of Finnish managers visiting or assigned to the unit. Lahtinen's interviews exposed a range of reactions. Some Italians were comfortable as they had English-language skills due to working in parts of the acquired company's international operations. Others were angry that language training had not been provided earlier when they were younger and 'now I am too old', or 'about to retire so why bother'. Others pointed to the fact that top managers were provided with language classes during their working hours, while the rest were expected to take the classes in their own time. Female employees reported that devoting time to learning a language was too difficult as they were already juggling competing time demands between work and family.

LANGUAGE AND THE HR DEPARTMENT

The above sections have considered the effects that language may have on the employment process. We have taken a broad perspective, as the cross-functional, blurred nature of HRM means that much of the language-related aspects of people management involves others, both internal and external to the internationalizing firm, as well as the HR department. In this final section, we discuss the role of the HR department in influencing how language is managed.

Despite concerted efforts of some proponents within the HRM field to push for a seat at the strategy table – that is, for HR managers to be included in the top executive team – it would seem that what Welch et al. (2009) term the HR zone of influence remains relatively small compared to that of areas such as finance and marketing. This is borne out in a recent survey by Ernst & Young. Like other global consulting firms, Ernst & Young undertakes annual surveys of trends relating to global mobility (moving staff internationally). Its 2012 survey data indicate a continuing limited zone of influence resulting in a disconnection between those who make selection decisions (line managers) and those who handle the consequences (HR managers). Assignment policies are generally set by HR at headquarters and cover areas such as relocation, remuneration (compensation) and entitlements. The dilemma for HR is that line managers play an active role in the selection of expatriates and may promise more than the standard package in order to persuade an individual to accept an international assignment. Inequitable treatment may be a source of disquiet if, at the same location, some expatriates are provided with entitlements (such as subsidized housing, or payment of local language classes) while others are not. Consistency of treatment lessens tensions that may have an adverse effect on expatriate performance, and makes it easier for HR at headquarters and at the subsidiary level to address expatriate concerns. Thus standardized policies can be an effective management tool provided that there is general compliance. It should be noted that the HR department's zone of influence will vary due to factors such as the national approach to employee management, the philosophy of the top executive team, and the regard with which an individual HR manager is held by colleagues.

As we have mentioned earlier, the international context introduces another layer of managerial complexity – the relationship between global headquarters and the various subsidiaries in terms of centralization of decision-making and standardization of procedures and practices. Based on our interaction with various HR professionals, global and regional meetings between headquarters and subsidiary HR managers form an integral part of designing standardized policies and procedures. One can assume that fluency in the corporate language facilitates attendance at global meetings, and input into procedure development would also be language-dependent. HR's role in the design, implementation and maintenance of a corporate language policy and language audits will be addressed in Chapter 9.

Devising, communicating and monitoring policies and procedures that affect employee behaviour and welfare necessitate careful attention to language, so that the intended meaning is conveyed. Subsidiary HR staff may re-translate information to ensure the message is communicated as intended. One example comes from a presentation in 2000 to a class of MBA students in Australia. The then HR manager in the Australian subsidiary of the Swedish telecommunications firm Ericsson informed students how she would check for what they called Swenglish. Documents translated from Swedish into English, the corporate language, would sometimes contain peculiar words and phrases that made little sense to Australians, so she or one of her staff members would rewrite such documents.

Technology can provide a useful service for the HR department but can be a mixed blessing. As mentioned earlier, Heikkilä and Smale (2011, 309) investigated the acceptance and use of e-HRM systems in two European multinationals. They report that e-HRM adoption affected the role of the HR department. The impact goes beyond the use of information technology within the confines of the HR department. The subsidiary HR managers who were interviewed reported that access to the e-HRM system required English skills, thus restricting its reach due to variable language competence. This meant a 'significant amount of translation work' for some HR managers, and that the need to provide 'extensive language support' negated one of the aims of the system: freeing HR to concentrate on more strategic tasks. However, there was a subtle power aspect. Subsidiary HR managers had discretionary power in determining what parts of the new e-HRM system they would support based on their perceptions of the end-user (blue-collar workers' likelihood of having English fluency, for example), and could assume a gatekeeping role due to the translation service they provided.

CONCLUSION

As Luo and Shenkar (2006, 335) comment in their article on language in the multinational context, 'global human resource management is inextricably linked with the process and practice of language systems'. They argue for further investigation of how 'training, motivation, recruitment and rotation, among others, can help improve the effectiveness of language systems'. By taking the employment process as the framework, we have been able to explore the connection between human resource management and language, drawing on the emerging research into various areas, including those identified by Luo and Shenkar, some of which predated their own article.

The question for management is how to ensure that language considerations are included in HR activities, whether through the HR department or more generally. We return to this aspect in Chapter 9, where we address language policy issues.

NOTES

1. Comparative HRM is a distinct yet related area of scholarship that considers such national differences.
2. For those wanting a more detailed account of the employment process and/or cross-cultural employment aspects, most HRM textbooks provide an accessible, succinct treatment of the topics covered in this chapter.
3. Some recent HRM textbooks refer to these as resourcing strategies, and include the use of part-time and contract workers. For our purposes, we assume full-time, continuing positions.
4. Most HRM textbooks treat the selection decision in great depth, including a discussion on 'best person' and 'cultural fit', malleability and cross-cultural aspects.
5. This is taken from an interview conducted in 2008 by one of the authors with the then regional HR manager. The name of the company is withheld due to a confidentiality agreement.

REFERENCES

Allen, N.J. and J.P. Meyer (1990), 'The measurement and antecedents of affective, continuance and normative commitment to the organization', *Journal of Occupational Psychology*, **63** (1), 1–18.

Arthur, M.B. and D.M. Rousseau (1996), *The Boundaryless Career: A New Employment Principle for a New Organizational Era*, Oxford: Oxford University Press.

Bellak, N. (2014), *Can Language be Managed in International Business? Insights into Language Choice from a Case Study of Danish and Austrian Multinational Corporations (MNCs)*, PhD Thesis, Copenhagen: Department of International Business Communication, Copenhagen Business School.

Benito, G.R.G., O. Dovgan, B. Petersen and L.S. Welch (2013), 'Offshore outsourcing: a dynamic, operation mode perspective', *Industrial Marketing Management*, **42** (2), 211–22.

Blazejewski, S. (2006), 'Transferring value-infused organisational practices in multinational companies: a conflict perspective', in M. Geppert and M. Mayer (eds), *Global, National and Local Practices in Multinational Corporations*, Basingstoke: Palgrave Macmillan, pp. 63–104.

Bloigu, K. (2008), *Russian or English? Examining the Role and Importance of the Russian Language in the Russian Business of Finnish Companies*, Master's Thesis, Helsinki: Helsinki School of Economics.

Boudreau, J.W. and P.M. Ramstad (2007), *Beyond HR: The New Science of Human Capital*, Boston, MA: Harvard Business School Press.

Caldwell, R. (2008), 'HR business partner competency models: re-contextualising effectiveness', *Human Resource Management Journal*, **18** (3), 275–94.

Caligiuri, P. and I. Tarique (2012), 'International assignee selection and cross-cultural training and development', in G. Stahl, I. Björkman and S. Morris (eds), *Handbook of Research in International Human Resource Management*, Cheltenham, UK and Northampton, MA, USA: Edward Elgar, pp. 321–42.

Charles, M. and R. Marschan-Piekkari (2002), 'Language training for enhanced horizontal communication: a challenge for MNCs', *Business Communication Quarterly*, **65** (2), 9–29.

CILT (2006), *ELAN: Effects on the European Union Economy of Shortages of Foreign Language Skills in Enterprises*, Brussels: European Commission.

Collings, D.G. and K. Mellahi (2009), 'Strategic talent management: a review and a research agenda', *Human Resource Management Review*, **19** (4), 304–13.

Crick, D. (1999), 'An investigation into SMEs' use of languages in their export operations', *International Journal of Entrepreneurial Behaviour and Research*, **5** (1), 19–31.

Ernst & Young (2012), *Driving Business Success: Global Mobility Effectiveness Survey*, Switzerland: EYGM Ltd.

Farndale, E. and C. Brewster (2005), 'In search of legitimacy: personnel management associations worldwide', *Human Resource Management Journal*, **15** (3), 33–48.

The Financial Times (2013), 'The multilingual divide'. Online publication, 13 March, (www.ft.com/intl/cms/s/0/3fd31c1a).

Fixman, C.S. (1990), 'The foreign language needs of U.S.-based corporations', *Annals of the American Academy of Political and Social Science*, **511**, 25–46.

Forbes Insights (2011), 'Reducing the impact of language barriers', September, 1–9.

Fredriksson, R. (2005), *Effects of Language Diversity in an MNC*, Master's Thesis, Helsinki: Helsinki School of Economics.

Hagen, S. (2011), *Report on Language Management Strategies and Best Practice in European SMEs: The PIMLICO Project*, Brussels: European Commission.

Heikkilä, J.-P. and A. Smale (2011), 'The effects of "language standardization" on the acceptance and use of e-HRM systems in foreign subsidiaries', *Journal of World Business*, **46** (3), 305–13.

Heikkonen, M. (2012), *The Rationale and Effectiveness of Recruitment Outsourcing*, Master's Thesis, Helsinki: School of Business, Aalto University.

Inkson, K. (2006), 'Protean and boundaryless careers as metaphors', *Journal of Vocational Behavior*, **69** (1), 48–63.

Inkson, K., H. Gunz, S. Ganash and J. Roper (2012), 'Boundaryless careers: bringing back boundaries', *Organization Studies*, **33** (3), 323–40.

Klitmøller, A. and T. Bjerregaard (2013), 'Practice transfer in the MNC: an extended case study of local socio-economic strategies', in A. Klitmøller, *(Re)Contextualizing Cultural and Linguistic Boundaries in Multinational Corporations: A Global Ethnographic Approach*, Doctoral Thesis, Aarhus: Aarhus University, pp. 108–33.

Koho, M. (2007), *Hjälper språkkunskaper att få jobb? En studie om språkkunskapernas betydelse vid rekrytering på den finländska arbetsmarknaden – med fokus på nyutexaminerade från högskolor. (Do Language Skills Help in Getting a Job? A Study of the Role of Language Skills in Recruitment on the Finnish Job Market – a Focus on the Newly Graduated University Students)*, Master's Thesis, Helsinki: Hanken School of Economics and Business Administration.

Lahtinen, U. (2000), *Language Skills in Inter-Unit Communication of an Internationalising Company*, Master's Thesis, Helsinki: Helsinki School of Economics.

Lazarova, M.B. and J.-L. Cerdin (2007), 'Revisiting repatriation concerns: organizational support versus career and contextual influences', *Journal of International Business Studies*, **38** (3), 404–29.

Lehtovaara, H. (2009), *Working in Four Official Languages: The Perceptions of OGB Employees on the Role of Language in Internal Communication*, Master's Thesis, Helsinki: Helsinki School of Economics.

Lewis, R.E. and R.J. Heckman (2006), 'Talent management: a critical review', *Human Resource Management Review*, **16** (2), 139–54.

Lincoln, J., H.R. Kerbo and E. Wittenhagen (1995), 'Japanese companies in Germany: a case study in cross-cultural management', *Industrial Relations: A Journal of Economics and Society*, **34** (3), 417–40.

Lu, W. (2014), *Localization of Human Resource Management Practices in China: A Qualitative Comparative Analysis Approach*, Doctoral Thesis No. 6/2014, Helsinki: School of Business, Aalto University.

Luo, Y. and O. Shenkar (2006), 'The multinational corporation as a multilingual community: language and organization in a global context', *Journal of International Business Studies*, **37** (3), 321–39.

MacDonald, S. and M. Cook (1998), 'An exploration of the use of language training in exporting firms: case studies from Northamptonshire', *Local Economy*, **13** (3), 216–27.

Marschan-Piekkari, R., D.E. Welch and L.S. Welch (1999), 'Adopting a common corporate language: IHRM implications', *International Journal of Human Resource Management*, **10** (3), 377–90.

Mirchandani, K. (2012), *Phone Clones: Authenticity Work in the Transnational Service Economy*, Ithaca, NY: ILR/Cornell University Press.

Muukari, K. (2008), *The Influence of Language Competence on Individuals' Career Paths in a MNC*, Master's Thesis, Helsinki: Helsinki School of Economics.

Mäkelä, K., I. Björkman and M. Ehrnrooth (2010), 'How do MNCs establish their talent pools? Influences on individuals' likelihood of being labeled as talent', *Journal of World Business*, **45** (2), 134–42.

Neeley, T.B. (2013), 'Language matters: status loss and achieved status distinctions in global organizations', *Organization Science*, **24** (2), 476–97.

Neeley, T., P.J. Hinds and C.D. Cramton (2012), 'The (un)hidden turmoil of language in global collaboration', *Organizational Dynamics*, **41** (3), 236–44.

Ng, T.W., K.L. Sorensen, L.T. Eby and D.C. Feldman (2007), 'Determinants of job mobility: a theoretical integration and extension', *Journal of Occupational and Organizational Psychology*, **80** (3), 363–86.

Nousiainen, A. (2011), *The Relationship between Language and Careers in Multinational Corporations*, Master's Thesis, Helsinki: School of Economics, Aalto University.

Osman-Gani, A.M. (2000), 'Developing expatriates for the Asia-Pacific region: a comparative analysis of multinational enterprise managers from five countries across three continents', *Human Resource Development Quarterly*, **11** (3), 213–35.

Peel, M.J. and H. Eckart (1997), 'Export and language barriers in the Welsh SME sector', *Small Business and Enterprise Development*, **4** (1), 31–42.

Peltokorpi, V. (2007), 'Intercultural communication patterns and tactics: Nordic expatriates in Japan', *International Business Review*, **16** (1), 68–82.

Peltokorpi, V. and E. Vaara (2012), 'Language policies and practices in wholly owned foreign subsidiaries: a recontextualization perspective', *Journal of International Business Studies*, **43** (9), 808–33.

Piekkari, R., P. Nell and P. Ghauri (2010), 'Regional management as a system: a longitudinal case study', *Management International Review*, **50** (4), 513–32.

Piekkari, R., E. Vaara, J. Tienari and R. Säntti (2005), 'Integration or disintegration? Human resource implications of a common corporate language decision in a cross-border merger', *International Journal of Human Resource Management*, **16** (3), 330–44.

Pohjanen-Bernardi, K. and K. Talja (2011), *Language Strategies in Finnish Small and Medium Enterprises*, Master's Thesis, Helsinki: School of Economics, Aalto University.

SanAntonio, P. (1987), 'Social mobility and language use in an American company in Japan', *Journal of Language and Social Psychology*, **6** (3–4), 191–200.

Selmer, J. (2006), 'Adjustment of business expatriates in Greater China: a strategic perspective', *International Journal of Human Resource Management*, **17** (12), 1994–2008.

Stahl, G.K., I. Björkman and S. Morris (2012), *Handbook of Research in International Human Resource Management*, 2nd edn, Cheltenham, UK and Northampton, MA, USA: Edward Elgar.

Stiles, P. (2012), 'The International HR department', in G.K. Stahl, I. Björkman and S. Morris (eds), *Handbook of Research in International Human Resource Management*, 2nd edn, Cheltenham, UK and Northampton, MA, USA: Edward Elgar, pp. 36–51.

Strauss, G. (2001), 'HRM in the USA: correcting some British impressions', *International Journal of Human Resource Management*, **12** (6), 873–97.

Sullivan, S. and Y. Baruch (2009), 'Advances in career theory and research: a critical review and agenda for future exploration', *Journal of Management*, **35** (6), 1542–71.

Sulonen, J. (2011), *International Organisations in the Linguistic Context of Quebec*, Master's Thesis, Helsinki: School of Economics, Aalto University.

Sørensen, E.S. (2005), *Our Corporate Language is English*, Master's Thesis, Aarhus: Aarhus School of Business.

Tapscott, D. (2009), *Grown up Digital: How the Net Generation is Changing Your Work*, New York: McGraw-Hill.

Tienari, J. and R. Piekkari (2011), 'Z ja epäjohtaminen' (Generation Z and non-management), Helsinki: Talentum.

Tietze, S. (2004), 'Spreading the management gospel – in English, language and intercultural communication', *Language and Intercultural Communication*, **4** (3), 175–89.

Ulrich, D. (1997), *Human Resource Champions*, Boston, MA: Harvard Business School Press.

Welch, D.E., A. Steen and M. Tahvanainen (2009), 'All pain, little gain? Reframing the value of international assignments', *International Journal of Human Resource Management*, **20** (6), 1324–40.

Wright, C., F. Kumagai and N. Bonney (2001), 'Language and power in Japanese transplants in Scotland', *Sociological Review*, **49** (2), 236–53.

Yamao, S. and T. Sekiguchi (2014), 'Employee commitment to corporate globalization: the role of English language proficiency and human resource practices', *Journal of World Business*, http://dx.doi.org/10.1016/j.jwb.2014.03.001, published online 27 March 2014.

Yoshihara, H. (2001), 'Global operations managed by Japanese and in Japanese', in J. H. Taggart, M. Berry and M. McDermott (eds), *Multinationals in a New Era*, Basingstoke, UK: Palgrave, pp. 153–65.

7. Language and international marketing

> If I am selling to you, then I speak your language, aber wenn du mir etwas verkaufst, dann mußt du Deutsch sprechen. (Willy Brandt, former German Chancellor, in Hagen, 2011)

In the book so far, we have concentrated on the role of language within the internationalizing firm. The focus has been on internal interactions between headquarters and the various subsidiary units, teams and individuals. We now turn our attention to the role of language in connections between internal organizational members and external parties. Obviously, marketing, or more specifically international marketing, is at the forefront of an internationalizing firm's interactions with foreign institutions, groups and individuals, involving communication with customers, intermediaries, government agencies and the like. How the organization handles these external interactions will have a critical impact on its ability to penetrate foreign markets.

The importance of language considerations for international marketing effectiveness is confirmed in a wide range of studies, some of which we identify in this chapter. Earlier chapters of this book have shown the myriad ways in which language effects play out in different communication forms, within and between organizations and individuals, potentially altering, distorting, filtering or blocking messages. For marketers, such effects are at the heart of marketing processes. In addition, lack of relevant language fluency in a foreign market can affect the ability of a firm's representative to collect relevant marketing information. This also demands communication proficiency (such as conversing with potential customers), and translators are only a partial answer. On-the-spot investigations are often a prelude to foreign marketing activity, and such direct market research action can be seriously restricted with respect to information collection and interpretation, and the quality of the information gathered.

The need to deal with language differences is often the first aspect of an international marketing attempt by a firm. As we have seen from examples in earlier chapters, when handled badly, language can hinder or prevent communication. In many cases, particularly for small and medium enterprises (SMEs), the firm does not possess the requisite foreign language skills among its employees, so it has to decide whether to simply leave it up to its foreign customer to handle the communication in whatever way it can, or find the resources necessary to have the information converted into the foreign customer's language. The results of a survey of German SMEs are indicative of the extent of the problem (Coleman, 2002, 21):

> Sixty per cent of those interviewed have no business connections with enterprises in the UK, but if they were to establish them, 80 per cent would prefer to correspond in German. Only 20 per cent would even be prepared to use English. Of those who trade with the UK in English, half said that they would look more favourably on UK companies that have made the effort to learn German.

The German perspective shines a language light on the contrasting viewpoint of some companies from English-speaking countries that English will be enough to deal with the international marketing demands of foreign expansion, as illustrated by the position of a 'typical respondent' in a survey of Irish exporters (Clarke, 2000, 83): 'English is the universal language of business; other languages are useful on a social or personal level, but we find that all our foreign customers speak fluent English.' Similarly, Swift (1993) found among UK executives that the major reason claimed for not learning foreign languages was the universality of English competence.

For many exporters, initial communication in foreign markets may involve dealing with potential intermediaries (see Chapter 8) in an effort to interest them in the possibilities of handling the exporter's product. In markets where such entities are experienced in handling discussions with exporters in a foreign language, such as German intermediaries dealing with UK exporters, the language question may not arise until direct interaction with end-customers is required. In contrast, Internet sales generally negate the need for an intermediary, so exporters may be confronted with end-customer enquiries in another language in a very direct form, and at an earlier stage.

Company responses to the need to cross the language barrier, and who is responsible for the exercise, vary. At various steps in the international marketing process, companies may have to resort to the use of translators, such as preparing multilingual brochures for distribution at international trade fairs; or acting as interpreters in negotiation situations. But translation assistance cannot help in many foreign-marketing situations, including important social interaction (Ellis, 2000). And the quality of on-the-spot, direct translation has been shown to be variable (Swift, 1991). Intermediaries often perform the translation function in the foreign market as part of their normal role in servicing their principals' businesses as they visit end-customers and the like. This is an important reason for many exporters preferring to use intermediaries. However, if the exporter has to use its own international marketing staff in the foreign market, these individuals will typically need a relatively high level of language competence to function effectively without a translator. At a broader company level, language difference in international markets poses questions regarding the appropriate extent of responsiveness and adaptation in different parts of a company's operations to the foreign language context. Language difference throws up a marketing barrier, and responding to it involves effort and cost. On the other hand, having appropriate language-proficient staff to deal with international marketing encounters can turn language difference into a marketing advantage relative to other foreign competitors.

INTERNATIONAL MARKETING ISSUES

Figure 7.1 summarizes the main international marketing issues that crossing into another language is likely to engender. In the following sections we explore how language affects these international marketing demands.

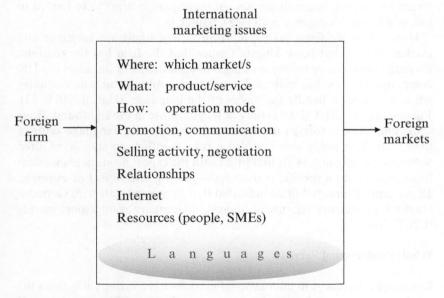

Figure 7.1   International marketing issues and language

Where: Choice of Foreign Market/s

As noted in Chapter 1, research has shown how language is an important part of measures of the psychic or cultural distance between countries (Johanson and Wiedersheim-Paul, 1975; Dow, 2000). Cultural distance influences choices made as to which foreign markets are interesting for international marketing purposes. Managers tend to be drawn to markets that are more readily accessible, with existing products, services and marketing programmes, reducing the extent and cost of adjustments that have to be made in order to ensure marketing effectiveness. Language clearly is an important element of the perceived attractiveness of different foreign markets, and dealing with language has cost implications. Particularly in the early stages of a firm's international marketing efforts, the convenience and comfort of not having to cross language barriers is an appealing proposition. Research has also shown that communication and contact patterns surrounding cultural similarity increase the likelihood of fortuitous foreign contact for exporters (Wiedersheim-Paul et al., 1978; Welch and Wiedersheim-Paul, 1980). There are many examples of exporters going to countries initially because they can use the same marketing material, in the same language, including television advertisements, without the need to make adjustments. Similarly, language influences have been found for other forms of foreign operation. For example, with respect to foreign direct investment, research has shown that Spanish firms have tended to follow a Spanish-language path (see Chapter 1).

However, some firms take a more proactive stance on language and market choice; that is, seeking to ensure that the firm has the requisite language competence before entering a new market. For instance, the UK company, Nikwax, has indicated that it 'only embarks on a new country when it is able to handle the basics of the language' (Hagen, 2011, 33). Further, as the CILT (2006) study of language use in the EU found, firms sometimes choose foreign markets on the basis of the language skills of their staff. This study also revealed a reverse influence: staff were hired with specific language skills that fitted with the export needs of respondent firms, often with a specific market focus driving selection. For example, 18 per cent of surveyed firms indicated that they hired staff with German-language proficiency because of interest in Germany as an export market (CILT, 2006, 27).

What: Products and Services

Language differences in international markets have various effects on the marketing process with respect to products and services. Branding is a good example. Zhang and Schmitt (2001, 313) argue that 'whenever a company introduces a product into a foreign market, one of its critical entry decisions is the choice of a local brand name . . . in the global marketplace, local names can add to – or destroy – established brand equity'. A basic issue is whether to adjust the brand name to the language used in a foreign market: simple translation may generate distortion or confused meaning. International marketing textbooks are replete with examples of firms having negative outcomes from direct translation without adjustment for language and cultural nuance (see, for example, Czinkota and Ronkainen, 2001). Brand name adjustment for the foreign language context may be a significant step for many internationalizing firms given the time, cost and effort associated with development of a global brand, and then the additional cost of adapting it for different markets. Additionally, there may be government constraints on how foreign brands can be used and presented in the foreign market, providing a further overlay of language adjustment demands (Czinkota and Ronkainen, 2001).

The branding issue is particularly fraught in a market such as China, but important nonetheless elsewhere, and even large multinationals with strong, globally established brand names have wrestled with how to handle it. Francis et al. (2002, 100) point out that 'the mind translates words into sound and brand names are likely to be said, not just read, [so that] the linguistic components of brand names, such as how pleasing it is and its connotations, can have a significant impact on the success of a brand name'. In their study of the extent of adaptation of international brands to Chinese markets (China and Hong Kong) by Fortune 500 companies, Francis et al. (2002) found that the bulk of brand names were adapted, with only 10 per cent retaining an English language name. These authors additionally point to research showing that 'Chinese localized brand names are also expected to have more positive connotations than the original brand names because of the Chinese cultural norm of imbuing names with special (positive) or lucky meanings'.

Similarly, Alon et al. (2009, 132, 124–5) maintain that 'for Chinese consumers to fully accept [international] brand names, the brand names should be translated into ideographic characters'. They describe the problems Coca-Cola had in translating the brand name into Chinese: to try to retain something of the sound of Coca-Cola from the original English but at the same time to ensure an acceptable meaning in the form of Chinese characters. The ultimate Chinese version literally back-translated as 'to allow the mouth to be able to rejoice', a compromise but a positive outcome in terms of the message promulgated. On the other hand, the authors refer to the unfortunate translation of Toyota's Prado vehicle into Chinese characters which literally translated as 'the mighty rule' or 'rule by force', which, given the history of Japanese wartime occupation of China, led to public and government outrage and reaction.

In their study of how foreign companies handled the issue, Alon et al. (2009, 133–4) found that, of 122 international brand names of companies in Shanghai, 62 per cent used 'transliteration without meaning' (Chinese and English names sound similar, but the Chinese characters have no discernible meaning) while 22 per cent used 'transliteration with meaning' (similar sound and the Chinese characters have a meaning that is reflective of the brand). Some companies seek to retain the appeal of a strong global brand name by including, for example, the English and Chinese versions of the name on the product (Zhang and Schmitt, 2001). More specifically, brand names of Fortune 500 companies in the study by Francis et al. (2002, 110) 'attempted to capture some product benefits in English, Chinese, or both languages'. A recent example of the role of language in global brand advertising was the use of the opportunity provided by having a Chinese woman, Li Na, competing in the 2014 Australian Open tennis tournament. One of the event's sponsors, the Australian bank ANZ, was aware of the high interest in the event back in China, so used Chinese signage around the tennis court whenever Li Na, the eventual winner, was playing. This was a way of promoting its name in the Chinese market. As an ANZ executive explained, 'The broadcast numbers are magnificently huge in China. And we are leveraging the numbers we get when Li Na plays' (Innis, 2014, 11).

Language is also an issue with respect to product labelling and packaging, and is critical to any associated instructional material regarding product use. Which language or languages should be used on the product, on the package and in usage instructions and/or product manuals? As most of us are aware, multiple languages are often used on packages and in product manuals and instructions as a way of dealing with the demands and costs of selling across multiple language zones. In the resulting communication clutter, there is a danger that the marketing message may be lost. The use of a foreign language, at least in part, may be useful in conveying an international image for the product concerned (for example, to emphasize French or Italian design in the UK). In Australia, for industrial products, German manufacture is highly regarded and can be supported by the use of German words. However, there is also the danger that it will convey an unacceptable level of foreignness to customers in the target market.

Services

Much of the research surrounding the effect of language on international marketing activities has focused on exporters of manufacturing products rather than services. The qualities of a product are often more readily apparent, and can be assessed by sight, feel and touch – and sometimes trial before purchase – so it can be argued that products are relatively less sensitive to language issues. While non-complex products may be easier to sell, and their features explained, in another language, this may not apply to more complex products, which require greater attendant communication, including some technical knowledge (Crick, 1999). However, in the activities surrounding the delivery and maintenance of many products, services are an important part of the total product package – for example with respect to large-scale capital equipment.

While the difference between products and services is often overdrawn, distinguishing service characteristics such as intangibility and perishability are often stressed (Czinkota and Ronkainen, 2001). Of importance, though, services tend to be more sensitive to language and cultural differences, due to the direct interaction between the service supplier and the client or customer in service delivery situations (Surprenant and Solomon, 1987; Cicic et al., 1999). Direct, face-to-face communication is often difficult to avoid, such as in the provision of health, legal, education and consulting services, ensuring that language becomes a key concern in service provision. For example, in health care, which has been subject to increasing internationalization, there has been growing recognition of the importance of language facility in the effective treatment of patients. Piekkari et al. (2013, 781) have noted that 'some multinationals have responded by providing patients with interpreter services and written translations, and making sure that clinicians and staff are linguistically concordant' (see also Brach and Fraser, 2002). In the international marketing of health services, language facility is likely to be critical to the ability of providers to interest potential customers in a health service available in another country, even before the actual provision, in whichever country that occurs – the patient's or the provider's. Some health organizations have regarded the marketing of linguistically and culturally aligned services as a way to increase market share (Betancourt et al., 2005).

As an illustration of international market development in health services, Russians have increasingly been going to other countries in order to have various forms of medical treatment, including major surgical operations. For example, one Helsinki hospital, Orton Orthopaedic Hospital, has had growth in Russian patients of about 65 per cent in the last few years. Promising as such numbers are, Finland overall attracts only a very low proportion of the total number of Russians travelling abroad for medical services. An industry investigation concluded that the 'key problem . . . was language and unless advertising, marketing and all contact are all in Russian, then the Russians will not go to that country'

(*International Medical Travel Journal*, 2013). While services are offered in Russian by Orton, there are various points where translators may be required, and this brings additional costs for Russian patients. Finnish health service providers have attempted to deal with this issue by building Russian-language skills among staff dealing with Russian patients and through Russian-language websites.

A study of language use in service encounters in Finland and Canada found that consumers' first language was important in high-involvement service encounters but of low importance in low-involvement encounters (Holmqvist, 2009). This research also indicated that consumers would be prepared to pay a higher price if the service were delivered in their first language, even for bilingual consumers. The importance of language in service encounters was consistent across four consumer groups studied: English-speaking Canadians, French-speaking Canadians, Swedish-speaking Finns and Finnish-speaking Finns. Holmqvist (2011, 188) also concluded that 'language is not merely a neutral tool of communication; rather it represents a sense of personal identity ... consumers have an emotional attachment to the use of their first language that transcends the practical aspects of communication with a service provider'. It can be argued that this will have an intangible benefit of greater confidence in the service provider.

A further illustration of the intrusion of language into the communication processes surrounding international service provision is provided in the study of 100 Scottish hotels by Martin and Davies (2006) of the handling of telephone enquiries from callers using a language other than English. They found that the level of language skills possessed by Scottish hotel operatives was poor, and this limited their ability to answer queries. Martin and Davies focused only on French and German as these two tourist groups were important to the region. They examined three stages of communication: employees' reaction to the foreign caller; their ability to reply in the foreign language; and their attempts at service recovery when unable to respond in the foreign language. Overall, 29 per cent were able to reply in French and 19 per cent in German. Of those not able to reply in either French (27 per cent) or German (23 per cent), staff tried to find someone who could take the call. The disturbing finding was the number of hotel operatives who simply hung up the phone or left the caller on hold until the caller hung up! Clearly, lack of an effective language response to foreign callers using a language other than English was leading to a loss of business, although the extent of loss would be difficult to gauge. This is one of the general problems in trying to bring greater attention to language issues in international business: losses due to language-based communication problems are not always apparent and may be hidden by those employees experiencing them. A similar point is stressed by MacDonald and Cook (1998). They point to the neglect of language training for office staff given the importance of their role in responding to telephone enquiries.

The tourism sector, given the rise of international tourism, is one where language represents an important consideration, and with a somewhat different context than that typically found in international business encounters. Cohen and Cooper (1986, 533, 537–8) stress 'the high temporariness of the foreigners [in international tourism encounters] and the high degree of linguistic accommodation of the locals to them'. Further, they argue that 'whereas in most of the local–foreigner situations subjected to socio-linguistic analysis it is the foreigner who tries to learn the locals' language, in touristic situations, this rarely takes place'. This dictum does not always apply, though, particularly in countries where English is the mother tongue, as noted in the Scottish study above (Martin and Davies, 2006). As Japanese and Korean tourist numbers increased in Australia in the 1990s, this strained the ability of providers to deliver services in Japanese and Korean languages rather than English. Both groups of tourists expressed their dissatisfaction with the extent of translation provided, including signage at appropriate points (Reisinger and Turner, 1998). It has been argued that a lack of language accommodation in the UK tourism industry is reinforced in tourism courses by a lack of stress on the importance of language training (Leslie and Russell, 2006). This stood in contrast to the higher regard for language training among non-UK tourism students. The attitude among many UK students could be summarized as 'most Europeans speak English anyway so why invest in language training?'.

In general, linguistic accommodation is particularly evident in institutionalized tourism situations where a tour leader is expected to be able to deal with the language diversity of tour participants, and companies may separate tour groups on the basis of language. 'Language performance' may be an important influence on the level of satisfaction with an international tourism encounter (as noted above). In many cases it is a basic feature of enjoyment. On the fringes of institutionalized mass tourism programmes, retailers sometimes advertise their language skills as a way of attracting customers, for example by placing a country's flag on a brochure or prominently displaying it in a retail outlet or eating establishment.

Choice and Use of Foreign Operation Modes

A basic international marketing question is: what operation mode should be used in the foreign market? The choice is important in terms of what marketing activities the entrant foreign firm will be responsible for, and the extent to which it will be required to function in the foreign language. It may be possible to leave a foreign intermediary or partner firm in the foreign market to carry out much of the interaction with customers in the local language, reducing the extent of the *language burden*. We take up this important point in Chapter 8 where we deal with the interactive effects between language and foreign operation modes.

International Marketing Communication

Firms use a multitude of avenues to communicate with customers and other relevant organizations and individuals in foreign markets. These include promotional literature such as catalogues or brochures; utilization of the Internet and social media such as Facebook and Twitter; advertising; negotiations; and network interactions (for example, government and other institutional players). Where these necessitate the crossing of language boundaries, how this process is handled can have substantial effects on the quality and outcome of international marketing efforts, and ultimately on the viability of the international venture. As Francis et al. (2002, 99) argue, 'language difference is critical, because language is the fundamental medium through which marketing communications such as advertising messages and brand names are delivered'. The problem is not just about communicating a product and service offering to a foreign customer in the customer's language. Longer-term damage may be generated by a reduced ability to understand a customer's needs and to build effective relationships and trust (Swift, 1991; Holden, 1998).

Despite this somewhat obvious fact, a study by Wright and Wright (1994) found that only about 50 per cent of UK firms exporting to Europe produced documentation in the language of their customers. The language deficit was even more pronounced when it came to personal contact between the UK exporters and their European customers. The language deficiency was not only because of the lack of language-qualified staff at the exporters. There was also a problem in effectively using the language skills of their staff: 41 per cent of staff with some French competence 'never use it', while the figure was 55 per cent for those with German competence. The authors concluded that language deficiency, which affected UK firms' ability to communicate with potential and actual customers, was hurting the export performance of UK firms in Europe.

In another study of UK SMEs, awareness of the importance of languages within most firms was evident, but this was not matched by their use or in recruitment and training policies (Crick, 1999). The perception that English was widely spoken and used in foreign markets was a factor in this. Not surprisingly, this study found that the use of foreign languages was strongest in the areas of sales and marketing, where the main activities, in order, were personal selling, trade fairs and promotion (Crick, 1999, 27). A similar result was found in a study of Irish exporters: 86 per cent of respondents indicated that foreign language skills were 'important, very important or essential' for exporting success (Clarke, 2000, 82). However, again, this position was not backed up by action. About two-thirds of companies in this study conducted their exporting business entirely in English, despite significant activity in non-English-speaking European countries. In addition, there was limited language training or language-focused recruitment. Not surprisingly, use of foreign languages in communication tasks (mainly telephone calls) occurred on an infrequent basis. Telephone calls to the office in a foreign language pose a particular problem for companies with a limited range of language skills: they are often neglected or ignored. MacDonald and Cook (1998, 225) relate the comment of one interviewee in their study of mainly SMEs in Northamptonshire (UK): 'I am always very impressed if I ring up a lot of German companies or French companies, immediately they answer the telephone they switch into English . . . I wish that I had people here who could do that' (see also Martin and Davies, 2006).

At the Tourism Service Centre, a call centre in Switzerland set up in the 1990s by various Swiss organizations dealing with tourists, the ability to respond to enquiries from other parts of Europe in multiple languages is critical. This is reflected in its staff selection policy that potential employees should be proficient in at least three languages. Multilingualism in this context is seen as a 'financial advantage for companies as it is cheaper and more practical, for example, to have employees who are able to answer phone calls in more than one language' (Duchêne, 2009, 4). Duchêne (2009, 12) refers to the experience of one call centre employee in responding to an enquiry in Dutch who commented: 'they are simply delighted when someone speaks [back to them in] Dutch'. In such circumstances multilingualism becomes an important marketing asset. Further, 'offering clients the opportunity to express their wishes in their own language will shorten the length of the call and hence its cost'. A similar pattern is reflected in the experience of Convergys, a US firm, which is a major operator of call centres providing outsourcing services (e.g. in human resources) for international clients. It pays more for its workers in Hungary than in India because of their 'multilingual skills that Indians do not have. Convergys provides services to clients in 15 countries and in 10 European languages' (Dolan, 2006, 31).

A study by Marcella and Davies (2004) of 13 Scottish food and drink companies marketing to French customers illuminates the many international marketing communication demands of language difference, and of the difficulty in responding to them. The authors considered various aspects of the communication process, including advertising, packaging, branding, logos, catalogues, trade fairs, Internet websites, public relations, face-to-face meetings and oral presentations. While the firms in the study recognized the importance of communicating in French, achieving this in practice was difficult: 'Present practice tends to be publication in English, relying on the customer to make the effort to translate the data' (Marcella and Davies, 2004, 1393, 1386–7). The authors found that only four of the case firms had a language strategy in place, such as part-time employment of foreign nationals, or hiring graduates with combined language and marketing skills. One respondent in this 'aware' group commented: 'the use of the customer's language is a fundamental principle of marketing practice . . . it's part of reaching out to the customer'. For the language-aware firms, language proficiency was important for more than sales and marketing. It was also important for the firm's administrative processes and quality assurance. That is, the need for language went deeper into the internal workings of the firm. In contrast, some Scottish firms were unconvinced about the need for a language strategy. Respondents indicated that using French did not make a discernible difference to service quality. One went so far as to say that 'it does not matter which language you speak as long as you can communicate'. This comment was said to have reflected others in the Scottish study: languages were viewed as less important than other marketing communication skills. Indeed, there seemed to be considerable self-justification of the respondents' lack of language skills.

A survey by Vandermeeren (1999, 289) of exporting companies located in Germany, France and the Netherlands investigated the use of English in written communication. Pre-sale documents (e.g. advertising catalogues and offers) were more frequently written in the customer's language than post-sale documents (e.g. confirmations of orders and invoices). Perhaps not surprisingly, companies that adapted to the client's language achieved higher export performance. French companies (the sellers) using German when corresponding with German companies sold more than those who operated in English. Vandermeeren concluded that adapting language to the foreign customer's requirements contributes to export performance. That is, 'linguistic adaptation to its clients can make the difference between failure and success in establishing and maintaining a business relationship'. These findings reflect those of Wright and Wright (1994). Their results showed that UK firms committed to using the language of their customers experienced a much larger increase in profits (about double) compared to those without such a commitment.

International Sales Force Activity

As we detail in Chapter 8, rather than using intermediaries in the foreign market, exporting firms often use their own sales staff (referred to as direct exporting). Inevitably, these people perform a variety of activities: selling, product and service promotion, market research, negotiation, trouble-shooting, attending trade fairs, and relationship cultivation. Even if exporters use foreign intermediaries to handle most of the marketing in the target market, they will still need to monitor intermediary activities, gather market information and handle key relationships. It is also not uncommon for exporting firms to undertake sales activities alongside those handled by their intermediaries – sometimes dealing directly with major customers (referred to as dual distribution; see Welch et al., 2007).

A consequence of an exporting firm using its own international marketing staff is the amount of foreign travel involved (Welch et al., 2007). Regardless of advances in information and communication technology, face-to-face communication remains important. Surveys indicate that, even in the aftermath of the global financial crisis, international business travel has been maintained because of the importance attached to dealing face to face with foreign market stakeholders. As we stressed earlier, the ability to conduct meaningful dialogue requires a shared language and, despite the inroads made by English as the international business language, studies show how important it is for salespeople to be able to operate in the language of the foreign client/customer.

Negotiation

In a study of the international activities of 1261 SMEs in the UK, France, Germany and Spain, Hagen (1999) found that negotiation, mainly in oral form, was one of the key tasks that demanded foreign language expertise. This was confirmed in a case study investigation of a small group of UK exporters (MacDonald and Cook, 1998). Some firms stressed that they needed foreign language skills in negotiations with foreign partners and customers, and this demanded a high level of language fluency to be effective. Foreign language issues obviously come to the fore when negotiations are held between parties who normally use different languages and therefore choices have to be made as to which language or languages should be used in negotiations (Swift, 1991), as illustrated in Figure 7.2. As a marketing manager at a Finnish SME explained regarding the firm's international marketing experience, 'language skills are one of the prerequisites for starting negotiations' (Pohjanen-Bernardi and Talja, 2011, 82). Parties could agree that one of their languages, or a shared language such

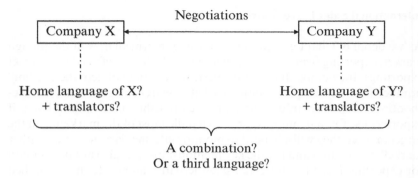

Figure 7.2   Which language in negotiations?

as English, should be used. Alongside such a solution a translation facility could be employed – for example someone sitting in or simultaneously translating through headphones. Answers to these questions are important for the conduct and efficiency of the negotiation, but they also have implications for power and dependence in relationships and the notion of psychological advantage.

Adler and Graham (1989, 517) have noted that 'when individuals interact with people from different cultures, the differences become salient ... moreover, when people in interpersonal situations confront these actual differences, they tend to exaggerate them'. However, important as language choice may be, research on international business negotiations shows that it is part of a broad exchange process, alongside influences such as organization-related factors, negotiator characteristics (including language), the negotiation content and context, inter-negotiator interaction and the ability to handle compromise (Reynolds et al., 2003). Language choice and language use in prior communication and the negotiation are part of the adaptation process between the parties that research has shown is important in achieving positive negotiation outcomes (Francis, 1991).

Schneider and Barsoux (1997, 195) point out that choice of language can create 'winners or losers as language dominance is often associated with power and influence'. Swift (1991, 44) cites the example of a UK sales executive operating in the Spanish market who noted the psychological disadvantage of conducting negotiations in English, seemingly to his advantage as the native speaker, and yet, as he explained: 'I am aware that sometimes they revert to their own language just to get an edge. Even when we are negotiating in English, they talk between themselves in their native tongue. I would love to know what they are saying.' A similar reaction is often reported by Australians negotiating in Japan. Such asides during a negotiation may be innocent: the Spanish or Japanese merely comparing their interpretations of what is being said in English, rather than a negotiation ploy.

Language acts as an exclusionary as well as an inclusionary agent, as we mentioned in earlier chapters. Apart from the mediation effect, language sets the atmosphere of exchange, signalling preparedness to establish common ground, and the surrounding socialization processes. An important part of negotiation is the small talk preceding and around the formal processes. Westerners negotiating in Asian markets sometimes encounter at least a day of preliminary activities such as visits to factories, other institutions or tourist sites before any formal negotiation takes place, so that language use in a social setting immediately has to be accomplished. Some Western countries require a similar approach to negotiation. As the Slovenian firm, Bisol, indicated: 'Operating in the Russian and Bulgarian markets demands great investments of time, personal communication, gift-giving, social chitchat about non-business topics, generous time arrangements for negotiations' (Hagen, 2011, 105). Of course, there is a considerable difference between negotiation as part of an initial exchange between the parties and that between parties with long-standing relationships. Considerable language accommodation in one form or another may have developed (e.g. via the insertion of personnel with appropriate language skills) to the point where language is less of a factor in the atmosphere and conduct of the negotiation.

Relationships

Much of international marketing is about establishing, building and managing relationships with key stakeholders in foreign markets: intermediaries, customers, government officials, suppliers, marketing agencies and the like. As we discussed in Chapter 5, researchers in this area have been heavily involved with seeking to understand relationship dynamics and their effects on firms' international operations. The research carried out by the IMP Group since the 1970s demonstrates how language aspects are often asymmetrical in buyer–seller exchanges: not surprisingly, sellers are more likely to seek to adjust to the language of potential buyers than vice versa (Håkansson, 1982; Håkansson and Snehota, 1995). For example, industrial buyers in the UK, France, Germany, Italy and Sweden generally did not find language to be a problem in cross-country exchanges, whereas suppliers experienced difficulties. Adjustment by the seller to the language of the buyer provided evidence of commitment and adaptability. Overall, the IMP studies demonstrated that, when information was provided in the buyer's language, distance between the parties was reduced, and the supplier gave evidence of likely commitment and responsiveness to potential foreign customers. One of the early findings was that lack of language proficiency hampered the ability of buyers and sellers to develop closer actor bonds. According to Turnbull and Cunningham (1981, 86), 'about half of the marketing respondents [in their study of industrial marketing exchanges across France, Germany, Sweden and Italy] said it caused them difficulties in dealing with the UK. Indeed for 25 per cent of all respondents, language creates a serious obstacle.'

As social exchange is recognized as a critical element of buyer–seller interaction, it is not unexpected that proficiency in the buyer's language is deemed essential to the development of closer personal relationships. As the manager at a medium-sized UK manufacturer commented: 'I think what is important though is that when you are trying to build up personal relationships with a customer you can answer questions but you can't get to know them unless you understand their own language. That's what we try to do' (MacDonald and Cook, 1998, 221). The ability to establish social relationships not only enhances buyer–seller interaction, but assists in reducing business uncertainty (Håkansson and Wootz, 1979). As we discussed in Chapter 5, effective communication is important in building trust, which is a critical component of relationships. For trust to be established between the sender and the receiver of knowledge, a relationship has to be built. Roberts (2000, 434) stresses face-to-face contact and socialization as important in this process, especially in the context of communication difficulties that arise from 'differences in culture and language'. A case study of a Norwegian firm by Welch et al. (2002) is illustrative of the importance of the personal side of buyer–seller relationships. They relate a comment by one of the Norwegian interviewees: 'Personal contacts were so important that during the first three years [of] dealing with the Russians, I had between 50 to 100 trips to Russia, talking to suppliers and maintaining the personal network.'

Similarly, the exporting literature demonstrates how the use of personal networks contributes to foreign-market expansion. In his review of 35 exporting studies, Leonidou (1995, 40) concluded that access to foreign-market information had 'the greatest inhibiting effect on the firm's ability to initiate or develop exports'. The use of personal networks as trusted sources of information in the uncertain decision context of export entry has been shown to be important in various exporting and entrepreneurship studies (see, for example, Ambler and Styles, 2000; Harris and Wheeler, 2005). Ellis and Pecotich (2001) explore the link between social networks, antecedent social ties and export initiation through an exploratory case study investigation of 31 export initiations by eight Australian SMEs, involving a wide range of foreign countries and languages. They

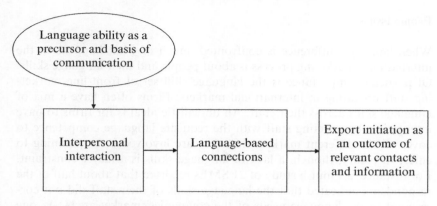

Figure 7.3   Language, networks and export initiation

concluded that the international social network of decision-makers was critical in delivering information about export opportunities vital to export initiation.

The link between networks and export initiation is shown in Figure 7.3. Only basic conversation is possible between two individuals who have a limited shared language facility that will inevitably constrain the development of any relationship and the depth of information and knowledge exchange (Sunaoshi et al., 2005). In instances involving a third party (for example, a foreign intermediary) as the language go-between, the resultant dyadic relationships will be between buyer and translator (intermediary), and seller and translator. This limits the development of direct buyer–seller relationships as it is difficult to build relationships and trust at arm's length through a third party. The frustration of the language barrier in restricting the ability of an exporter to connect with end-customers only via the foreign intermediary was expressed by one company in the following terms: 'Whilst the German distributors speak excellent English, you go out visiting the customers out there – it's so difficult – they don't speak English at all. Most of them speak a smattering of it, but sit down in a meeting to have a conversation to try and do it in English is very difficult' (MacDonald and Cook, 1998, 221).

In general, foreign language competence on the part of the seller in the foreign market enables the salesperson or firm to build closer relations with end-customers, rather than going through language-competent intermediaries (agents, distributors). As a result, the seller is able to monitor market developments more effectively and reduce reliance on the intermediary. This may be particularly important in the lead-up to a move to replace the intermediary with a firm's own sales subsidiary (Petersen et al., 2000).

People Issues

When language difference is confronted, much of what happens in the international marketing process is about people and their language skills. Of particular importance is the language skill set of front-line marketing staff operating in international markets. Firms often have a mix of language skills across their staff. An unrealistic ideal is for firms to have international marketing staff with the requisite language competence to cover all the different markets that they are involved in or planning to enter. In reality, though, a lack of language skills is a major constraint. For instance, a Finnish study of 21 SMEs reported that about half of the respondents indicated that the language skills of their staff did not correspond to the language needs of the companies' market areas. As one respondent noted, 'we should have a Chinese-language Internet store, but nobody knows the language' (Pohjanen-Bernardi and Talja, 2011, 50). A similar finding is reported in a study of SMEs across EU countries. A lack of staff with appropriate language skills was the main factor driving loss of business due to deficiencies in foreign language competence. Moreover, 13 per cent of companies indicated that the language skills of their staff had influenced the choice of export markets (CILT, 2006).

However, as discussed in Chapter 6, language considerations are not always taken into account in human resource decisions. Arguably, international marketing efforts are tied to recruitment and training steps to build language competence. For example, in the CILT study (2006, 39) mentioned above, one French respondent commented: 'We have been employing for two years a trainee who is Chinese. It is essential for us because she can contact people directly and help us to stay in touch in China.' Ultimately, marketing strategy needs to be in harness with an internationalizing firm's language resources and human resource practices.

SMEs and Language Resources

In our discussion of languages in international business, there has been a weighting towards the multinational. However, we would not like to give the impression that language matters only in such firms. In fact, it is difficult for SMEs to avoid the language challenge that dispersed internationalization brings. At the same time, SMEs typically face additional issues connected with their small size and lack of human and financial resources. In a survey of Welsh manufacturing firms, small companies (fewer than 50 employees) indicated that lack of financial resources was a significant export impediment – rated as well above that of language constraints (Peel and Eckart, 1997). Larger companies in the study regarded financial resources as far less important, but considered language constraints to be more important in restricting exports than smaller firms. Resource constraints such as adequate finance affect the ability of SMEs to cope with an expanding language challenge if they enter increasingly distant markets. A UK study of a small group of exporters by MacDonald and Cook (1998) illustrates this. Respondents recognized the advantage of having foreign language competent staff in their exporting operations, but commented that lack of resources constrained their ability to take corrective action. In Peel and Eckart's (1997) study, small firms exported to, and imported from, significantly fewer countries than either medium-sized (50–100 employees) or large firms. Consequently, they indicated significantly less need for translation services or foreign language training, and had significantly fewer employees with foreign language skills.

The potential consequences of a lack of language resources within SMEs for the ability to pursue international expansion are graphically highlighted by Crick (1999, 21). He cites the example of a UK firm that went into receivership. The receivers found a letter in a filing cabinet that had gone unnoticed as it was written in German. It contained 'an order of such volume that it would have saved the company'. A similar case is highlighted by Knowles et al. (2006, 634). A UK printing firm was approached about printing a catalogue for a Norwegian furniture manufacturer: 'Of course, it would all have been in Norwegian and we're not terribly fluent in that language . . . So we decided not to pursue it any further.'

Limited resources may also engender a bias toward countries with similar languages. The resources constraint on language responsiveness to potential customers was mentioned by some Finnish respondents with regard to website translations: 'Although desirable, it is impossible for a small company to keep the website updated in many languages'; and 'We had translated our old website into several languages. Our aim is to translate the website again into more languages, but at the moment we don't have [the] resources' (Pohjanen-Bernardi and Talja, 2011, 85–6).

An overview of language concerns in the EU from an SME perspective is provided by the CILT study of European SMEs (CILT, 2006). Nearly 2000 exporting SMEs were included in the study, covering 29 European states, plus 30 multinationals to provide a counterpoint in perspectives on language. In 15 of the 29 countries, at least 50 per cent of the SMEs claimed to have a language strategy. Eleven per cent reported that they had lost a contract as a result of the lack of language skills, though many were reluctant to indicate the size of that lost contract. In the Finnish SME study, six of the 21 firms reported that a lack of language skills had led to the loss of international business in terms of the inability to enter new markets (Pohjanen-Bernardi and Talja, 2011).

The difference between UK and Finnish SME perspectives is evident in their approaches to the role of languages and international operations: the UK with English as its mother tongue and a global business language versus Finland operating as a dual-language society, with Finnish and Swedish having limited use beyond Finland (apart from Estonia and Sweden respectively). International operations for Finnish firms inevitably mean an early need to deal with other languages. A 1996 UK government study of northern English exporting SMEs revealed that 33 per cent had encountered language or cultural barriers, a figure almost twice as high as firms in comparable regions in Spain and Germany (cited in Crick, 1999). In Crick's (1999) study, referred to above, of 185 UK SMEs, ranging from very small (1–9 employees) to medium-sized (100–249 employees), firms were asked in which business departments or functions they used foreign languages and to what extent. The main area that emerged was that of sales and marketing. Further, in response to a follow-up question on the aspects of sales and marketing, the main areas in order of importance were: personal selling, exhibitions, public relations and promotional literature. This result applied for all firms, regardless of size. Reasons proffered for not using foreign languages were: English widely spoken, and the lack of skills within the company. In contrast, a survey of 21 Finnish SMEs by Pohjanen-Bernardi and Talja (2011) found that there was a high level of awareness of language as a pressing issue. Fourteen companies in the study reported that they had offered language training to their staff members during the previous three years.

International Marketing, the Internet and Language

From the earliest stages, the marketing potential of the Internet has been enthusiastically welcomed for its contribution to such activities as selling, research and dialogue with the full range of market players. This enthusiastic response was not always matched by consideration of all the language and cultural implications that would still have to be dealt with. For example, in 2000, the then Asia-Pacific head of Visa, the credit card company, advised Australian companies to develop websites in languages other than English, due to the influence of the proliferation of non-English-language websites. This seems a simple, somewhat obvious, step, but what he did not say was, among the many languages, which one or ones? How would the choice be determined – for example, simple demand from customers? There are other flow-on issues as well, such as having language competent people who can follow up website enquiries in the relevant languages. In fact, and particularly for smaller firms embarking on international sales with limited resources, language demands for the whole company may change dramatically, with significant resource implications. In other words, while the Internet opens up the whole world in a seeming instant, resource constraints still apply, with important implications for the ability to handle language questions.

As many have pointed out, the easy response is to translate a website into another language, or multiple languages, thereby achieving rapid localization (Petersen and Welch, 2003), but the difficult part is the follow-up. Figure 7.4 illustrates some of the questions posed by multilingual responses to a website: inevitably they create demand for responses in multiple languages, thereby creating the need for suitably language-competent staff, effective machine translation systems or the resort to outsourcing. Some companies may decide to ignore multilingual enquiries, given the cost of such responses. For those companies with rich and diverse language resources, there is an incentive to use these as part of the appeal to diverse markets via the language profile of their websites.

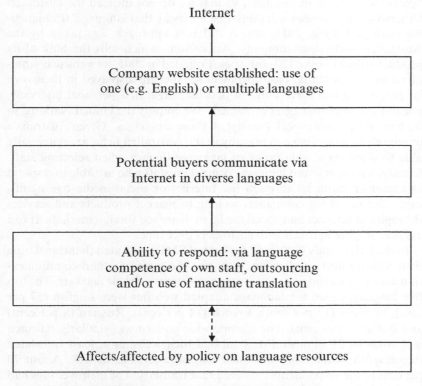

Internet

Company website established: use of
one (e.g. English) or multiple languages

Potential buyers communicate via
Internet in diverse languages

Ability to respond: via language
competence of own staff, outsourcing
and/or use of machine translation

Affects/affected by policy on language resources

Figure 7.4   Internationalization, language and the Internet

As shown in Figure 7.4, the language issues and responses thrown up by website creation and diversity of foreign markets include a company's language resources policy. Once a company decides to mount a response to the language demands created by foreign buyers seeking to communicate in their own language, resources will need to be allocated to support the response in whatever form that takes. This may provoke the development of a deliberate policy regarding the assembly of an appropriate level of language resources for its Internet-based international marketing activities.

Many small companies, because of limited resources to mount a meaningful multi-language response, may be better off operating only in English as a signal to potential customers about their true language competence, rather than raise false expectations. Having a website in multiple languages is a clear signal to potential foreign customers using those languages that the firm will be able to respond in the languages listed. As one Finnish SME indicated: 'If we have brochures in different languages, we start getting inquiries in those languages. We should write something like "please write to us in English", so that we do not mislead the customer. Otherwise the customer will think that we speak that language' (Pohjanen-Bernardi and Talja, 2011, 86). A different approach was taken by the Australian underwear company, AussieBum, which sells the bulk of its product online to over 120 countries. Founded in 2001, its website is structured so that potential customers will see the site displayed in their own language, and can correspond in that language. In a personal interview, one of the owner/managers explained, 'We employ the United Nations, so we have people who speak [nearly] all those languages.' Given Australia's immigration programme over many years, Australian firms are potentially able to draw on a wide range of language fluency when selecting staff. Clearly, having relevant language competent staff who are able to respond to customer enquiries through the Internet or social media has significant advantages for companies seeking to market products and services through the Internet and social media in dispersed foreign markets. It can assist in staying in touch with customers over time.

In the CILT study (2006), 62 per cent of SMEs indicated that translating their website into another language was the most common communication action in adapting to the language diversity of their markets. The top five languages used for language-adapted websites were English (57 per cent), German (15 per cent), French (14 per cent), Russian (8 per cent) and Italian (7 per cent). The Europe-wide pattern was similarly reflected in a study of 21 Finnish SMEs: all had their websites at least translated into English, while most had other-language versions as well. About 70 per cent of the respondents indicated that translation of their websites had resulted in increased business (Pohjanen-Bernardi and Talja, 2011).

Developments in machine translation technology, which we addressed in Chapter 2, have provided some way around the need to set up websites in multiple languages, but this places the burden of translation back on to potential customers. In marketing terms, the aim should be to make the buying process as comfortable as possible for prospective buyers.

CONCLUSION

International marketing is a critical part of a firm's ability to achieve success in international expansion. In Chapter 1, we demonstrated how companies can avoid foreign language demands for some time by following a same-language path in foreign market choice, particularly if the home country has English as its mother tongue. However, our discussion in this chapter has shown that, once international marketing crosses language boundaries, language demands affect all aspects and stages of the foreign-marketing process, and sometimes powerfully so. And the Internet, with its instantaneous global reach, is ensuring that the world, with its mix of languages, is arriving at the doorstep of even those companies that seek to remain monolingual. The reality is that, however interesting the product and service offering of a company is to potential customers, they normally prefer to conduct business in their own language. Thus the pressure soon builds to develop a response in the language of the customer, whatever the foreign-market expansion strategy.

Some of the responses in dealing with the language demands of international marketing activities are shown in Figure 7.5. We have shown that companies can partially respond to the language issue through third parties, which is where agents/distributors, foreign partners and the like perform not only a selling role in foreign markets but a key language role in many cases. Companies have long used outsourcing as a way of coping with foreign language demands. At the least, external translators are often used, accompanying the foreign company's salespeople in sales visits or assisting in negotiation sessions. At some stage, though, if foreign language demands grow in line with market growth and expansion into new markets, firms are likely to consider different internal responses as a way of developing their own language operative capacity. This may involve language training of some, particularly marketing, staff involved in dealing directly with foreign counterparts in customer firms. Or the issue could be handled through language-driven recruitment of new staff. In general, having staff with market-appropriate language skills is a major advantage in international marketing, which points to the importance of the link to a company's human resource management policies and actions.

Responses

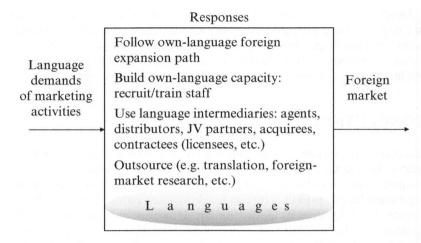

Figure 7.5   *Potential responses to language demands in marketing activity*

In the following chapter, we extend our analysis into an important aspect of the international marketing process: the interplay of the choice and use of various foreign operation modes and language.

REFERENCES

Adler, N.J. and J.L. Graham (1989), 'Cross-cultural interaction: the international comparison fallacy?', *Journal of International Business Studies*, **20** (3), 515–37.

Alon, I., R.F. Littrell and A.K.K. Chan (2009), 'Branding in China: global product strategy alternatives', *Multinational Business Review*, **17** (4), 123–42.

Ambler, T. and C. Styles (2000), 'The future of relational research in international marketing: constructs and conduits', *International Marketing Review*, **17** (2), 492–508.

Betancourt, J.R., A.R. Green, J.E. Carrillo and E.R. Park (2005), 'From the field: cultural competence and health care disparities – key perspectives and trends', *Health Affairs*, **24** (2), 499–505.

Brach, C. and I. Fraser (2002), 'Reducing disparities through culturally competent health care: an analysis of a business case', *Quality Management in Health Care*, **10** (4), 15–28.

Cicic, M., P.G. Patterson and A. Shoham (1999), 'A conceptual model of the internationalization of services firms', *Journal of Global Marketing*, **12** (3), 81–106.

CILT (National Centre for Languages) (2006), *ELAN: Effects on the European Economy of Shortages of Foreign Language Skills in Enterprise*, Brussels: European Commission.

Clarke, W.M. (2000), 'The use of foreign languages by Irish exporters', *European Journal of Marketing*, **34** (1/2), 80–90.

Cohen, E. and R.L. Cooper (1986), 'Language and tourism', *Annals of Tourism Research*, **13** (4), 533–63.

Coleman, A. (2002), 'Speaking in tongues', *Director*, **55** (11), 21.

Crick, D. (1999), 'An investigation into SMEs' use of languages in their export operations', *International Journal of Entrepreneurial Behaviour and Research*, **5** (1), 19–31.

Czinkota, M. and I. Ronkainen (2001), *International Marketing*, 6th edn, Orlando, FL: Harcourt College Publishers.

Dolan, K. (2006), 'Offshorers go offshore', *Business Review Weekly*, 27 April–3 May, 30–31.

Dow, D. (2000), 'A note on psychological distance and export market selection', *Journal of International Marketing*, **8** (1), 51–64.

Duchêne, A. (2009), 'Marketing, management and performance: multilingualism as commodity in a tourism call centre', *Language Policy*, **8** (1), 27–50.

Ellis, P. (2000), 'Social ties and foreign market entry', *Journal of International Business Studies*, **31** (3), 443–69.

Ellis, P. and A. Pecotich (2001), 'Social factors influencing export initiation in small and medium-sized enterprises', *Journal of Marketing Research*, **38** (1), 119–30.

Francis, J.N.P. (1991), 'When in Rome? The effects of cultural adaptation on intercultural business negotiations', *Journal of International Business Studies*, **22** (3), 403–28.

Francis, J.N.P., J.P.Y. Lam and J. Walls (2002), 'The impact of linguistic differences on international brand name standardization: a comparison of English and Chinese brand names of Fortune 500 companies', *Journal of International Marketing*, **10** (1), 98–116.

Hagen, S. (1999), *Business Communication across Borders. A Study of Language Use and Practice in European Countries*, Stirling: CILT/Languages NTQ.

Hagen, S. (2011), *Report on Language Management Strategies and Best Practice in European SMEs: The PIMLICO Project*, Brussels: European Commission.

Harris, S. and C. Wheeler (2005), 'Entrepreneurs' relationships for internationalization: functions, origins and strategies', *International Business Review*, **14** (2), 187–207.

Holden, N. (1998), 'International marketing studies – time to break the English strangle-hold?', *International Marketing Review*, **15** (2), 86–100.

Holmqvist, J. (2009), *Language Influence in Services*, Doctoral Thesis No. 194, Helsinki: Hanken School of Economics.

Holmqvist, J. (2011), 'Consumer language preferences in service encounters: a cross-cultural perspective', *Managing Service Quality*, **21** (2), 178–91.

Håkansson, H. (1982), *International Marketing and Purchasing of Industrial Goods: An Interaction Approach*, New York: John Wiley.

Håkansson, H. and I. Snehota (1995), *Developing Relationships in Business Networks*, London: Routledge.

Håkansson, H. and B. Wootz (1979), 'A framework of industrial buying and selling', *Industrial Marketing Management*, **8** (1), 28–39.

Innis, M. (2014), 'As Li heads to finals, ANZ aims ads at her fans in Asia', *International New York Times*, 25–26 January, 11.

International Medical Travel Journal (2013), 'Finland care promotes health tourism to Russians', http://www.imtj.com/news./entryid82=405904, accessed 3 March 2013.

Johanson, J. and F. Wiedersheim-Paul (1975), 'The internationalization of the firm: four Swedish cases', *Journal of Management Studies*, **12** (3), 305–22.

Knowles, D., T. Mughan and L. Lloyd-Reason (2006), 'Foreign language use among decision-makers of successfully internationalised SMEs', *Journal of Small Business and Enterprise Development*, **13** (4), 620–41.

Leonidou, L.C. (1995), 'Empirical research on export barriers: review, assessment, and synthesis', *Journal of International Marketing*, **3** (1), 29–43.

Leslie, D. and H. Russell (2006), 'The importance of language skills in the tourism sector: a comparative study of student perceptions in the UK and continental Europe', *Tourism Management*, **27** (6), 1397–407.

MacDonald, S. and M. Cook (1998), 'An exploration of the use of language training in exporting firms: case studies from Northamptonshire', *Local Economy*, **13** (3), 216–27.

Marcella, R. and S. Davies (2004), 'The use of customer language in international marketing communication in the Scottish food and drink industry', *European Journal of Marketing*, **38** (11/12), 1382–95.

Martin, A. and S. Davies (2006), 'An evaluation of the language skills in Scottish hotels', *Journal of Hospitality, Leisure, Sport and Tourism Education*, **5** (1), 4–15.

Peel, M.J. and H. Eckart (1997), 'Export and language barriers in the Welsh SME sector', *Small Business and Enterprise Development*, **4** (1), 31–42.

Petersen, B., D.E. Welch and L.S. Welch (2000), 'Creating meaningful switching options in international operations', *Long Range Planning*, **33** (5), 688–705.

Petersen, B. and L.S. Welch (2003), 'International business development and the Internet, post-hype', *Management International Review*, **43** (Special Issue 1), 7–29.

Piekkari, R., D.E. Welch, L.S. Welch, J.-P. Peltonen and T. Vesa (2013), 'Translation behaviour: an exploratory study within a service multinational', *International Business Review*, **22** (5), 771–83.

Pohjanen-Bernardi, K. and K. Talja (2011), *Language Strategies in Finnish Small and Medium-Sized Enterprises*, Master's Thesis, Helsinki: School of Economics, Aalto University.

Reisinger, Y. and L. Turner (1998), 'Cross-cultural differences in tourism: a strategy for tourism marketers', *Journal of Travel & Tourism Marketing*, **7** (4), 79–106.

Reynolds, N., A. Simintiras and E. Vlachou (2003), 'International business negotiations', *International Business Review*, **20** (3), 236–61.

Roberts, J. (2000), 'From know-how to show how? Questioning the role of information and communication technologies in knowledge', *Technology Analysis and Strategic Management*, **12** (4), 429–43.

Schneider, S.C. and J.-L. Barsoux (1997), *Managing Across Cultures*, Hemel Hempstead, UK: Prentice Hall.

Sunaoshi, Y., M. Kotabe and J.Y. Murray (2005), 'How technology transfer really occurs on the factory floor: a case of a major Japanese automotive die manufacturer in the United States', *Journal of World Business*, **40** (1), 57–70.

Surprenant, C.F. and M.R. Solomon (1987), 'Predictability and personalization in the service encounter', *Journal of Marketing*, **51** (2), 73–80.

Swift, J.S. (1991), 'Foreign language ability and international marketing', *European Journal of Marketing*, **25** (12), 36–49.

Swift, J.S. (1993), 'Problems with learning foreign languages for international business', *Journal of European Industrial Training*, **17** (10), 35–42.

Turnbull, P. and M.T. Cunningham (1981), *International Marketing and Purchasing: A Survey among Marketing and Purchasing Executives in Five European Countries*, London: Macmillan.

Vandermeeren, S. (1999), 'English as a lingua franca in written corporate communication: findings from a European survey', in F. Bargiela-Chiappini and C. Nickerson (eds), *Writing Business: Genres, Media and Discourses*, Harlow, UK: Pearson, pp. 273–91.

Welch, D.E., L.S. Welch and V. Worm (2007), 'The international business traveller: a neglected but strategic human resource', *International Journal of Human Resource Management*, **18** (2), 173–83.

Welch, L.S., G.R.G. Benito and B. Petersen (2007), *Foreign Operation Methods: Theory, Analysis, Strategy*, Cheltenham, UK and Northampton, MA, USA: Edward Elgar.

Welch, L.S., G.R.G. Benito, P.R. Silseth and T. Karlsen (2002), 'Exploring inward–outward linkages in firms' internationalisation: a knowledge and network perspective', in S. Lundan (ed.), *Network Knowledge in International Business*, Cheltenham, UK and Northampton, MA, USA: Edward Elgar, pp. 216–31.

Welch, L.S. and F. Wiedersheim-Paul (1980), 'Initial exports: a marketing failure?' *Journal of Management Studies*, **17** (3), 333–44.

Wiedersheim-Paul, F., H.C. Olson and L.S. Welch (1978), 'Pre-export activity: the first step in internationalization', *Journal of International Business Studies*, **9** (1), 47–58.

Wright, C. and S. Wright (1994), 'Do languages really matter? The relationship between international business success and a commitment to foreign language use', *Journal of Industrial Affairs*, **3** (1), 3–14.

Zhang, S. and B.H. Schmitt (2001), 'Creating local brands in multilingual markets', *Journal of Marketing Research*, **38** (3), 313–25.

8. Language and foreign operation modes

> I have to admit that international sourcing is not very well organized because of language problems. We have one person who is responsible for sourcing, and then he has one assistant buyer who sources only from domestic sources due to the lack of language skills. (Interview with a manager of a Finnish SME, in Korhonen, 1999, 174)

Internationalizing firms use a variety of modes or methods when operating in foreign markets. These include exporting; contract-based operations; and different forms of foreign direct investment (FDI) that involve the establishment, or acquisition, of a firm in the target foreign market, perhaps in partnership with a local company and/or another foreign firm. At first glance, an obvious question is: what has this to do with language? In this chapter we show how there is a surprisingly intimate connection between language and the ways in which companies carry out their foreign operations. This connection runs in both directions. The type of mode or mode combination chosen, and the way it is put into practice, affects the nature of language demands created for the firm; and, in reverse, there are also situations where language influences the type of modes chosen and used in the foreign market (see Figure 8.1). The type of foreign operation mode used by a company has a major influence on management, and contact activities involving the internationalizing firm and various entities in the foreign market. As Welch et al. (2007, 5) point out, 'the nature and character of the management process, including aspects like control, coordination and staffing, are driven by the type of foreign operation'.

As an example, a firm might set up a foreign sales office in a particular foreign market to handle exports to that market because it has an indi-

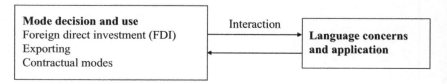

Figure 8.1   Language and foreign operation modes

vidual on staff with the relevant foreign language skills (and other relevant cultural and/or market knowledge): thus language influences the foreign operation mode decision. In many cases, the person's foreign language facility has been derived from being a native of that country or having lived there for some time (Welch et al., 2007). Language may be an important aspect of the ability of immigrants to return to their country of origin, as we now see for many Chinese returnees. There is an obvious incentive to use such skills when a relevant foreign opportunity arises. In countries such as Canada and Australia, with substantial numbers of immigrants, companies often find a diverse range of language skills as a result of having employees who were born overseas, or the children of the overseas-born, for whom the foreign language has been maintained in the family home.

In the other direction, as a result of using a particular mode to establish operations in a target foreign market, such as through exporting, a firm may become 'language aware' through having to deal with foreign customers, suppliers and government officials in their local language. Mode use thus influences management thinking about the need to develop appropriate language resources. In general, though, language tends to have limited impact on the mode decision, driven as it is by other internal and external influences that are viewed as having a more immediate and powerful impact on firms' international sales and profitability (Welch et al., 2007).

However, we know little about the language–mode connection because there has been very little research conducted on this topic, particularly when it comes to contractual modes of operation such as licensing, franchising and management contracts. This stands in contrast to the important place of foreign operation modes in international business (IB) research in general. Research on language and international marketing (mainly covering exporting; see Chapter 7) has led the way in trying to take account of language because of a natural interest in trying to ensure marketing effectiveness in foreign markets, but such research has not been extended into a specific consideration of the language–mode connection. Thus, in this chapter we explore this connection. We begin by outlining the range of foreign operation modes used by internationalizing firms. A brief overview is provided in the following section. For a comprehensive treatment of modes and their characteristics, and the implications for internationalizing companies' strategies and management, see the work of Welch et al. (2007). We then explore the language–mode connection, demonstrating the types, and extent, of influence and interaction that play out over time.

It should be stressed that firms often use combinations of modes or mode packages in servicing foreign markets. For example, licensing is frequently used as an add-on to FDI (Benito et al., 2011). Such combinations or mode packages are an additional consideration in the exploration of languages and foreign operation modes, and may change the nature of language demands.

TYPES OF FOREIGN OPERATION MODES

Figure 8.2 summarizes the foreign operation mode options that companies might employ in foreign operations. The double-headed arrows indicate that they are often used in combination. The different modes, and how they are used in the foreign market, may result in considerable variation in the type and extent of direct involvement by companies, and this is an important factor in the kind of language demands faced. Cooperation agreements are shown in a separate box, and may vary from informal understandings of, for example, mutual market assistance without a contract, through to substantial cooperation at many levels such that the arrangement has many of the features of a formal alliance.

As we now outline, within each of the broad categories shown in Figure 8.2 there are many different forms, which allows for quite fine-grained variations from one foreign market situation to another.

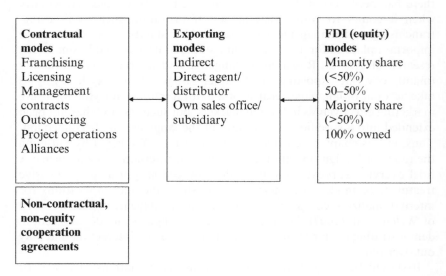

Figure 8.2   Options of major foreign operation modes

Foreign Direct Investment (FDI)

FDI is typically defined as occurring when the level of ownership via equity in a foreign enterprise reaches a level at which the investing company acquires a significant influence, whether exercised or not, over the key policies of the foreign entity, through a long-term investment (Welch et al., 2007). Many countries use 10 per cent equity as the defining level of FDI for statistical purposes. In global terms FDI is a significant factor in global business activity, and the sales generated by companies' FDI far exceed the gross value of global exports of goods and services. Investment activity may be enacted via two main paths: acquisition of an equity stake, part or full, in an operating company within the target market; or establishment of a new company, with or without partners, and operations from scratch – a so-called 'greenfield' investment. An in-between form has been referred to as 'brownfield' investment. In brownfield cases, a local enterprise and its assets in the target foreign market are acquired, but then the investing company undertakes major restructuring of, and new investments in, the acquired entity to the point where it comes to resemble a greenfield operation. Acquisition might be enacted via a merger or takeover: put simply, a merger refers to two companies agreeing to join as one firm, in the foreign location, whereas an acquisition is a takeover of one firm by another, although the distinction is often a fine one, as many so-called mergers are in reality takeovers because of the stronger position of one of the parties, based on relative size or other features. As we later discuss, the power positions can be underlined through the choice of language used across the merged organization as an integrative mechanism.

Contractual Modes

Contractual modes come in many forms, as shown in Figure 8.2, and we outline the different characteristics of each form in more detail later in this chapter. Whatever the form, though, they are governed by a contractual agreement covering what is being transferred between the parties, who undertakes what activities in fulfilment of the contract, and the type and extent of compensation paid by the recipient to the foreign provider. There is considerable variation in the extent of direct involvement in the foreign market across the different contractual modes and depending on how they are managed over time. Contractual modes often end up being highly relationship-intensive and requiring close oversight – meaning heavier direct involvement in the foreign market than many firms anticipate when choosing such modes at the outset.

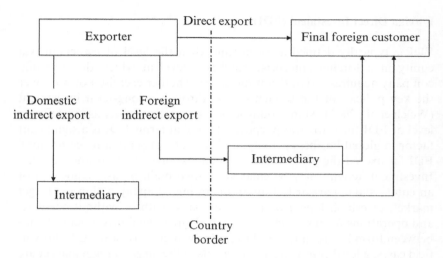

Figure 8.3   Export operations

Exporting

As illustrated in Figure 8.3, exporting is handled in three main ways, For some firms, the exporting act is fully handed over to an intermediary (for example a trading company) in the firm's home (domestic) market. As such, the sale is much like any other sale at home, and the 'exporter' may have no direct dealings at all with the foreign market. Trading companies still perform a major role in the world trading system, providing an important service for companies of all sizes, but particularly many smaller companies. Most firms involved in exporting play a more substantial part in the exporting act, through using intermediaries in the foreign market (agents or distributors). Such intermediaries typically handle marketing and sales activities in the foreign market, although there is a wide variation in the nature and extent of involvement of exporters alongside their foreign intermediaries. Exporting directly to the foreign market without the assistance of intermediaries is less common, but is still an important part of the total exporting picture. Some studies show direct exporting to be as high as 30 per cent or more of total exporting activity (Burgel and Murray, 2000; Dimitratos and Lioukas, 2004). In the direct form, the exporter takes on the full demands of marketing and servicing in the foreign market, with all its language implications if a different language is involved. In addition, exporting is often carried out under the umbrella of FDI. Indeed, some FDI is carried out with the sole purpose of supporting exporting activities, in the form of foreign sales subsidiaries or sales offices. Important as it is, however, we treat this activity as part of FDI.

Mode Combinations

The fact that foreign operation modes are frequently used in combination adds a further layer of mode complexity that can affect how the language issue is dealt with (Benito et al., 2011). For example, FDI is often used alongside contractual modes and export operations, providing mutual support in seeking to achieve diverse goals apart from the general objective of foreign market sales, such as using a licensing agreement to ensure control of the firm's intellectual property. In general, language tends not to be a consideration in the construction of mode combinations or packages, and the packages themselves may evolve over time with mode additions and deletions on the basis of experience in specific foreign markets, but language may come into play in various ways as a factor in how and when foreign market entry is accomplished, managed and advanced over time.

Inward/Outward Operations

Foreign operation modes are used for inward as well as outward international activities: many companies start their international activities via inward operations. In the process, the firm begins to learn about the demands of international involvement, including language aspects. It establishes foreign networks, some of which can be employed to assist in later outward internationalization (Welch and Luostarinen, 1993). Importing is an example, as is international outsourcing, the product of which is often brought back into the originating company's home market, as we discuss later in this chapter.

At first glance, it might seem that inward operations are just a mirror image of outward operations, so that any language issues will similarly be reflected on the inward side. To some extent this is the case, but there is an important difference: on the inward side companies are buying, in some form, from foreign sources. This means sales for the foreign supplier firm. The evidence shows that, in such situations, the foreign supplier firm will normally do as much as possible to accommodate the language base of the buying firm: there is often substantial asymmetry in the approach to language by the seller and buyer.

These points are illustrated by Bloigu's study of Finnish firms in Russia (2008, 83–4). English might be used as a link language in some Finnish–Russian inter-company interaction, but could not be taken far in the Russian context. One of Bloigu's Finnish interviewees commented: 'A Russian customer wants to do business in his/her mother tongue even though he/she would know English. The motto is you can buy in any language but if you want to sell you'd better speak the language of your customer.' Another respondent commented (Bloigu, 2008, 84):

> Customers want all written etc. material in Russian because the organization does not possess adequate language skills, interpretation [translation] causes great problems and unnecessarily slows down information flow. In addition, some kind of neo-nationalism is prevailing – only Russian communication is right and English brochures are often not even accepted.

Put simply, operating in Russia, or communicating with Russians, generally required the use of Russian, and foreign firms would not be able to avoid this reality at some stage in any attempt to penetrate the Russian market. This business reality frames many of the language responses on the inward side, but it is not as simple as the Russian example might imply.

There are many situations where a buyer might be the one prepared to undertake *language accommodation*. For example, a company may have noted an interesting franchise concept in a foreign market and be keen to bring the system to its own market, instigating contact and trying to persuade the foreign franchisor to agree to a franchising relationship. Thus the buyer becomes the supplicant in the relationship, ensuring a different approach to language use. This will often happen in licensing situations too if the potential licensee is seeking to obtain what is viewed as a particular, unique technology that is owned by, and only available from, a foreign firm. Such technology could be embodied in capital equipment that the buyer may be particularly keen to obtain, again being prepared to accommodate the language of the seller. Clearly, it is difficult to generalize on the language front simply on the basis of the side of the sales exchange that a firm finds itself on. To some extent each case is different and has its own language nuance. What can be said in general is that, whether buying or selling, the process will proceed more readily if either party in the potential exchange is willing and able to bridge the language divide; and of course, if both sides share this approach, the process may be accelerated even further.

DIFFERENT MODES, DIFFERENT LANGUAGE DEMANDS

Our overview of the modes that firms use in international operations shows something of the extent of variation of their direct involvement in the foreign market, depending on the type of mode employed. Likewise,

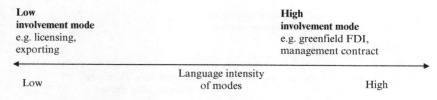

Figure 8.4   Foreign operation modes and language intensity

this variation affects the extent to which internationalizing companies may be called on to bring language resources to bear, through their own staff or externally, to effectively service the foreign market. Clearly, some modes, such as licensing or the use of a foreign distributor to handle the exporting activity, allow a company to minimize the need to use directly the language of the foreign market. This is shown in Figure 8.4 as a low-involvement mode from the firm's perspective, generating low need for language skills. Modes in this category also tend to be low-control; that is, they require low levels of direct management, leaving the management of activities in the foreign market to the foreign partner in whatever form that takes.

At the other extreme, modes such as a greenfield FDI or a management contract arrangement require a much more involved approach by the internationalizing company to both language and management aspects. Indeed, in their early foray into the UK via FDI, Japanese companies showed a strong preference for entry via greenfield operations rather than acquisitions of already established companies. By so doing, the Japanese entrants felt that they would be able to control the development of their own companies' culture at the UK unit, rather than inherit an existing one.

Management and other activities carried out in the foreign unit will generally, although not in all situations, have to be carried out in the local language, assuming language difference. Thus higher, locally specific language intensity will be required. Many of these demands will not be able to be outsourced, requiring the appointment or transfer of language-competent staff to the foreign unit. Modes in this category are generally high-control operations.

While different foreign operation modes call on different language responses in character and extent, the connection may be substantially moderated by the overlap in language abilities within the companies con-nected by the relationship created by the mode used in foreign market entry, as illustrated in Figure 8.5. If there is substantial overlap, the lan-guage demands of the operation, whether small or large, can be readily accommodated. Of course, language accommodation might be handled

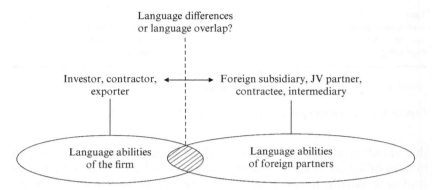

Figure 8.5   Company language abilities and interaction with foreign partners

primarily on one side of the relationship, for example by the foreign licensee. This might seem to be a comfortable arrangement for the licensor, but it delivers substantial control of information flow from the foreign market into the hands of the licensee (Petersen et al., 2000). As we discuss later in this chapter, in the longer term, this may be seen as a negative.

FDI

In this section, we consider three major forms of FDI: mergers and acquisitions, greenfield investments and equity joint ventures.

Mergers and acquisitions (M&As)

These are major ways in which FDI is enacted, sometimes with important differences in language effects. Whatever the resulting level of foreign ownership of the acquired/merged foreign unit, the extent of direct involvement in management of the new unit may vary widely, with corresponding variation in how language differences are handled. Some of the language management variations resulting from foreign acquisitions are illustrated in Figure 8.6. We stress that the examples referred to are illustrative rather than exhaustive.

In Situation 1, the existing management group at the acquired unit might be left in place, so that the direct language demands for the acquiring company within the relevant foreign market remain relatively unchanged. The Finnish bakery and confectionery company Fazer Group acquired a minority holding in St Petersburg-based bakery, Hlebnyi Dom, in 1998 and continued to increase its shareholding in the company until it reached full ownership in 2000 (Karhunen, 2008). Fazer decided to

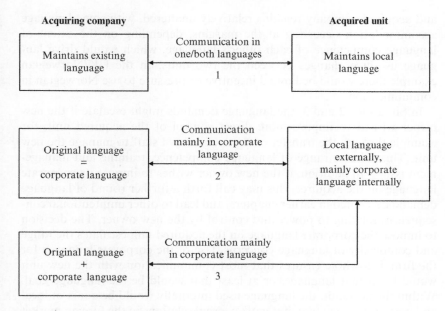

Figure 8.6   Language choice after an acquisition

keep the old management team headed by the former owner of Hlebnyi Dom, Mr Fedorenko. The communication between the headquarters in Finland and the Russian operation was undertaken mostly in English, Fazer's corporate language. Within the Fazer Group in the confectionary division, however, Swedish was also used alongside English because of the merger between Fazer Confectionery and the Swedish Cloetta AB in 2000. Quite a few managers at Fazer's headquarters studied Russian in order to be able to communicate informally with their new colleagues in St Petersburg. The younger generation of Russian managers, who were around 35 years old, were able to communicate in English but the older managers lacked the requisite fluency in English (Karhunen, 2008).

As the example of the Fazer Group suggests, the language demands of communication between management in the acquired unit and the acquiring firm depend on the extent of language difference and relevant language competence on both sides. For example, for a UK firm, an acquisition in Norway would pose limited communication difficulties given the high level of English language competence within Norway, so that the extent of language difference would have limited effects. The same could not be said for an acquisition in Japan or Korea. Thus, in the first example shown in Figure 8.6, the approach to language in both the acquiring and acquired company remains relatively unaltered, with some language accommodation occurring at the margins, depending on the extent of language competence of each other's language, which would drive language use in exchanges between the two units. In the UK/Norwegian example there would be limited incentive or pressure to use Norwegian in communication.

In Situations 2 and 3, the language demands might escalate if the new owner wished to impose more direct control of the acquired unit, for example through the transfer of some of its own staff to manage the new unit. This raises a range of language competence, training and management issues. In addition, if the new owner wishes to impose its corporate language on the acquiree, this may call forth a further round of language demands, as noted in earlier chapters, and lead to other unintentional consequences relating to power and control by the new owner. The decision to impose the corporate language on the acquired unit escalates the range and complexity of language concerns. Use of the corporate language for the firm as a whole ensures that most communication with the new unit would be in that language, or at least that would be the language goal. Within the new unit, the language used internally would be a mix of local and corporate languages, but with external relations in the foreign market being handled in the local language. Bloigu (2008) found that, for Finnish companies with operations in Russia, there could be some interchange between the Russian unit and the Finnish parent in English, but only Russian could be used in the local market. It would be some time before English competence in the Russian units was so widespread that English could be the dominant language in inter-unit exchanges.

The choice of language in a merger/acquisition can affect how participants see themselves in relation to the new organizational construct, and can affect the type and quality of relationships between the different groups as the language divide is crossed. Birkinshaw et al. (2000) stress the importance of human integration in ensuring acquisition success but point to its complexity. Language is an under-appreciated component of this in many cases. The language decision could be contentious in political terms: an acquisition can be seen as an instance of the takeover of one nation's business by that of another, which would then be reinforced by the decision to use the acquiring firm's language. An important aspect of this issue is whether the corporate language of the acquiring firm is the same as the original language of the owner. When these differ, as shown in Situation 3 (Figure 8.6), the corporate language, often English, in many instances is a language-neutral one, as in the takeover of a Norwegian company by a Swedish firm. In an interview study of two Finnish–Swedish mergers, Louhiala-Salminen (2002) found that having to use a foreign language was the main source of communication problems between individuals across the merged organizations. For many of the Finnish staff the concern was the increased need to use English and Swedish rather than Finnish, particularly given that the bulk of internal firm communication was in oral form.

A study of the merger between two Nordic banks (Merita, Finland and Nordbanken, Sweden) in 1997 revealed that there may be other issues consequent on language choice (Piekkari et al., 2005; Vaara et al., 2005). Following the merger, the new organization, MeritaNordbanken, chose Swedish as its common corporate language (CCL). This resulted in a major divide between the groups of employees. The study focused on the Finnish side of the merger, and showed how many of the Finnish staff felt a negative impact from having to use Swedish. Interviewees noted a sense of having their professional competence impaired and a reduction in career prospects compared to native Swedish speakers. Subsequently, the language issue was substantially resolved following further mergers with the Danish bank Unidanmark and the Norwegian bank Christiana Bank og Kreditkasse in 2000. A decision was made to use English as the CCL, accompanied by a change in the company name to Nordea.

The above examples demonstrate the difficulties some individuals may encounter if suddenly forced to deal with new language demands generated by a merger or acquisition, bearing in mind the time and effort it takes to become even basically competent in a foreign language. And these problems may be accentuated if the merger/ acquisition introduces new 'company speak'. For example, the US-based corporation, General Electric, acquired the Finnish company, Instrumentarium, in 2003. Not only did the employees of the Finnish unit need to expand their use of English, but they also had to quickly pick up the codes and abbreviations widely used in communications within General Electric (Lovio et al., 2003). The example also illustrates the interaction of the layers of language we mentioned in Chapter 1 (Figure 1.1).

As we have shown in earlier chapters, language differences are not removed by the use of a CCL. After a merger or acquisition, language differences make it harder to transfer people and knowledge, and to inculcate a corporate value system. In a study of 35 acquisitions by Western companies in Hungary, the Czech Republic, Slovakia and Poland, Villinger (1996, 200) found that

> Language problems are clearly perceived to be the dominant barrier to successful learning following a western acquisition in central eastern Europe. Although interpreters can be used to ease this problem, a real understanding of the true, underlying meanings is frequently impossible, if no means of direct communication, i.e. common language, are available.

So far we have been discussing examples of mergers/acquisitions in which one party joins with, or takes over, another. However, in some cases more than two companies from different countries, with different languages, merge. A case in point is Scandinavian Airlines (SAS), based in Sweden, Denmark and Norway. SAS did not formally adopt a CCL as this was seen, in part, as potentially disturbing the power balance between the three nations (Bruntse, 2003). The three Scandinavian languages had equal status within the organization. However, in much of the internal communication so-called '*sas*peranto' was used, constituting a mixture of Scandinavian languages (sometimes referred to as parallel multilingualism). '*Sas*peranto' is dominated by Danish words but has some Swedish words and a Swedish touch to it. Bruntse (2003) reports that, while many SAS employees were able to cope with this construction, a large group experienced difficulties in comprehension, particularly during company presentations and telephone calls, and some admitted to experiencing loss of face, and avoided making necessary telephone calls to foreign colleagues.

Greenfield investments

M&As on a global basis constituted almost 50 per cent of total FDI in the period leading up to the global financial crisis. Since 2007, though, there has been a notable fall in M&As in absolute terms and in relation to greenfield investments. UNCTAD (2013) data indicate that in 2012 global greenfield investment projects were about double the value of M&As. A recovery of M&As, however, can be expected as world economic growth continues to develop, and as companies from countries such as China and India seek to penetrate world markets via the acquisition of Western multinationals, as in the case of the Chinese company Lenovo acquiring parts of IBM. Nevertheless, it is clear that greenfield investment remains an important FDI path for internationalizing firms, and will continue to do so.

Many of the issues around language and M&As discussed above apply with respect to greenfield investments. In general, these revolve around how the new investment in a foreign country is organized and managed over time, with the extent of direct involvement in the running of the foreign operation being crucial. Inevitably, though, because the investing company develops the foreign investment itself, albeit with the help of outsiders such as consultants in the foreign market, it has to deal with language issues from the very outset. Therefore it can be argued that it should be more conscious of such aspects, more language aware, as it makes decisions regarding how the foreign operation ought to be structured and managed over the long term.

Equity joint ventures
As a form of FDI, international equity joint ventures exist when two or more companies have a share in the ownership of another company in a foreign location, and the owners could be all foreign or a foreign/local mix. International joint ventures (IJVs) potentially create a more demanding language situation, depending on the languages employed by the owners as they enter the IJV. The levels of ownership by the partners in the IJV are a consideration. In the case of an IJV that has a local and foreign partner and the foreign investor has less than 50 per cent equity in the new organizational entity, the foreign firm may not be in a position to determine what language or languages are designated for use at the joint venture. Language may be a constraint on the ability of the foreign investor to fit the IJV into its wider global operations. The parties will still need to communicate, even if the local operations are mainly handled by the local IJV partner, although this would be made more difficult if there are few members of both management teams that have shared language capabilities. This would also constrain the ability to transfer knowledge in both directions. Of course, in situations where the foreign investor has more than 50 per cent equity, it is in a stronger position to control language and other policies, but this is by no means absolute. Again, much depends on the extent and level of shared language capabilities.

To some extent, answers to the language question will be driven by the broader global context of the foreign investor and what this means in a language sense. If it is a widely dispersed multinational with a CCL, such as English, the IJV partner may be happy to fit into this framework, particularly if it has a reasonable level of English competence among its staff. More problematic is the reverse situation, in which the foreign investor has a less common language than its new foreign partner, and may even regard the IJV as providing a *language bonus*.

As Chinese companies proceed into the international arena via FDI, whether through acquisitions or other forms of foreign establishment, they face difficult language questions. The reality is that there is limited competence in the Chinese language that they can draw on in equity IJVs or through M&As. It is not surprising that many have resorted to the adoption of English as a quasi- or near-full CCL. As was earlier found for Japanese firms following their initial FDI forays into the USA and the need to deal with English in those operations, the language bonus for Chinese internationalizing firms may be delivered as an ability to operate more effectively in other foreign markets where English is widely used (Welch et al., 2001). A striking example of this potential development is the Chinese multinational Lenovo. English is now its official language, and some of its senior executives are foreign. The language question could not be avoided after it acquired IBM's personal computer business in 2005 – a business that was roughly twice its size at the time. The current CEO, Yang Yuanqing, 'spoke little English at the time of the deal, moved his family to North Carolina to immerse himself in American ways' – and in the English language (*The Economist*, 2013, 53). In a similar case, Hiroshi Mikitani, CEO of the Japanese online shopping company Rakuten, with global operations, adopted English as the CCL in 2010, even though only about 10 per cent of staff could function in English at the time. Between the ages of seven and nine, Mikitani had lived in the USA with his parents, and returned later to undertake an MBA at Harvard University (Neeley, 2011). However it emerges, CEO language awareness may be an important factor in the development of language strategies alongside internationalization and mode choice.

Contractual Modes

As noted above, contract-based operations such as licensing or franchising may be favoured because they are seen as posing limited language demands. Nevertheless, it is still hard to avoid language concerns when the language divide has to be crossed, even when working through a contractee (that is, the contracted firm) in the foreign market. First, finding potential contractees and then initiating contact will normally require use of the local language. Then a language for negotiation has to be agreed between the parties. Translation of key documents will be required (see Chapter 2). Knowledge transfer has to be undertaken, which, as noted in Chapter 4, tests both sides' ability to handle language differences; and successful training in an appropriate language is critical to the foreign contractee's performance. From a language perspective, however, by using a foreign contractee, in whatever form, to undertake operations in the foreign market, an internationalizing firm is able to avoid most of the day-to-day language demands of foreign involvement.

Franchising
Franchising is a well-used, contract-based operation form in international business, often associated with the global activities of multinational companies (MNCs) such as McDonald's and Subway. Such companies use business format franchising, which is 'characterized by an ongoing relationship between franchisor and franchisee that includes not only the product, service and trademark, but the entire business format – a marketing strategy and plan, operation manuals and standards, quality control, and continuing 2-way communication' (International Trade Administration, 1987, 3). Franchising is often not used as a single mode,

but as part of a mode package, in association with an IJV or wholly owned subsidiary in the foreign market which undertakes on-the-spot management of the process of rolling out the franchise system – including choice of franchisees, training, marketing, franchising package modifications, franchisee audits and the like (Welch et al., 2007). Also, it is common for the foreign unit to set up company-owned operations, for example retail outlets, as a prelude to the franchising roll-out; for training; as a model for incoming franchisees; and to sort out the potential need for local adjustments because of different local laws regarding employment and different cultural biases, such as product content and decor of outlets (see Figure 8.7).

One of the advantages of using franchising is that much of the local 'work' in the foreign market is carried out by the franchisee. Key activities such as customer interaction and delivery of products and/or services are handled by the franchisee. In that sense, use of the local language is largely taken out of the equation as an issue for the entrant firm within the foreign market. But it does not disappear and may still pose significant demands in that a high level of communication tends to be required between the franchisor and its foreign unit as the franchising package is transferred and inculcated in the new foreign unit and passed on to franchisees. Which language should/can be used if a language divide exists? If the language divide between the parties is substantial, then it becomes a factor in building the relationship at the outset through personal interaction when negotiating the initial deal and settling on the franchising contract. It might even cause the relationship to flounder before it gets started. Even after establishment of the franchising operation, management and maintenance of the franchising operation require continuing transfers of technology, and marketing knowledge and materials, from the foreign investor.

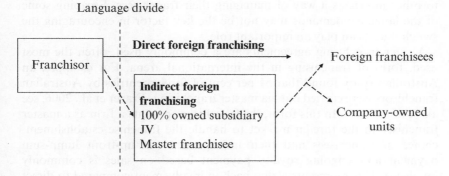

Figure 8.7   Franchising modes and language

Franchisors typically seek to ensure a high degree of standardization in their franchising activities and content when expanding internationally. This has important implications in terms of quality and consistency of documentation, marketing, training and managerial control. For example, the translation of documents and promotional material (see Chapter 7) can be critical if consistent meaning is to be maintained across language boundaries. Key questions relating to training are: who should undertake the activity and what language should be employed in the process?

Language may interpose in a multitude of ways if franchising companies decide to handle the activity directly rather than through some form of intermediary when it uses direct franchising in the foreign market (see Figure 8.7). Direct foreign franchising remains a commonly used form of foreign operations for franchisors (Welch et al., 2007). In a recent study of Spanish franchisors' operation form in emerging markets (including Mexico, Argentina, Brazil and China), direct franchising constituted almost 40 per cent of total franchising operation forms (Baena, 2009). With direct franchising, the franchisor appoints and manages each individual franchisee in the foreign market, rather than working through another entity (compared with the other three forms noted in Figure 8.7), and therefore is fully exposed to any language difference. The franchising package has to be translated, potential franchisees sought and normally dealt with in the foreign language, a legal agreement has to be negotiated and established in the foreign language, and individual franchisees have to be managed by the franchisor's staff, through visits and the like. These call on the full range of language-related personal and HRM issues noted in earlier chapters. The process of managing individual franchisees from a distance is difficult, and grows increasingly so as the number of individual franchisees in the foreign market rises; when language poses a barrier the difficulty is all the greater. It is not surprising that many franchisors shift to other modes as a way of managing their franchisees. Escaping some of the language demands may not be the key factor in encouraging the switch, but it can play an important role.

Master franchising agreements are a commonly used, often the most used, form of franchising in the international arena. For example, an Australian study found that 51 per cent of foreign entries by Australian franchisors were carried out via master franchising (Frazer et al., 2006; see also Alon, 2006). In this form, the franchisor appoints a firm as a master franchisee in the foreign market to handle the franchise establishment, choice of franchisees and their management (an up-front lump-sum payment and ongoing royalty payment based on sales is commonly involved). This represents a step back in involvement compared to direct franchising. One of the obvious attractions is that this form allows the franchisor to limit its commitment in terms of resources employed in the project, including language resources.

Communication and knowledge transfer are mainly confined to the interaction of the franchisor and foreign master franchisee, thus limiting the extent of language demands, but, again, not removing them. To some extent, though, the nature and scope of the language question will be determined by the relative language abilities of key staff on both sides of the arrangement. A master franchisee with strong language capabilities among its staff in the franchisor's language is likely to limit the language demands for the franchisor even further. Franchisors from English-speaking countries are often able to take advantage of the widespread use of English in many markets as a second or business language. But this does not apply in all markets.

Of course, whether the franchisor is prepared to cede so much power and control to the master franchisee within the foreign market because of language deficiencies on its side is another question. Without adequate facility in the relevant language, the franchisor may find it difficult to monitor the situation in the foreign market and effectively evaluate the master franchisee's performance. Staying in control of foreign operations comes at a price, and building appropriate language resources is part of the exercise. However, franchisors may not be aware of this need until some time after the master franchising arrangement has begun, as many such agreements come about as a result of approaches to the franchisor by potential foreign master franchisees (Welch et al., 2007). If the initial approach and negotiation process is undertaken in the language of the franchisor, it is easy to settle into an arrangement on this basis, lulled into *language complacency* with potentially long-term negative consequences. Language can readily become the forgotten factor in international franchising, as in many other aspects of foreign operations (Marschan et al., 1997).

Licensing

This mode has been defined as a 'sale of the right to use certain proprietary knowledge (so-called intellectual property) in a defined way' (Luostarinen and Welch, 1990, 32). The key words here are 'the right to use'. It is not a sale *per s*e. The proprietary knowledge may take the form of trademarks, designs and patents, and technical, commercial and administrative 'know-how'. In many respects, licensing shares characteristics with franchising, and is also frequently used alongside FDI or with different forms of exporting. It should be stressed that, when used on this accompanying basis, licensing may be performing diverse roles that have little to do with direct involvement in the foreign market and more to do with lowering taxation (for example via charging a subsidiary for technology transfers in the form of royalties) or seeking to move funds out of a subsidiary or as part of a cross-licensing arrangement that delivers interesting foreign technology, and language may minimally intrude into these forms of licensing (Welch et al., 2007).

It is not uncommon for companies to start international operations via licensing, because it tends to be viewed as a low-cost way of expanding internationally, and, like franchising, can ensure that the bulk of the 'work' in the foreign market is undertaken by the licensee. As with franchising, this may also mean the ability to limit the language demands of foreign involvement for the licensor. However, it may not be so simple, depending on the type of relationship and extent of language divide between the licensor and licensee.

As shown in Figure 8.8, the strength of the relationship between licensor and licensee influences and is influenced by the type and extent of transfers and common activities undertaken by the parties to the relationship. If the licensor seeks to ensure that technology and marketing know-how are effectively transferred and used in the foreign market, this typically requires greater involvement by the licensor and has implications for language use. With a large difference in language between the parties, greater language resources may need to be inserted into the transfer process, while the quality of the language response will affect the quality of the transfer process and ongoing relationship.

A substantial language divide means that language will be a factor at all

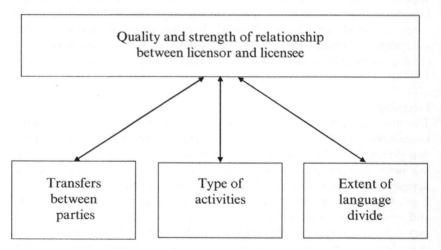

Figure 8.8   Licensing relationship and language

stages of the licensing process: initial contact; negotiation of an agreement (which can take a long time); transfer of relevant knowledge and associated materials; and then, depending on the length of the agreement, long-term management of the licensing relationship. As noted in Chapter 2, the translation alone of key documents relating to knowledge transfer can be demanding and costly (Buckley et al., 2005). And licensing is not a one-way street from the licensor to the licensee: successful licensing has been shown to depend in part on the quality of the relationship between the parties. The licensee often comes up with improvements in the original licensed technology as a result of applying it in a different context, or simply as a result of the way it is implemented within the licensee firm. For positive technological and marketing developments to flow from a licensing arrangement there has to be meaningful interaction, emphasizing the importance of how any language divide is dealt with. Translation is a part solution but is limited in dealing with the need for personal interaction. For instance, Russians show a strong preference for personal dealings in their business relationships with foreign partners (Bloigu, 2008). Facility in the Russian language is a key to these. As with contractual modes in general, it is somewhat paradoxical that licensing is typically based on a formal licensing contract, and therefore seemingly controlled by it with limited flow-on language considerations thereafter. But this is not the case, as relationships, with all their language implications, tend to be critical to long-term licensing success (Welch, 1985).

Management contracts
The attraction of contractual modes such as franchising and licensing is the potential to use a foreign entity (master franchisee or licensee) to carry out basic activities in the foreign market on behalf of the foreign firm, that is, to delegate these activities in a way that is akin to outsourcing. But this is not the case for management contracts. In fact, it is almost the reverse: direct involvement in the foreign market is at the core of this operation. The contractor manages an organization in the foreign market on a contractual basis rather than through an equity arrangement for a specified period of time and fee.

In some industries management contracts are an extensively used foreign operation mode. For example, a large global study of foreign operation mode choice by hotel chains found that management contracts were the most important individual mode used, constituting 37 per cent of total foreign hotel arrangements (Contractor and Kundu, 1998). When Philippine Airlines ran into financial troubles in the late 1990s, it turned to the German airline Lufthansa for assistance in managing the operation, under the terms of a management contract (*The Australian*, 1998).

Because the contractor has a direct role in managing the foreign operation and training local staff, using the local language is central to the
contractor's ability to perform its role. In many cases indigenization is a
key goal for the contractor, driven by the local host government. That is,
at the end of the contract, locals should be able to manage the operation
with minimal continuing help from the contractor, although this has been
shown to be difficult to achieve in many situations, such that management
contracts are frequently rolled over into an extension. By their very nature,
management contracts typically require the transfer of staff from the contractor to the foreign operation, with full language implications if there
is a language divide, and this may be written into the contract (Al-Husan
and James, 2003). It is therefore difficult for a company to contemplate
using this mode if it cannot call on staff with language skills appropriate for certain foreign markets. Employing outsiders with the relevant
language profile (language of contractor and contractee) is an option, but
such people may not possess the relevant technical or commercial knowledge, and lack critical knowledge of the contractor's systems and way of
operating, making it difficult to undertake training and other key activities
at the foreign location.

Outsourcing
International outsourcing occurs when a company transfers some of its
operations, for example the production of a component or the internal
creation of a service, to an independent supplier in a foreign location. By
so doing, a company is able to tap into the production or service provision
capacities of the foreign supplier, rather than undertake the activity itself
(Benito et al., 2013). International outsourcing is heavily used in firms'
global operations, although frequently not with the purpose of penetrating foreign markets. Instead, the aim is to benefit from cheaper sources of
supply, enabling the company to become more competitive in the home
market. In this case, outsourcing leads to imports from the foreign market.
Although commonly associated with consumer products, such as clothing
and shoes, or call centres, it has increasingly come to be used in areas such
as research and development, and product design where skilled or intellectual labour, rather than simply lower labour costs, is important (Manning
et al., 2008).

The case of the Danish financial software multinational SimCorp is
illustrative of how the language question might emerge with outsourcing
(Benito et al., 2013). Because of a shortage of software development professionals in Denmark at the time, the company decided to try outsourcing
some of the software development work as one way around the problem.
It eventually reached agreement with two Ukrainian companies to act as

contractees. Given the nature of the service, software development, close liaison with SimCorp headquarters was necessary, and because of the lack of facility in Ukrainian among SimCorp's staff, this dialogue had to be conducted in English. But on the Ukrainian side there were few staff with strong English fluency. To overcome this deficiency, at one of the Ukrainian contractees (Infopulse), 'management offered English courses at the company's expense for upgrading language skills if SimCorp found technically appropriate candidates among Infopulse staff who lacked English communication skills' (Benito et al., 2013, 219). There was an added bonus for SimCorp in that it was seen as an attractive company to work for, including international work prospects, so that contractee employees were keen to undergo the training to raise their level of English proficiency (see Chapter 6).

As with the other modes, how international outsourcing is carried out may change the nature of the language question. Even the act of appointing a suitable foreign supplier and management of the ongoing outsourcing activity itself can be outsourced to an intermediary that handles the whole operation. A major player in this area is the Hong-Kong-based multinational, Li and Fung (Welch et al., 2007; Benito et al., 2013). As such, the instigator of the outsourcing activity can avoid almost all the responsibility for crossing the language divide. The relationship is with the outsourcing intermediary, and typically such intermediaries can communicate in the language of the outsourcing instigator. However, where the end product of outsourcing is important to the contractor – for example as part of a major, larger product – the concern to assure the quality, reliability and efficiency of the foreign contractee may lead the contractor to pursue a long-term, close relationship with the foreign contractee (supplier), thus bringing any language difference into play. As with other operation modes, the downside of avoiding language issues tends to be some loss of control over what is happening in the foreign market, whether on the buying or selling side.

Project operations
As a distinct form of international business operations, project operations are somewhat loose in scope and difficult to define with precision due to the diversity of forms and activities. Broadly speaking, the industry comprises two sectors: commercial projects (such as construction of mines, dams, roads, airports and railways) and international aid and development projects (such as schools, hospitals, water and sanitation, funded by agencies like the World Bank). Projects can involve multiple suppliers and subcontractors, along with financiers, regulators, consultants and local stakeholders. Complexity is thus a common feature, along

with high risk and uncertainty around the final contract, start date and building process. The negotiation process preceding the award of a major project to a principal organizing firm (the supplier) can take many years, involving multiple rounds of bid submissions and renegotiation. There is also an element of discontinuity, as each project is a temporary organization and this affects the work flow of the supplier firm. Despite all this, those in the project business consistently stress that it is a network and relationship business (Welch et al., 1996; Cova et al., 2002; Skaates et al., 2002). A high degree of interaction between project client and supplier during project implementation is normally required, making customer management an important skill for project staff. It is also a heavily human resource dependent industry, with projects generally awarded on the basis of the skills and expertise of the people to be deployed. For instance, funding agencies such as the World Bank have stringent rules regarding the technical skills and international expertise of the people whose names appear on the bidding document, and supplier firms are locked into those individuals. As a reflection of the dependence on their personnel, supplier firms in the industry refer to themselves as 'body shops'. In their study of the HR implications of international project work, Welch and Welch (2012, 601) relate a comment by a senior project manager: 'All that [project companies] have is their human capital and intelligence, and at the end of the working day, all that walks out the door and you only hope that it all walks back in the next day.' Project workers rely on their network connections to gain and maintain employment – moving from project to project.

The project operation label represents a very broad umbrella of mode content. There may be elements of FDI (joint ventures are common); contracts covering the transfer of technology (covered by a licensing deal); product, system and service exports/imports; and may include training as part of the project contract. For major project suppliers, typically the mix alters during the project cycle (Welch et al., 2007).

Given the importance of relationships and personal interaction at all stages of the project development process, despite their appearance of being hardware-driven, projects can be highly language-affected. The demand for highly specialized skills means that project teams may be drawn from multiple organizations, professions and countries, with some team members geographically dispersed. Some may be permanent employees of the supplying firm, others contractors employed from various countries for varying lengths of time, and there will be a local component. Thus multicultural and multilingual project teams are a common phenomenon. Many projects are undertaken in countries where little-used languages in an international context have to be confronted, and cross-language solutions devised in order for projects to proceed. For example, a major concern for project firms, particularly those involving infrastructure, is work safety. Making sure that all team members adhere to strict safety guidelines involves language. One of the firms in the Welch and Welch (2012) study had a large infrastructure project in Iceland that involved a multilingual project workforce using between five and seven languages. This posed considerable communication challenges. To deal with these, visual aids and translators were used to ensure that messages about safety were understood. Individuals interviewed who worked on international aid projects in remote locations, such as Mongolia, would often rely on a local counterpart who could act as an interpreter.

Exporting Operations

The last major category of foreign operation mode is that of export operations (see Figures 8.2 and 8.3). Under the umbrella of the term 'exporting' a wide range of activities and forms can be identified. While the term exporting was used originally with respect to foreign sales of physical goods, it has come to be used also as applying to services and we follow this broader usage. As noted in our description of the main mode options, there are three basic approaches to undertaking exporting activity: using local intermediaries; using foreign intermediaries; or exporting directly to a foreign market. Exporting often starts as a result of a potential exporter being contacted by interested foreign companies, some wanting to buy the relevant product or service or to represent the exporter. The Internet has increased the possibility of such enquiries, frequently unsolicited (Petersen and Welch, 2003). In addition, as noted above, exporting may emanate from prior inward international activities and networks, smoothing the path to a particular form of exporting.

Given such wide variation in paths to and forms of exporting, one cannot generalize about the language implications of exporting. However, it can be argued that the greater the direct involvement in the foreign market by the exporter, whatever the form of exporting, and the greater the language divide, the more exposed the exporter will be to language influences on the exporting operation (see Figure 8.4 above). As noted in Chapter 7, this may range across many marketing activities, including negotiation, communication, advertising, personal visits and selling. Many of these activities and their language implications can be passed on to a foreign intermediary, in which case the intermediary plays an important language node role for the exporter, and the ability to do so (for example fluency in the exporter's language and the local language) may be a key factor in intermediary choice. Thus the form of exporting and how it is handled may influence, and be influenced by, language considerations and responses. Readers interested in the language–exporting mode connection should refer to Chapter 7 for a more extended treatment of this topic.

For many firms operating in the international arena, agents and distributors remain critical to exporting operations. They also represent a potential answer to the many language questions that may be posed by exporting to foreign markets using a different language from that of the exporter's home market. An intermediary in the foreign market, with the necessary local language base, can readily undertake the language conversion role, in conjunction with its sales function. As a marketing manager from a Finnish SME explains, 'we would not manage [to handle language demands in foreign markets] without our agents and the help of our subsidiaries' (Pohjanen-Bernardi and Talja, 2011, 82). The managing director of another Finnish SME commented: 'we make an effort to find partners whenever language skills are seen as a prerequisite for success. We have English speaking partners in Korea, Japan and China. They act as a buffer between us and local companies and authorities' (Pohjanen-Bernardi and Talja, 2011, 81). In a study of Hong Kong toy exporters, Ellis (2000, 461) found, somewhat surprisingly, that 'more than two-thirds of early entries into the EU were to non-English speaking countries such as Germany and Italy'. However, almost 90 per cent of these connections were not initiated by the Hong Kong manufacturer. Rather, the buyer or third parties (such as trading companies) intervened, often through trade fairs, assuming the responsibility for bridging the language divide.

The two main forms of foreign intermediaries acting for exporters are agents and distributors. Agents provide a basic selling function and sometimes a range of other services, such as after-sales service, for exporters in the foreign market. They do not take title to the products; that is, they act for the exporter. An important aspect of the agent's role is often to provide connection through language between the seller and the buyer in the foreign market. In a study of Finnish SMEs, 57 per cent of respondents indicated that 'they use local agents in their export markets in order to compensate for their staffs' "limited language skills"' (Pohjanen-Bernardi and Talja, 2011, 81–2). It is a basic reality of foreign business that customers prefer to do business in their own language. This extends beyond the initial enquiry. As one of the interviewees in the Finnish study commented, 'We want someone who speaks the [local] language. We want the agent to do the job that is hard for us to do, such as contacting clients and architects, visiting, showing our products, and marketing.' For these reasons, we extend the use of the term intermediary as commonly used in international marketing texts to include the 'language role'. The importance of the language role of agents can distort the evaluation and monitoring processes by exporters. Research by Crick (1999) indicated that some UK exporters were choosing agents as much for their English skills as for their marketing capacity. Little is known about whether exporters are getting good value out of agents chosen on this basis, but it illustrates how important the language role of agents is regarded by many exporters.

In contrast to agents, distributors buy from the exporter, taking title over the products, with the legal implications that this entails, and undertake a full sales and perhaps product servicing role. Thus the distributor typically undertakes the full language role involved in engaging with customers. In many respects, the exporter outsources the language task to the distributor. However, exporters are not always happy to leave all aspects of selling and customer relationships to their distributors, because of the implications for long-term success in the foreign markets in question. In simple terms, exporters generally have less control over marketing aspects such as pricing when operating via distributors than when using agents (Welch et al., 2007). There are times when exporters want more detailed information about what is happening in foreign markets with respect to their products than distributors, or agents, are willing or capable of providing (Petersen et al., 2000). As a result, the management of relationships with distributors and agents, and the attempt to garner more market-sensitive information without a local sales office in the foreign market, typically means that travelling staff must be employed. Relationships with the agents/distributors may be readily handled in the language of the exporter because of language skills within the agent/distributor. However, other activities, such as chasing market information, talking to end-customers and dealing with other market players, typically demand relevant foreign language skills on the part of the exporter's travelling sales staff, or the resort to translation services. In general, independent market monitoring and information collection activities in the foreign market are much more difficult when language dependence on the agent/distributor is strong. As one UK exporter commented:

> Whilst the German distributors speak excellent English, you go visiting the customers out there – it's so difficult – they don't speak English at all. Most of them speak a smattering of it, but sit down in a meeting to have a conversation to try and do it in English is very difficult. (MacDonald and Cook, 1998, 221)

CONCLUSION

In this chapter we have explored the relationship between language considerations and the foreign operation modes that companies employ in the process of penetrating foreign markets. We stress that under the umbrella of three basic categories of foreign operation modes – exporting, contractual modes and foreign direct investment – multiple variations are feasible. Research has shown that these multiple variations are used in the search for foreign market penetration effectiveness. Further, firms have to respond to the action of potential buyers and foreign partners with business offers that have mode implications. As a result, it is difficult to be definitive about the mode–language connection.

We have shown in this chapter that there is an interaction process between language aspects and modes and, importantly, that influence runs in both directions. Nevertheless, this influence is variable, particularly, but not only, across modes. The type of mode matters in terms of language consequences because of the extent of direct involvement that different modes imply. The use of particular modes may allow companies to avoid most of the direct foreign language demands of operating in a foreign market. However, much depends on how particular modes are used. The use of foreign intermediaries is common for exporters, and they can be important language intermediaries as part of their role. But, even so, exporters in many cases still try to be involved in the foreign market (for instance because of an interest in moving to an alternative operation form), and dealing with language difference is part of such involvement. Additionally, there may be a variety of language benefits of using particular modes in foreign markets with different languages. For example, MacDonald and Cook (1998) cite the case of a Japanese company with a subsidiary in the UK sending trainees from Japan for training, part of which involved *in situ* tuition in the English language: a language bonus from FDI in this form. Being more involved in the foreign market and having to deal with the need to cross the language divide may, in the end, build a stronger foreign language perspective and associated resources – a language capability that makes a company more fit for other foreign markets.

We have argued that, in general, language is not a strong influence on mode choice and use, but this does not always apply: inability to function in a foreign language may bias mode choice towards forms that limit direct foreign involvement, and thereby foreign language proficiency demands. On the other hand, though, possession of particular foreign language skills among staff can bias both the country and mode choice. There are examples of companies establishing a foreign sales subsidiary to facilitate exporting operations because of the ability to send a staff member with appropriate language skills to set it up and run it in the foreign market in question. Thus, while *language delegation* may be a short-term attraction in the use of certain foreign operation modes and the way that companies relate to their foreign partners, it may not be in their best interests in the longer term. Comfort with the situation where the foreign partner is handling the front-line language issues may lead to *language complacency* and under-investment in the development of language resources. To some extent, language delegation may cede control in the foreign market to a firm's foreign partner. Whatever the mode used and how it is managed in the longer term, relevant language ability on the part of the entrant foreign firm helps with control of the local operation. The concern about a *language deficiency* in relation to use of a given foreign operation mode may grow over time as the entrant firm finds that it has become dependent on its foreign partner for appropriate market information, local contacts and relationships with local customers. *Language dependence* can breed mode and partner dependence. Control over a foreign operation may be strongly linked to language proficiency.

The wide range of potential influence running both ways between language and mode is further moderated by the relative language abilities on both sides of the foreign operation mode relationship. When an internationalizing firm is entering a country in which there is a different main language, but a high level of competence in the entrant firm's language at the partner firm, it can more readily dismiss the language question in choosing its operation mode.

REFERENCES

Al-Husan, F.B. and P. James (2003), 'Cultural control and multinationals: the case of privatized Jordanian companies', *International Journal of Human Resource Management*, **14** (7), 1284–95.

Alon, I. (2006), 'Market conditions favoring master international franchising', *Multinational Business Review*, **14** (2), 67–82.

The Australian (1998), 'Lufthansa flies to rescue of PAL', 2 June, 27.

Baena, V. (2009), 'Modeling global franchising in emerging markets: an entry mode analysis', *Journal of East–West Business*, **15** (3–4), 164–88.

Benito, G.R.G., O. Dovgan, B. Petersen and L.S. Welch (2013), 'Offshore outsourcing: a dynamic, operation mode perspective', *Industrial Marketing Management*, **42** (2), 211–22.

Benito, G.R.G., B. Petersen and L.S. Welch (2011), 'Mode combinations and international operations: theoretical issues and an empirical study', *Management International Review*, **51** (6), 803–20.

Birkinshaw, J., H. Bresman and L. Håkanson (2000), 'Managing the post-acquisition integration process: how the human integration and task integration processes interact to foster value creation', *Journal of Management Studies*, **37** (3), 395–425.

Bloigu, K. (2008), *Russian or English? Examining the Role and Importance of the Russian Language in the Russian Business of Finnish Companies*, Master's Thesis, Helsinki: Helsinki School of Economics.

Bruntse, J. (2003), *It's Scandinavian: Dansk–Svensk Kommunikation i SAS*, Master's Thesis, Copenhagen: Institut for Nordisk Filologi, University of Copenhagen.

Buckley, P.J., M.J. Carter, J. Clegg and H. Tan (2005), 'Language and social knowledge in foreign-knowledge transfer to China', *International Studies of Management & Organization*, **35** (1), 47–65.

Burgel, O. and G.C. Murray (2000), 'The international market entry choices of start-up companies in high-technology industries', *Journal of International Marketing*, **8** (2), 33–62.

Contractor, F.J. and S.K. Kundu (1998), 'Modal choice in a world of alliances: analyzing organizational forms in the international hotel sector', *Journal of International Business Studies*, **29** (2), 325–58.

Cova, B., P. Ghauri and R. Salle (2002), *Project Marketing: Beyond Competitive Bidding*, Chichester, UK: John Wiley & Sons.

Crick, D. (1999), 'An investigation into SMEs' use of languages in their export operations', *International Journal of Entrepreneurial Behaviour and Research*, **5** (1), 19–31.

Dimitratos, P. and S. Lioukas (2004), 'Greek perspectives of international entrepreneurship', in L.-P. Dana (ed.), *Handbook of Research on International Entrepreneurship*, Cheltenham, UK and Northampton, MA, USA: Edward Elgar, pp. 455–80.

The Economist (2013), 'From guard shack to global giant', 12 January, 52–3.

Ellis, P. (2000), 'Social ties and foreign market entry', *Journal of International Business Studies*, **31** (3), 443–69.

Frazer, L., S. Weaven and O. Wright (2006), *Franchising Australia 2006 Survey*, Griffith University: Franchise Council of Australia.

International Trade Administration (1987), *Franchising in the Economy 1985–87*, Washington, DC: US Department of Commerce.

Karhunen, P. (2008), 'Human resource management in Russia: Fazer Group', unpublished teaching case prepared for the course 'International Business and Institutional Change in Russia', Helsinki: Helsinki School of Economics.

Korhonen, H. (1999), *Inward–Outward Internationalization of Small and Medium Enterprises*, Doctoral Thesis A-147, Helsinki: Helsinki School of Economics and Business Administration.

Louhiala-Salminen, L. (2002), 'Communication and language use in merged corporations', Working Paper W-330, Helsinki: Helsinki School of Economics.

Lovio, R., A. Jalas and M. Laakso (2003), 'Patient revolution: Instrumentarium's transformation to a multinational healthcare technology business', in P. Mannio, E. Vaara and P. Ylä-Anttila (eds), *Our Path Abroad*, Helsinki: Taloustieto Oy, pp. 421–38.

Luostarinen, R.K. and L.S. Welch (1990), *International Business Operations*, Helsinki: Export Consulting KY.

MacDonald, S. and M. Cook (1998), 'An exploration of the use of language training in exporting firms: case studies from Northamptonshire', *Local Economy*, **13** (3), 216–27.

Manning, S., S. Massini and A. Lewin (2008), 'A dynamic perspective on next-generation offshoring: the global sourcing of science and engineering talent', *Academy of Management Perspectives*, **22** (3), 35–54.

Marschan, R., D.E. Welch and L.S. Welch (1997), 'Language: the forgotten factor in multinational management', *European Management Journal*, **15** (5), 591–8.

Neeley, T. (2011), 'Language and globalization: "Englishnization" at Rakuten', Harvard Business School teaching case, No. 9-412–002.

Petersen, B., D.E. Welch and L.S. Welch (2000), 'Creating meaningful switching options in international operations', *Long Range Planning*, **33** (5), 688–705.

Petersen, B. and L.S. Welch (2003), 'International business development and the Internet, post-hype', *Management International Review*, **43** (Special Issue 1), 7–29.

Piekkari, R., E. Vaara, J. Tienari and R. Säntti (2005), 'Integration or disintegration? Human resource implications of the common corporate language decision in a cross-border merger', *International Journal of Human Resource Management*, **16** (3), 333–47.

Pohjanen-Bernardi, K. and K. Talja (2011), *Language Strategies in Finnish Small and Medium-Sized Enterprises*, Master's Thesis, Helsinki: School of Economics, Aalto University.

Skaates, M.A., H. Tikkanen and J. Lindblom (2002), 'Relationships and project marketing success', *Journal of Business and Industrial Marketing*, **17** (5), 389–406.

UNCTAD (2013), *World Investment Report 2013*, New York and Geneva: United Nations.

Vaara, E., J. Tienari, R. Marschan-Piekkari and R. Säntti (2005), 'Language and the circuits of power in a merging multinational corporation', *Journal of Management Studies*, **41** (3), 595–623.

Villinger, R. (1996), 'Post-acquisition managerial learning in Central East Europe', *Organization Studies*, **17** (2), 181–206.

Welch, C.L. and D.E. Welch (2012), 'What do HR managers really do? HR roles on international projects', *Management International Review*, **52** (4), 597–617.

Welch, D.E., L.S. Welch and R. Marschan-Piekkari (2001), 'The persistent impact of language on global operations', *Prometheus*, **19** (3), 193–209.

Welch, D.E., L.S. Welch, I. Wilkinson and L. Young (1996), 'Network development in international project marketing and the development of external facilitation', *International Business Review*, **5** (6), 579–602.

Welch, L.S. (1985), 'The international marketing of technology: an interaction perspective', *International Marketing Review*, **2** (1), 41–53.

Welch, L.S., G.R.G. Benito and B. Petersen (2007), *Foreign Operation Methods: Theory, Analysis, Strategy*, Cheltenham, UK and Northampton, MA, USA: Edward Elgar.

Welch, L.S. and R. Luostarinen (1993), 'Inward–outward connections in internationalization', *Journal of International Marketing*, **1** (1), 44–56.

9. Language strategy and management

Language strategy has been defined as 'the planned adoption of a range of techniques to facilitate effective communication with clients and suppliers abroad' (Hagen, 2011, 4). What is still somewhat unknown is at what stage, if ever, internationalizing firms develop such formal language strategies. What we can say, based on our treatment of language in earlier chapters of this book, is that, whether the language is formal or not, internationalizing firms develop varied responses to language demands over time. Collectively, these may be referred to as their evolving language strategies.

It is not the objective of this chapter to provide a full review of how firms design strategies to further their global intentions.[1] However, we present a brief summary as a necessary context for those not familiar with the area of business strategy. In business, there are several schools of thought regarding strategy, with various definitions, most of which are derived from the military context. The common thread is that strategy consists of two parts: formulation (deciding what to do) and implementation (achieving desired results). The formulation stage involves setting goals and objectives and plotting a business path to their eventual achievement. Activities include global scanning; and country, industry and competitor assessment. These inform the planning process through the use of a variety of managerial techniques, such as SWOT analysis (of strengths, weaknesses, opportunities, threats). As Figure 9.1 indicates, the process includes making strategic choices across a wide range of issues relating to: location; mode of operation; structure and intra-company relationships; production and procurement; finance; marketing; technology transfer; human resource management; and host-government relations.

While strategic formulation and planning are stressed in management texts, in reality, plans often go awry as a result of changing circumstances, particularly in the volatile global environment. Thus, as Dyer (1983) pointed out, strategic adaptation better describes the process whereby an opportunity or crisis prompts managerial intervention in order to capitalize on or cope with the situation. He estimated that 70–80 per cent of strategies are an outcome of strategic adaptation. Thus firms need to be flexible – able and prepared to change strategies as conditions evolve. The means to change is critical. It has been argued that strategic flexibility needs to be

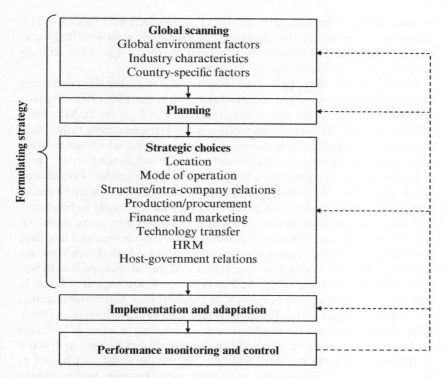

Figure 9.1 The strategy process

built in through such means as including in the initial negotiations with foreign partners the option to change mode of operation or the contractual agreement, as market circumstances alter (Petersen et al., 2000).

Implementation is effectively strategic execution. Management needs to delegate responsibility, that is, indicating who implements what and where. Processes and systems may need adjustment or realignment. Allocation of necessary resources is essential for success. Business is often criticized for being too focused on the formulation and planning stage, and not paying enough attention to ensuring successful implementation. Percy Barnevik, the former CEO of the Swedish–Swiss multinational Asea Brown Boveri (ABB), was often quoted as saying that 10 per cent of strategy was in its formulation and planning stage, whereas the remaining 90 per cent was its implementation. This is the difficult stage, as much depends on how the execution process is handled and whether or not implementation is interrupted by events outside management control, or that could not have been forecast. As the Scottish poet Robert Burns said: 'the best laid schemes of mice and men are bound to go astray' (translated into English). This sentiment encapsulates the challenges of executing a well-crafted strategy. Performance and monitoring represent the final stage of the strategy process and we return to this aspect later.

For most firms, the approach to language seems, rather than deliberate or planned, more an *ad hoc* response as the firm expands internationally and confronts the reality of language diversity (see Chapter 1). Mintzberg and Waters (1985) contend that strategies are often emergent rather than deliberate or intended. 'Emergent strategies are those which are realized despite, or in the absence of, intentions: a form of unintended order. There is an absence of preconception but a pattern is discernible' (Welch and Steen, 2013, 796). What starts out as an *ad hoc* process can later be recognized as an appropriate strategy, formalizing what is already in practice.

Further, internationalization is a dynamic process. Firms move in and out of markets as a result of global expansion and exit decisions, and language requirements are altered as a result. Take the case of the French retailer Carrefour. In 2005, it withdrew from Japan, and traded (swapped) its hypermarkets in the Czech Republic and Slovakia to its UK competitor Tesco, in exchange for Tesco's stores in Taiwan. In the same year, Carrefour acquired retail operations in Poland, Brazil, Italy and Turkey (*The Economist*, 2005). What would have been the implications for Carrefour in terms of language at the end of this exercise, where the multinational was moving in and out of different language regimes? Similarly, as we discussed in Chapter 8, mode changes will bring new language challenges. Our point here is that the need for a language strategy is a consequence of the firm's overall strategy, including its global operations. Language issues are unavoidable. That is the nature of the multinational. However, as Figure 9.2 indicates, language strategy is typically at the back end of strategic thinking – almost forgotten, an afterthought. It tends to be well behind in terms of consideration compared to other corporate strategy components.

It is not clear at what stage in the internationalization process companies see the need to develop more formalized responses to language diversity. Our language path concept indicates the impact of the language of the country of origin (see Chapter 1). It would appear that internationalizing companies can function for some time without recognizing the need for formalization through an articulated strategic response. As our KONE case study showed, the decision to adopt English as the common corporate language (CCL) was easy, given that it was effectively the operating language once the firm moved beyond its Nordic boundaries. But it still took a considerable period of time before that decision point was reached. In essence, this is perhaps indicative of the way in which language is viewed, particularly given that KONE was based in a language-aware society.

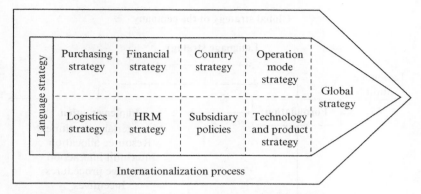

Figure 9.2   Language, internationalization and global strategy

Finland as a bilingual country has a nationally recognized dual-language policy.

FORMULATING A LANGUAGE STRATEGY

Language planning has been defined as 'a corporation's conscious effort to determine the status and function of multiple languages for particular forms of spoken and written communication' (de Groot, 2012, 256; see also Thomas, 2008). We see language strategy as more than language planning. It is broader as it involves both planning and managerial responses to the multifaceted dimensions of international operation discussed above. Language strategy is enfolded by the firm's international strategy. Figure 9.3 depicts the various stages and components of a language strategy. It illustrates that if a firm seeks to develop an effective language strategy, it will have to acknowledge the pervasive nature of language.

Throughout this book, we have discussed the reasons for, and consequences of, language standardization. Table 9.1 summarizes the strengths and weaknesses of language standardization identified in previous chapters. Clearly, the strengths noted are important reasons for management to adopt a CCL. They address the need for information flow and communication throughout the global entity. However, as our list of weaknesses indicates, a CCL introduces unintended consequences, some of which may contribute to implementation problems, generating inefficiencies and interfering with the control and coordination mechanisms that the CCL was introduced to facilitate. These consequences may be hidden from management because of language differences at the subsidiary level, thus creating a *language screen* that people can hide behind. This may foster

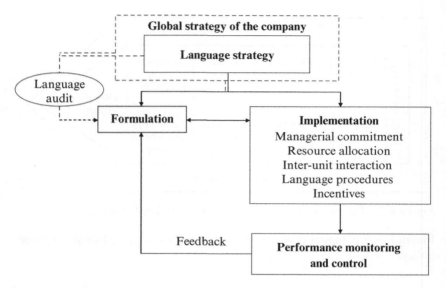

Figure 9.3   Developing a language strategy

errant, even illegal, behaviour, effectively acting as a shield to protect from headquarters' scrutiny (Welch et al., 2005). The potential for communication distortion and knowledge transfer barriers remains in spite of, or because of, the CCL (see Chapters 3 and 4).

As we have pointed out in other parts of this book, the adoption of a CCL can lull top management into a false sense of security. Picking up on this point, Steyaert et al. (2011, 271) remark that 'there seems to be a growing consensus that the adoption of a common corporate language is not the endpoint of a language policy but forms one of the possible anchor points around which to deal with multilingual complexity'. For example, language standardization provides uniformity, yet practical considerations may suggest a need to accommodate multilingualism. The reality is that a CCL is not a managerial panacea, and, as we now discuss, there are many other important aspects that should be considered when designing a language strategy.

Which Language?

In terms of language strategy, having decided to introduce a CCL, a key question for management is: which language or languages should it espouse? As we have already noted, this is often an unexceptional decision given that a particular language may have already 'emerged' as a conse-

Table 9.1   The impact of a common corporate language (CCL)

Strengths	Weaknesses
• Facilitates formal reporting between units in various countries	• Masks communication distortions
• Reduces the potential for miscommunication	• Disadvantages those without CCL fluency (e.g. career paths)
• Improves access to company information	• Allows individuals and subsidiaries to deliberately hide behind lack of CCL fluency
• Enhances informal communication	• Multilingual differences hidden
• Fosters a sense of belonging to 'global' family	• Managerial complacency
• Signals global outlook to external parties	• Creates language hierarchies
	• Becomes a knowledge transfer barrier

quence of international expansion. The act of specifying a CCL may well be merely the act of making official what is already occurring. For many firms, this may be recognizing the place of English as the default language, particularly in Western markets.

For those firms that do not have English as the home (parent) language, an important question becomes whether to concentrate solely on English or to allow two or more languages in parallel use. For example, some German companies may have both English and German as the official languages; and Spanish companies may have English alongside Spanish. A factor influencing the decision may be the company's internationalization pattern in language terms (see Chapter 1). Inevitably, for Spanish companies, expansion into Spanish-speaking markets will push them towards the dual adoption of Spanish and English as joint corporate languages once international expansion moves into non-Spanish-speaking markets.

Clearly, adjustments in language policy are a consequence of internationalization and the level and depth of business activities and investment in particular countries. As companies develop more business in China, for instance, the question of how to deal with the Chinese language (Mandarin) arises. Does the company need to add Chinese to the company language portfolio? Should it be exclusively Mandarin? If the proportion of Chinese business contribution to global revenue grows significantly, pressure will build to include Chinese. The choice of operation mode in various foreign markets is an additional factor. Deciding on a language policy is different when dealing with a cross-border merger compared to simple exporting; or between greenfield investments and acquisitions (see Chapter 8).

While these issues emerged from our early work on KONE, and in later case research of other firms, a recent broad survey has provided confirmation data. Harzing and Pudelko (2013) conducted a cross-sectional survey (partially online) between August 2008 and April 2010. Respondents (HR managers) were drawn from more than 800 subsidiaries across a wide range of countries and industries, and included English, European and Asian languages. The response rate was 13.8 per cent. The study reflected the subsidiary perspective on language standardization. Language barriers were influenced by a combination of home country language (that is, the parent's); host country language (subsidiary) and corporate language. Data were grouped into language clusters: Anglophone, Far Eastern Asian, small northern European, and larger continental European. Around half of the Asian firms did not mandate a corporate language. This was in contrast to the far higher use of a corporate language by firms from continental European countries (about 85 per cent) and Anglophone countries (75 per cent). Of the Asian companies that did have a corporate language, 60–70 per cent used the language of the headquarters.

While such studies provide a language snapshot, several issues remain unexplored. Harzing and Pudelko (2013), for example, suggest that multinationals that have linguistic duality, such as European firms, may have a competitive advantage over those that are monolingual. As we indicated in Figure 9.1, competitive assessment is a key component in devising a corporate-level strategy, and perhaps integrating language at this level may assist in raising the profile of language in the minds of top management. Another issue is that there may be a tendency to overvalue the CCL while undervaluing other languages in diverse foreign markets. The importance of a local language response remains, whatever an internationalizing firm decides will be the CCL. Awareness of the consequences of a CCL must be factored into decision-making. Hence the link between formulating a language strategy and the allocation of resources, such as provision of requisite language training, so that the CCL delivers the advantages set out in Table 9.1.

There may be external requirements to consider – again one of the preliminary steps in strategic formulation. For internationalizing firms, adherence to national legal requirements in some countries is often a harsh reality that forces strategic adaptation. A good example is provided by Sulonen (2011, 69) in her study of foreign firms operating in the Canadian province of Quebec. There is a stringent French-only language state policy requirement that is rigidly enforced, so much so that several of her informants used the term 'language police' when explaining why they could not publicly admit that English was the CCL. For example, when the interviewer said, 'So you would say that English is your official language', the HR manager at one of the case companies replied:

Yeah, you're right, but we don't say that. We don't want to have any trouble. But of course everything is done in English. But if I have to deal with people in Quebec, I will do it in French as well . . . We try to keep it as low profile as possible . . . because they [language police] can come here and decide that the button that says enter has to say something else, and they can go nuts . . . It's why we are really careful about never saying that our official language is English.

In an interview with a person from the government office responsible for French-language enforcement, Sulonen (2011, 78, 89) was told that there was a poster in one of the offices saying 'We [the enforcing office] came and seized a parrot because it only spoke English'. The legal requirement is such that any foreign firm that is not certified by the Quebec government as French language compliant cannot tender for government contracts. One CEO interviewed commented that the regulatory environment was a concern to the extent that if the authorities 'come to me and start putting pressure on me because of French, I won't think twice, I'll move out of Quebec'.

De Groot (2012) provides a similar experience with respect to the entity resulting from the 2004 merger of Air France and KLM airlines. English was adopted as the corporate language, but French people obtained a prominent position in company board meetings due to legal requirements, though English language summaries were allowed for non-French board members.

Language Audit

We indicate in Figure 9.3 that the conduct of a language audit is an essential step in the formulation of a language strategy. After all, one does not embark on planning an international move without adequate research to provide relevant information. For example, market research is normal as a prelude to foreign market entry and commitment. Yet anecdotal evidence suggests that audits of firms' own language capabilities are not undertaken before they enter new foreign markets. Similarly, we suspect that language audits are rarely conducted as part of the due diligence process preceding a foreign acquisition. The study by Vaara et al. (2005) shows how language can be a disruptive factor in foreign mergers and acquisitions that cross language boundaries and hinder the integration process.

We see the conduct of regular language audits as a similar essential step in determining the level of language proficiency across the organization so that informed management decisions can be made. In a sense, all aspects of language strategy flow from an understanding of language resources, their spread, and utilization arising from the language audit. As Dhir (2005) comments, a language audit could be seen as an element in a firm's strengths and weaknesses assessment as part of the planning process. In our HRM chapter (Chapter 6), we discussed the role of planning as an important first step in determining present and future employment needs. Another role for HR would be to monitor the effectiveness of company-sponsored language training, hiring practices and staff placement that utilizes language competence. This would inform a language audit, and feed back into strategic planning. External language service providers could be included as part of a comprehensive language audit.

IMPLEMENTING A LANGUAGE STRATEGY

As depicted in Figure 9.3, language strategy implementation involves many aspects of the operations of an internationalizing firm. In essence, if a language strategy is to make a difference, it needs to be substantial, comprehensive and pervasive. Making a managerial directive by itself is meaningless. There needs to be strong follow-through. However, what emerges from the work on language standardization is that policy directives from headquarters, despite their official status and codification in the CCL, are subject to implementation barriers. Peltokorpi and Vaara (2012) found, in their study of 101 subsidiaries in Japan, that MNC-level language policies and practices are seldom transferred intact, and transfer relies on key actors such as subsidiary managers. These findings confirm what was revealed in our original KONE study, particularly where key actors regard language as a contributor to their own power base. We found subsidiaries in KONE where subsidiary managers restricted communication, using tactics such as not investing in CCL training, ignoring HQ directives or not translating corporate policies into local languages that would enable wider access. In the case of the Italian subsidiary, the then subsidiary manager was fluent in English but those below had limited, if any, fluency (Marschan-Piekkari et al., 1999). We have highlighted throughout this book how a mandated CCL creates winners and losers to the extent that unintended outcomes may result. Managing the consequences of adopting a CCL is therefore a critical part of strategic implementation. In the following section, we elaborate on the various implementation components identified in Figure 9.3.

Managerial Commitment: Sensitizing the Organization

We argue that a starting point to having language seriously considered in strategic terms is for senior managers to clearly articulate its importance. To work as intended, language strategy should be backed by financial support and managerial commitment at all levels. A critical issue for management in any firm is to be seen to be matching rhetoric with action. A study of Irish exporters is a case in point. Clarke (2000, 86) comments: 'It would appear from the data that there is a major divergence between what Irish exporters say, and what they actually do in practice. They emphasise the importance of good language skills for success in exporting . . . but this is not matched [with practical measures].'

Of course, the ultimate language champion is the CEO. This is exemplified by the case of Rakuten, the Japan-based global e-commerce firm founded by Hiroshi Mikitani in 1997. Speaking in English for the first time to his assembled Japanese workforce in 2010, Mikitani announced that English would become the CCL. He commented: 'Our goal is to catch up with the global market. To step up to this challenge we must try to change our language from Japanese to English. This is going to be a long-term effort for us. Starting this month, my own speech will simply be in English' (Neeley, 2011, 1–2). Neeley further reports 'that only an estimated 10 per cent of Rakuten staff could function in English, his rapid and aggressive global expansion plans gave him little choice but to ask his workforce to relinquish their reliance on communicating exclusively in their own language'. Actions taken to ensure this language strategy was implemented included English language testing to audit employee progress, and mandatory reporting by managers of language competence progress of their employees to Mikitani personally. These were expected to arrive on his desk once a month. A threshold score of 650 in the Test of English for International Communication (TOEIC) for every employee was set, and those who failed to meet this standard were threatened with demotion. The rapid globalization of this Japanese company has continued since 2010, in line with the stated organizational objectives.

Another example is de Groot's (2012, 259) study of a Dutch–German merger where English was mandated as the 'common working language for documents and meetings involving cross-border communication'. English was chosen for its neutrality and the belief that there were sufficient numbers of English-competent employees. However, in interviews, it emerged that, while English was accepted as appropriate for written communication, each nationality preferred its own language for situations involving oral communication. This was despite the efforts of management to support the implementation of its language policy (see also Harzing and Pudelko, 2014). To some extent, what management needs to do is to embed the recognition of language into the organization's consciousness (psyche), in a similar way that corporate social responsibility (CSR) has been developed and championed. Actions by top management are therefore critical and may actually undermine the language strategy. This is perhaps graphically illustrated in one of the cases in a Danish study

Language in international business

examining CCL consequences. Lauring and Klitmøller (2013) recount watching the Danish CEO address staff at the yearly assembly held at headquarters. The authors were surprised when the CEO switched from English to Danish, despite the fact that foreign nationals represented about 8 per cent of those employed at headquarters. This was puzzling, given that the CEO had himself launched the policy designating English as the corporate language. One Dutch interviewee later explained to the authors that 'He does that every year. I can understand what he is saying in Danish but I know many that cannot. They are really annoyed with this. But his English is also not so good' (Lauring and Klitmøller, 2013, 93).

An important statement of managerial commitment would be the appointment of a designated language officer. The incumbent would be delegated the oversight of language-related policies and activities. The appointment would need to be at the highest level, and have the imprimatur of the CEO, given that a key task is to 'evangelize', that is, sell the need for, and value of, the language strategy. This position is important particularly in terms of key strategic decisions, such as mergers and acquisitions and entry into new markets, which have direct language implications and are influenced by language considerations. Such an appointment would be a way 'of raising the profile of language and its strategic importance, and as a means of managing language as a critical resource' (Marschan et al., 1997, 596). We see the language officer as akin to the idea of a knowledge officer, given that knowledge moves through language channels. Earl and Scott (1999) were early proponents of the position of a knowledge officer. A language officer would effectively be a *language champion*, delegated to articulate and manage the language strategy and its implementation. This would increase the chances of a language policy not only being adopted but also monitored. The danger would be in being seen as an enforcer (language police), rather than as an advocate.

Language standardization can have the effect of pushing language problems 'further down the hierarchy, and creating new centres of language power' in subsidiary units where managers can act as gatekeepers through their CCL language skills (Welch and Welch, 2008, 357). A language officer should be able to counter this, keeping language issues to the fore and ensuring that language policies continue to be developed, implemented and evaluated. The legitimization of the role of language officer would also require a formal designation in terms of the organization's hierarchical structure. For example, the firm may already have a translation department (see Chapter 2). One of the problems with having language aspects confined to a separate translation department is that language becomes invisible at the higher executive level and can easily be regarded as a low level issue. The appointment of a key executive at the highest level should prevent this. It is a very visible statement of the level of managerial commitment to ensuring its language strategy is effectively implemented.

Sensitizing the organization to the value of language involves more than the appointment of a language officer or the commitment of top management. Deciding on policies related to language may just be the start. An international firm is more than its headquarters. The identification of people within the multinational with specific language skills requires interaction between headquarters and the various subsidiary units. A language audit would probably be handled by HR departments – at headquarters as well as in the subsidiaries – with input from others such as functional and line managers (Pohjanen-Bernardi and Talja, 2011). While critical to implementation of language strategy, HR has an image problem, as discussed in Chapter 6. This is not necessarily helpful when trying to raise the status of language issues, a factor that reinforces the need to have a designated champion whose role is to sensitize the organization to the value of HR's contribution to the realization of the language strategy. The concept of language capital, introduced in Chapter 5, recognizes that language has value and should be considered as an asset. In a similar vein, Dhir (2005, 376) draws a parallel between language and currency: 'corporations can begin to think in terms of a portfolio of language assets much in the same way as it thinks of [a] portfolio of financial currency assets'. Given that companies do not have languages, people do, it would be logical to include HR managers in the formulation as well as implementation process (Bellak, 2014).

Sensitizing also means converting language strategy into a myriad of decisions and practices of managers on a day-to-day basis as a way of ensuring implementation occurs in an effective manner. For instance, managers may need to develop tactics to facilitate the introduction of language policies and practices. While the various research studies we review in this book reveal that a major challenge is the range of language fluency among employees, it would seem that this fact has yet to be internalized by many top managers in internationalizing companies and that the imposition of a CCL can mask this.

The variation in preparedness and ability to perform in the CCL may generate resentment, inhibition and withdrawal (as outlined in Chapter 3). Neeley (2013, 490) studied the adoption of English in a French multinational. She reports that some employees were reluctant to speak up in meetings conducted in English if native English-speakers were present. One person commented: 'I understand [English] because I am trained in English, but I might not say anything or may stop talking during the meetings [with US counterparts] because I am afraid of looking silly [and of] making mistakes.' Speaking at a seminar at Hanken, the Swedish business school in Helsinki (22 October, 2003), the then brand director for the chocolate manufacturer Cloetta Fazer provided an example. Recognizing that Finns have a high threshold in being prepared to speak up in public in a foreign language, due to feeling inadequate compared to counterparts, he would note who was unusually silent in meetings conducted in Swedish (its CCL at the time). He was aware that these individuals were professionally very competent and their input was important but in danger of being lost. He would therefore deliberately speak to these colleagues in their mother tongue during meeting breaks. Perhaps a better way would be for CEOs to publicly acknowledge that non-native speakers of the CCL face significant challenges and reassure people that they would not be judged negatively on the basis of CCL fluency compared to native speakers, nor to their language peers, who may have started with high fluency in the CCL.

Resource Allocation

Strategic implementation requires the allocation of adequate resources. That may seem an obvious statement, but the strategy literature abounds with examples of how good strategies failed due to lack of required resources. The likelihood of a language officer being appointed, for example, will depend on financial support. The reality is that budgets impose constraints. Hiring multilingual staff generally will cost more. Funding language training is another consideration, as is the provision of translation, whether in-house or outsourced. There is considerable cost involved in mounting an effective language strategy, but this should be weighed against the costs, often hidden or intangible, associated with non-provision of adequate resources. Such costs may include lost contracts, lower sales performance and lost productivity as employees seek assistance to deal with translation needs (Piekkari et al., 2013).

However, merely allocating resources does not ensure implementation. Resources may be spent in unintended directions; or overtaken by conflicting cost-cutting messages that reinforce language non-prioritization; or be diverted to other areas via what is popularly referred to as creative accounting. Deciding what deserves priority in terms of resource allocation is a perennial, difficult question. As part of prioritization, a decision has to be made about spending coming from the centre versus allocating resources and leaving it to the discretion of subsidiary unit management. It is not a simple decision. Our early work on KONE provides an example. At the time of the study, HR budgets included what the then KONE HR manager referred to as investments in language training (Marschan, 1996).

Top management could check whether subsidiaries were actually spending the allocated funds on language training, but there were no formal sanctions if language training targets were not reached. In this area, KONE employed what were described as soft control measures. The lack of sanctions allowed the Italian subsidiary to underinvest in CCL training, a situation that was not discovered for some time, to the public dismay of the Finnish parent.

Investment in language development produces returns in the medium to long term, but the difficulty is that the investment is primarily in people. If people exit the organization, the potential benefits are lost. Of course, through the hiring process, the same firm may gain employees who have received language training in another firm or organization (such as school or university). It is very difficult to determine the balance resulting from the entry and exit of language-competent employees. Also, it is difficult to identify the returns to the international firm from resources allocated to language, which further accentuates the difficulty in justifying such resource allocation to the firm at large. This is in the context of language issues having a low profile, and may reinforce the argument for language championship at the higher managerial level.

One of the few empirical studies that attempts to measure the return on investment in languages is the ELAN research (CILT, 2006). To investigate the language approaches of almost 2000 exporting SMEs operating across 29 countries, respondents were asked to provide data on four categories of language investment: language skills, language plan, employment of nationals, and use of translators. The authors conclude that those SMEs that had made investments in all four categories experienced substantially higher export sales than those that did not. The most important individual investment category was language skills.

Resource allocation can send a strong signal of strategic intent and managerial commitment. When Wärtsilä NS absorbed the Italian operation Grandi Motori Trieste, out of around 1000 employees, only four were fluent in English. Language training was provided at all levels and across all functions at the multinational's expense. One Finnish expatriate at the Italian operation commented: 'It's amazing that Wärtsilä is investing so much on this, but maybe they have realised it's really important' (Lahtinen, 2000, 112).

Inter-unit Interaction and Language

As we discussed in Chapter 3, internationalizing firms face the issue of determining what processes and practices can be globally implemented (standardization) and what should be nationally responsive (localization).

Individual managers in subsidiary units can interpret, intervene and counter policies – what could be called localization by stealth. Localization can be formally reinforced through the introduction of technology that brings units together, but can also divide. For instance, the use of machine translation attempts to further the global reach of communication transmitted in the CCL so that those lacking the language fluency can translate such communications, as a way of assisting inclusion. However, rather than encouraging adoption of the corporate language, machine translation software provides a mechanism for individuals to opt out of the CCL, thus reinforcing localization of languages (see Chapter 2). This may run counter to the managerial intentions behind language standardization.

By its very nature, a decision taken at headquarters to introduce a corporate language drives a language strategy that may have the effect of overriding subsidiary unit requirements. When formulating a language strategy, a challenge is to accommodate as far as possible the diverse requirements of different subsidiary contexts, particularly where national laws dictate local language policies. In other words, there is a need to provide some room for flexibility without compromising CCL objectives (see Table 9.1).

When it comes to implementation, then, what is the role of the subsidiary? In Ylinen's (2010, 78) study of 47 international organizations based in Finland, one interviewee commented that 'our subsidiaries use naturally their own language in their operations and translate and localise the needed materials'. This pattern was quite common across participating organizations. The emerging research we reviewed confirms the critical role of individual subsidiary managers, whether expatriates or locals. Their actions help or hinder the introduction and support of a language strategy as exemplified by the approach to the CCL, as outlined in earlier chapters.

What is pertinent, and perhaps less recognized, is the interaction between subsidiary units. Joint activities may involve cross-border teams and project work, for instance. These require a shared language, reinforcing the need for adequate language training, feeding back into resource allocation and supporting implementation of a language policy. As we have previously mentioned, lack of CCL skills can be a major inhibitor in joint activities at the regional or global level. But as our KONE work demonstrated, language drove inter-unit cooperation based on language clusters (Germany–Austria, for example), as the units concerned lacked CCL skills. These cooperative activities assisted in furthering technical skills and knowledge transfer, but came at the expense of language standardization and implementation of the stated CCL.

Much of the communication is conducted informally through

person-to-person interactions and therefore subject to negotiation between the parties as to what language will be used. This may run counter to stated policy, but the need to get the job done can prompt the use of whatever language works in a given situation. Inter-unit interaction is furthered through the actions of individuals who base responses on assessments of the appropriate language that fits the specific context – what could be called *language contingency*. For example, in Nordea, the Nordic-based bank, English was adopted as the CCL (see Chapter 2). In her study, Louhiala-Salminen (2002, 135) found that there was considerable flexibility in language use. As one Finnish-speaking interviewee commented, 'I use what is easiest in the situation. English, if Danes are present, but I do use Swedish, too, with the Swedes, especially in informal situations.' Another Finnish interviewee explained: 'Everything in writing should be in English, and it is certainly practical . . . But I do speak Swedish with the Swedes on social occasions.' A frank admission by one of the interviewees was that using Swedish, the other person's language, was a way of getting that person 'on side'. These examples illustrate that implementing a language strategy as intended by top management may be negated by work-related contingencies.

Language Procedures

Supporting directives set out how the language strategy is to be implemented. These generally take the form of procedures written in the CCL, though some firms will permit these to be translated into other languages. Formally specifying procedures can be seen as a way of ensuring indirect supervision, as it is impossible for management to personally oversee the introduction and monitoring of a language strategy across all units. But a chain is only as strong as its weakest link and, as the examples above show, what happens at the subsidiary-unit level is often contrary to managerial intent.

Procedures provide step-by-step guidelines. For example, procedures relating to employee selection may specify the hiring of language competent employees, and indicate the language in which the job advertisement is to be written. Provision of language training may cover aspects such as whether this is to be company sponsored; if individual employees can attend during work hours; and the allocation of supportive funds. A procedure may cover external communication, indicating the language or languages to be used in press releases and the like. Louhiala-Salminen (2002, 122) reports the procedure followed in the Finnish forestry multinational Stora Enso. Press releases were to be written first in English before being translated into Finnish, Swedish and often German. Initially British

English was specified, but later what was described as 'mixed English' was permitted. Practices are generally more loosely defined, leaving some areas for discretion, such as allowing for judgement calls made by specialists or operatives – situational factors that may require local adaptation or reaction to unusual circumstances. Of course, over time, procedures may be adapted as practices evolve and take on a more formal character.

Incentives

Aligning individual and organizational goals is a major managerial challenge. For individuals, investing in language capital may be linked with career goals and aspirations, and thus becomes a major incentive to maintain their language competency and even add to their language portfolio through acquisition of additional languages. Some insight comes from a survey of 581 Thunderbird alumni conducted by Grosse (2004). She asked respondents what were the rewards for acquiring foreign language skills during their studies. Their replies included travel opportunities (41 per cent); overseas assignments (33 per cent); written or oral recognition (30 per cent); promotion (18 per cent) and salary increase (14 per cent). Analysing data from the Finnish Association of Graduates, Velikodnaya (2011) found that there was a link between ability to speak English and salary level.

Retaining key employees is part of the managerial challenge, particularly if the individual employees have benefited from company sponsored and funded language training (see Chapter 6). One way may be to ensure that individuals are placed where their competence is seen to be valued. Language skills may become obsolete or outdated if not utilized, and language-aware employees may be inclined to leave the organization if there is a possibility of 'language decay'.

Important yet overlooked language resources are those individuals whom we have described as language nodes. These individuals play an important role as communication conduits between headquarters and subsidiaries. Lahtinen (2000, 119) provides an example in her study of Wärtsilä NSD and its Italian subsidiary, Grandi Motori Trieste, mentioned above. She reports that language nodes often developed informally. However, there was one case where a Finnish expatriate was deliberately sent to the Italian subsidiary to act as the communication conduit to ensure that product development was aligned between Finland and Italy. In this case, the actions taken formalized what had previously been informal practice. However, there seems to be little evidence that this important role was linked to either the individual's or the sending unit's performance management and incentive system. A possible way of recognizing the role

that key individuals play would be to specifically include language performance in the formal evaluation of the subsidiary manager as a strong
incentive to actively manage subsidiary language resources.

PERFORMANCE MONITORING AND CONTROL

In Figure 9.1, we indicated that the final stage of the strategy process is
that of performance monitoring and control. This could be described
as an essential feedback mechanism for managerial decision-making.
Control is about achieving consistency and compliance. Performance
management forms part of a firm's control system. For example, reporting systems, performance targets and budgets are ways in which management establishes formal control (see Chapter 3). The underlying objective
is to monitor how the firm's intended strategy is being implemented, and
whether intervention, correction or adaptation is required. Inherent is
appraisal of employee behaviour, and hence the stress on rewards, such
as salary increases and promotion. All levels – the individual, the unit and
corporate – are included, but of course internationalization brings additional challenges in terms of standardization, equity and transparency.
Behaviour is measured against predetermined targets and goals, ideally
clearly linked to the overarching corporate strategy. The challenge is that
as strategies are adapted to changing circumstances, performance bench-
marks may become out of date, and therefore inappropriate or irrelevant.

In this section we are concerned with where language strategy fits into
this process. By its very nature, language management is complicated.
At one level, it is relatively easy to test an individual's level of language
fluency, as we discussed in the section on employee selection (Chapter
6). By the same token, it is possible, although difficult, to fully track how
language resources are being utilized as part of a cost–benefit exercise. At
the corporate level, one could argue that the conduct of a language audit
is part of performance monitoring, in that it has the potential to provide
up-to-date information on the state of the organization's pool of language
capital.

A major managerial challenge lies in assessing how individuals are
using their language skills to communicate and further information and
knowledge flow in the firm's interest. Research has shown that informal
knowledge flows are difficult to manage and control. Indeed, the very
act of control may be counter-productive (Marschan et al., 1996). As
Macdonald (1996, 228) maintains, '[i]nformal information flow is, by
definition, beyond the control of the organization'. We stress that language is an individual level skill. People are in a sense in control of how

and when their language skills are employed. Individuals have to be prepared to use their skills as the organization intends. As we have already shown, having a CCL does not simply solve this issue. Contributing to the challenge is that, having introduced a corporate language, managers are often lulled into a false sense of complacency and so it is not surprising that there is limited awareness of the true state of affairs on the language strategy front. In addition, in the informal arena, other languages may be used to avoid control through language standardization. Imposing a standardized language adds an additional layer as individuals can hide behind what we label the language screen. Take the case of Nestlé, the Swiss multinational. In 2013, its website indicated that it was operating in 86 countries. This involved 468 factories, more than 2000 global and local brands; multiple joint ventures and about 330 000 employees. Controlling and monitoring such a global entity is almost beyond imagination and, when one adds the language issue, it is easy to see how language screens can readily be erected to shield subsidiaries from headquarters' scrutiny.

Feedback can be inhibited by the language strategy. An effective monitoring system relies on formal reporting and the garnering of appropriate information and data. The example of KONE's Italian subsidiary is a case in point. The reporting data being fed back to headquarters were not an accurate picture of the true state of the subsidiary's financial health. Accurate decision-making is made more complicated if information is not complete. An inability to translate information into the correct language, or not being aware of the need for particular data due to miscommunication or language-induced ignorance can exacerbate the situation. Apart from its contribution to control and performance management, feedback is essential for strategic learning. If management is convinced that the CCL is being implemented as intended, then it may be blind to information that may indicate otherwise.

Another aspect is the monitoring and control of language-related external providers. As indicated in Figure 9.4, implementation of a language strategy can involve outsourcing of some activities, such as the use of external translation firms, university or other language training agencies, and employee search firms. Though external, these services need monitoring. Generally speaking, the department or subsidiary that sanctioned the use of the external service provider will be expected to monitor performance against contractual expectations and costs. As discussed in Chapter 2, decisions to use an external provider may be an *ad hoc* response to periods of heavy demand that have overloaded the internal translation capacity. Long-term relationships can develop to the point where the providers may come to be seen as part of the firm's language capital and even

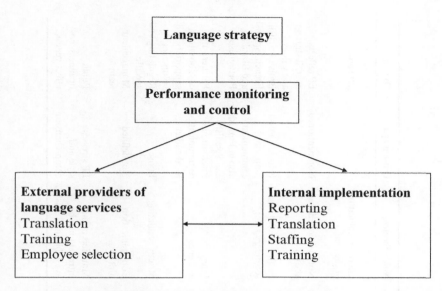

*Figure 9.4   Monitoring and controlling the implementation of language
strategy*

be included in a language audit. Monitoring is important because of such providers' role in language strategy implementation.

LANGUAGE STRATEGIZING IN PRACTICE

Given the limited knowledge about how language strategies evolve, it is interesting to note the results of a study of six Finnish firms (Kangasharju et al., 2010). The six firms involved indicated that they had a formal language policy and were prepared to allow these to be content-analysed. The policy documents mention the reasons for having a language policy. These include the aim to generate and maintain a shared corporate language (Nokia–Siemens), taking into account the different stakeholders and communication needs of various operating areas (Nordea, Oxfam), legal requirements (Itella, Oxfam), managing the costs of translation (Itella, Nordea), and needs related to language training (Itella, Oxfam). Table 9.2 highlights the key aspects that arose from the analysis. It should be noted that financial statements follow the European standard of using British English.

What emerged from the analysis was the lack of a strong strategic role for language. To the extent that strategy does intrude, it tends to be a

Table 9.2 Comparison of language policies

	Itella	Nordea	Nokia	Nokia Siemens	Outokumpu	Oxfam
Purpose of language policy (LP)	To define principles of language choices	To harmonize language choices and terminology	To stipulate internal and external use of language	To reflect international nature of the firm	Not mentioned	To give clear guidelines
Relationship between language policy and strategy	LP derived from goals, strategy and values	LP supports firm's strategy	LP aligned with Nokia strategy	Not mentioned (see above)	Not mentioned	LP reflects overall strategy and values
Official corporate language	American English, also partly Finnish and Swedish	British English	English	English (German a secondary role)	British English (important communications also in Finnish and Swedish)	British English, French, Spanish and Brazilian Portuguese
External parties included	Customers	Customers	Customers	International audience	International communications, local audiences	Partners and collaborators, supporters and volunteers
Enforcement	Quite loose	Quite detailed	Strictly regulating	Strictly regulating	Loose	Regulating and specific
Responsibility for language policy	HR and communication units jointly	Management team	Language and terminology unit	Communication unit	Not defined	Management team
Focus areas particular to the firm	LP stresses language training and skills development	Cost-efficiency, legislation and reputation criteria	Nokia Tone of Voice	Materials in the intranet must be available in English	LP stresses style and comprehension	Public openness, cost effectiveness

Source: Adapted from Kangasharju et al. (2010, 147).

one-way exercise. That is, corporate strategy (in its textbook use of goals, objectives and corporate values) influences the development of language policy, rather than language being first and foremost in the minds of the strategists. This brings language down to the level of guidelines and implementation in language-related areas such as translation, training and language-related technology.

As indicated in Table 9.2, Nokia established a dedicated unit with the specific responsibility for language policy. The policy was to be updated every one to three years, reflecting a concern for some stability. Oxfam had a similar approach, concerned with maintaining an up-to-date policy. For the remaining firms, responsibility varied in how it was devolved to parts within the organization: the management team (Nordea, Oxfam), the communications unit (Nokia–Siemens), HR and communications units jointly (Itella).

Kangasharju et al. (2010) found variation in the ways in which firms enforced the language policy. As can be seen from Table 9.2, some were rather loose while others were strict. Nokia, for example, permitted the use of local languages in order to ease communication, but the local language had to be complemented with the use of English. In contrast, Itella and Outokumpu were more flexible, permitting, even supporting, the coexistence of several languages. This acceptance of the parallel use of languages may not have been stated explicitly in the policy document.

Another interesting finding was the low level of general awareness of the existence of language policies in these firms. Kangasharju et al. (2010) noted that obtaining copies of the six firms' policy documents was a difficult exercise, both for the researchers and for those employees seeking to respond to the researchers' requests. They comment that simply having a policy is of little value unless it is widely circulated and enforced. Thus firms with language policies would benefit from communicating these to a wider audience. Rather than the reactive approach identified in this study, the authors suggest that a proactive approach to language policy is more appropriate as firms seek to accommodate the multilingual reality that global expansion brings. In general, it is clear that one language policy size does not fit all internationalizing firms.

Ylinen (2010, 42) also conducted a study of language strategies of 47 international organizations based in Finland, representing a wide range of industries and sectors, including non-profit organizations. She reports that 21 per cent had written language policies while 79 per cent did not. Of the latter, some organizations indicated that informal guidelines and practices existed but were not clearly documented. She provided an example of this from one respondent: 'We do not have a noteworthy strategy, but it has been stated that English is our official language. In addition, we have a so-called Tone of Voice document, which gives some guidelines also on language usage.' Simonsen (2009) undertook a similar study with Danish firms, although his purpose was different. He was concerned with how language policies were linked to corporate dictionaries and communication policies. Of the 65 Danish organizations in his sample, only 39 per cent had corporate language policies. This is compared to the 52 per cent who indicated that their organizations did not have such policies.

CONCLUSION

Throughout this chapter, we have stressed strategic flexibility as an important component of the strategy process. At the time when the initial decision to adopt a corporate language is taken, there may be an appropriate level of resource allocation to support the corporate language strategy. However, language needs alter as the firm internationalizes. As such, there are likely to be various aspects of existing strategy that need adjustment, but management may not recognize the need to change, particularly if language is given low priority. Our idea of a language officer would help to ensure a match between internationalization and language-related requirements. This raises the question of how much flexibility the internationalizing firm can allow, and how prepared management might be to accept solutions that may be contrary to existing procedures. For example, there may be an initial tolerance of parallel language use in headquarters–subsidiary communication, but this may not be sustainable over time as global expansion proceeds.

There is also a time element attached to language resource development. To produce the level of language capabilities through language training takes considerable time. Buying in suitably competent employees can assist in reducing the time required. Likewise, a decision to outsource activities such as language translation may seem a quicker and more convenient approach. In other instances, as Ylinen (2010) found, outsourcing may be a default strategy for dealing with language needs through external translation service providers. However, the end result may be the erosion of internal language capability. This can constrain the ability of the firm to respond to changing circumstances that demand a stronger set of language resources.

When formulating and implementing a language strategy, the main goal is to improve information and knowledge flow. Steyaert et al. (2011, 271) comment that language standardization is 'an administration management tool that helps global operations proceed efficiently'. Despite the fact that managers seek to control information flow and knowledge transfer, critical exchanges take place between people, often through informal interaction. It requires a fine balancing act to facilitate communication without introducing unintended impediments. This can only be achieved through a language strategy that permeates the whole organization, is championed by language-aware top management, and is supported by appropriate procedures practices, budgets and incentives.

NOTE

1. There are numerous global business strategy textbooks that provide comprehensive treatment for those interested in reading further on this topic.

REFERENCES

Bellak, N. (2014), *Can Language be Managed in International Business? Insights into Language Choice from a Case Study of Danish and Austrian Multinational Corporations (MNCs)*, PhD Thesis, Copenhagen: Department of International Business Communication, Copenhagen Business School.

CILT (2006), *ELAN: Effects on the European Economy of Shortages of Foreign Language Skills in Enterprise*, Brussels: European Commission.

Clarke, W.M. (2000), 'The use of foreign languages by Irish exporters', *European Journal of Marketing*, **34** (1/2), 80–90.

De Groot, E.B. (2012), 'Personal preference or policy? Language choice in a European-based international organization', *Corporate Communications: An International Journal*, **17** (3), 255–71.

Dhir, K.S. (2005), 'The value of language: concept, perspectives, and policies', *Corporate Communications: An International Journal*, **10** (4), 358–82.

Dyer, L. (1983), 'Bringing human resources into the strategy formulation process', *Human Resource Management*, **22** (3), 257–71.

Earl, M.J. and I.A. Scott (1999), 'What is a chief knowledge officer?', *Sloan Management Review*, **40** (2), 29–38.

The Economist (2005), 'Carrefour at the crossroads', 22 October, 67.

Grosse, C.U. (2004), 'The competitive advantage of foreign languages and cultural knowledge', *The Modern Language Journal*, **88** (3), 351–73.

Hagen, S. (2011), *Report on Language Management Strategies and Best Practice in European SMEs: The PIMLICO Project*, Brussels: European Commission.

Harzing, A.-W. and M. Pudelko (2013), 'Language competencies, policies and practices in multinational corporations', *Journal of World Business*, **48** (1), 87–97.

Harzing, A.-W. and M. Pudelko (2014), 'Hablas vielleicht un peu la mia language? A comprehensive overview of the role of language differences in head-quarters–subsidiary communication', *International Journal of Human Resource Management*, **25** (5), 696–717.

Kangasharju, H., R. Piekkari and R. Säntti (2010), 'Yritysten kielipolitiikka: missä se piilee?' (The language policy in international firms: where is it hiding?), in H. Lappalainen, M.-L. Sorjonen and M. Vilkuna (eds), *Kielellä on merkitystä (Language Matters)*, Helsinki: Suomalaisen Kirjallisuuden Seura, pp. 136–57.

Lahtinen, M. (2000), *Language Skilled Employees in Multinationals*, Master's Thesis, Helsinki: Helsinki School of Economics and Business Administration.

Lauring, J. and A. Klitmøller (2013), 'The effect of contextual factors on corporate language based communication avoidance in MNCs: a multi-sited ethnography approach', in A. Klitmøller, *(Re)Contextualizing Cultural and Linguistic Boundaries in Multinational Corporations: A Global Ethnographic Approach*, Doctoral Thesis, Aarhus: Aarhus University, pp. 80–107.

Louhiala-Salminen, L. (2002), 'Communication and language use in merged corporations', Working Paper W-330, Helsinki: Helsinki School of Economics.

Macdonald, S. (1996), 'Informal information flow and strategy in the international firm', *International Journal of Technology Management*, **11** (1/2), 219–32.

Marschan, R. (1996), *New Structural Forms and Inter-Unit Communication in Multinationals: The Case of KONE Elevators*, Doctoral Thesis A-110, Helsinki: Helsinki School of Economics.

Marschan, R., D.E. Welch and L.S. Welch (1996), 'Control in less-hierarchical MNC structures: the role of personal networks and informal communication', *International Business Review*, **5** (2), 137–50.

Marschan, R., D.E. Welch and L.S. Welch (1997), 'Language: the forgotten factor in multinational management', *European Management Journal*, **15** (5), 591–8.

Marschan-Piekkari, R., D.E. Welch and L.S. Welch (1999), 'Adopting a common corporate language: IHRM implications', *International Journal of Human Resource Management*, **10** (3), 377–90.

Mintzberg, H. and J.A. Waters (1985), 'Of strategies, deliberate and emergent', *Strategic Management Journal*, **6** (3), 257–72.

Neeley, T. (2011), 'Language and globalization: "Englishnization" at Rakuten', Harvard Business School Teaching Case, 9-412-002.

Neeley, T. (2013), 'Language matters: status loss and achieved status distinctions in global organizations', *Organization Science*, **24** (2), 476–97.

Peltokorpi, V. and E. Vaara (2012), 'Language policies and practices in wholly owned foreign subsidiaries: a recontextualization perspective', *Journal of International Business Studies*, **43** (9), 808–33.

Petersen, B., D.E. Welch and L.S. Welch (2000), 'Creating meaningful switching options in international operations', *Long Range Planning*, **35** (5), 688–705.

Piekkari, R., D.E. Welch, L.S. Welch, J.-P. Peltonen and T. Vesa (2013), 'Translation behaviour: an exploratory study within a service multinational', *International Business Review*, **22** (5), 771–83.

Pohjanen-Bernardi, K. and K. Talja (2011), *Language Strategies in Finnish Small and Medium-Sized Enterprises*, Master's Thesis, Helsinki: School of Economics, Aalto University.

Simonsen, H. (2009), 'Communication policy, corporate language policy and corporate information portal', *Journal of Communication Management*, **13** (3), 200–217.

Steyaert, C., A. Ostendorp and C. Gaibrois (2011), 'Multilingual organizations as "linguascapes": negotiating the position of English through discursive practices', *Journal of World Business*, **46** (3), 270–78.

Sulonen, J. (2011), *International Organizations in the Linguistic Context of Quebec*, Master's Thesis, Helsinki: School of Economics, Aalto University.

Thomas, C.A. (2008), 'Bridging the gap between theory and practice: language policy in multilingual organisations', *Language Awareness*, **17** (4), 307–25.

Vaara, E., J. Tienari, R. Piekkari and R. Säntti (2005), 'Language and the circuits of power in a merging multinational corporation', *Journal of Management Studies*, **41** (3), 595–623.

Velikodnaya, N. (2011), *Career Boundaries in the Boundaryless World*, Master's Thesis, Helsinki: School of Economics, Aalto University.

Welch, D.E. and A. Steen (2013), 'Repositioning global staff transfers: a learning perspective', *Human Resource Management*, **52** (5), 793–807.

Welch, D.E. and L.S. Welch (2008), 'The importance of language in international knowledge transfer', *Management International Review*, **48** (3), 339–60.

Welch, D.E., L.S. Welch and R. Piekkari (2005), 'Speaking in tongues: the importance of language in international management processes', *International Studies of Management & Organization*, **35** (1), 10–27.

Ylinen, A.-M. (2010), *A Comparative Study of Language Strategies in International Organizations*, Master's Thesis, Helsinki: School of Economics, Aalto University.

10. Conclusion

Treating language separately from culture has allowed us to demonstrate the pervasive, yet often downplayed or unappreciated, effects of language on the operations of internationalizing firms. As we noted in one of our earlier publications, 'language is not just an "add-on factor" for MNC management, which can be readily dealt with through employing a company language, as important as that step is in itself' (Marschan et al., 1997, 595). Language facilitates and impedes communication, and needs to be regarded as a key element of firms' international operations. If this importance is accepted, then language studies would seem to be more appropriately located alongside international business (IB) teaching and research. It could be argued that one of the reasons for the neglect of the impact of language is its typical separation from the business context. Language consciousness is less likely to emerge if it remains on the periphery for IB leaders of the twenty-first century. In this final chapter, we summarize key themes and issues that support our overall position on the role of language in internationalizing firms.

THE BROADER LANGUAGE CONTEXT

While our focus throughout this book has been on the internationalizing firm, we recognize that language is an issue that goes beyond the firm. As shown in Figure 10.1, language aspects are played out in a broader context. Firms do not control national education policies and thus may be constrained by host-country legislation (such as the situation in Quebec; see Chapter 9). Individual national governments' language policies matter as these affect what and how languages are taught – particularly in dual-language societies. There are genuine societal concerns about the survival of a local language – Icelandic for instance – when it is little used outside the national border. The fear is that it will be overwhelmed by dominant international languages, such as English, which are adopted by internationalizing firms as a corporate language. In cross-border mergers, the imposition of a common corporate language (CCL) may provoke accusations of a form of neo-colonialism (Vaara et al., 2005) – as can

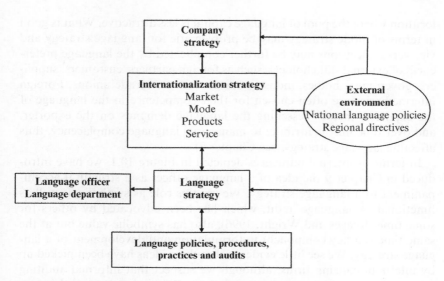

Figure 10.1   External and internal influences on language

the establishment of offshore call centres (Boussebaa et al., 2014). For these reasons, the introduction of a CCL can be a sensitive issue in some locations, for example English in France, and impede its effectiveness. Regional directives are important, as evidenced by EU policies. On the other hand, in countries where national language policies encourage foreign language learning at schools and universities, a wide pool of foreign language capacity is created on which an internationalizing firm may draw. Language capital is not just a firm level construct but extends well beyond its boundaries.

The external environment affects the company's strategy and thus elements of its internationalization strategy, as shown in Figure 10.1. For example, an important aspect of international operations is the choice of foreign markets. Our language path concept detailed in Chapter 1 demonstrates how a market strategy can be also regarded as a language strategy in that the choice of which country to enter drives the form and extent of language issues confronted by the internationalizing firm. As discussed in Chapter 8, choice of foreign operation mode has language strategy implications in that different modes may pose varied language demands. For instance, in the case of international mergers and acquisitions (M&As), there may be considerable variation in the availability of appropriate targets across different markets. Government policy in target markets may dictate whether this mode of operation is feasible. For greenfield investments, a foreign government might insist on establishment in a particular location where the pool of language capital is less attractive. What is good in terms of mode strategy may be problematic for language strategy and vice versa. Decisions may be further complicated by the language preferences of external stakeholders, such as foreign partners, customers, suppliers, government bodies, industry associations and trade unions. Foreign intermediaries are often chosen for their competence in the language of the exporter, thereby lessening the language demands on the exporter, and over time may contribute to managerial language complacency, thus affecting language strategy (see Chapter 7).

In terms of internal influences depicted in Figure 10.1, we have introduced in Chapter 9 the idea of a language officer as a structural accompaniment to a language strategy. We see this role as symbolic as well as functional. A language audit, which has been advocated by others for some time (Reeves and Wright, 1996), also has symbolic value but at the same time is a key component in formulation and development of a language strategy. We see little evidence that these ideas have been picked up by internationalizing firms, although we suspect that informal auditing may occur from time to time in some firms. What we can say is that language departments do exist, though are not necessarily given that name. For instance, the US multinational Medtronic has what it calls a 'multilingual core team' that handles translation (Welch et al., 2005). In other companies, such as Nordea, the designation is the translation department; in the Finnish company F-Secure, the unit is referred to as the translation and localization department.

LANGUAGE AND THE DIFFERENT LEVELS OF MANAGEMENT

We have mentioned the differences between how top management and those lower down in the organizational hierarchy view the language demands, particularly given the fact that in most cases top managers are comfortable operating in the CCL. There is another layer of management that we have not mentioned: the board of directors for firms that are publicly listed and within which there may be diversity of nationalities and mother tongues, and varying levels of proficiency in the working language used in board meetings. Research on the topic of language use in corporate board meetings reveals differences in how the language issue is resolved. For example, a study of the operations of the boards of nine Nordic listed companies found that some board members used the national language of the firm's headquarters; others used a mixed or blended approach. That is, members would use their own languages and other members' languages intermingled throughout the meeting. A final form was to adopt English as the vehicular language, even if it was not the corporate language, or any of the members' mother tongues. What was unexpected was that the entry of a foreign board member would not necessarily trigger a switch to a different working language. Another surprising finding was how ill prepared board members, including chairpersons, were for the language implications arising from internationalization (Piekkari et al., 2014).

Piekkari et al. (2014) develop the concept of a language ladder to describe how boards may approach the language issue over time, and with continued internationalization, as illustrated in Figure 10.2. The first rung of the ladder depicts those firms dealing with domestic matters and without foreign members, so that the national language is used. The second rung indicates that the composition of the board is more multilingual due to the presence of foreign board members. While translators could be used as a coping strategy, there may be occasions where, because of a background in the relevant language, the 'foreign' board member might be able to operate in the relevant national language without

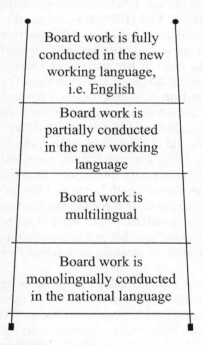

Board work is fully conducted in the new working language, i.e. English

Board work is partially conducted in the new working language

Board work is multilingual

Board work is monolingually conducted in the national language

Source: Adapted from Piekkari et al. (2014, 36).

Figure 10.2 Language ladder

assistance. This stage can be more *ad hoc*, with language responses emergent and dependent on each situation and board composition. On the third rung of the linguistic ladder, a new working language may be partially introduced but not fully embraced. The meeting could be conducted in a different language from that of documents, such as the agenda, supporting reports, other material and the minutes of the meeting. The final rung involves the full adoption of a new working language for the board (often English). Of course, positions on the language ladder should not be seen as always desirably upwards. Firms might stay on a particular rung, and even reverse position, depending on board composition, mix of languages and ownership.

LANGUAGE AS A RECONFIGURATION AGENT

Our treatment of language in the internationalizing firm goes beyond the more traditional cross-cultural communication approach. Work in semiotics has stressed the way in which language shapes and is shaped by its context. For example, Fiol (1989, 278) defines the study of semiotics as 'a formal mode of analysis used to identify the rules that govern how signs convey meanings in a particular social system'. Brannen (2004) used semiotics as the basis of her analysis of Disney's internationalization process to draw out language consequences. Transferring Disney's products, systems and programmes involved crossing cultural contexts that reshaped the intended meaning, inhibiting comprehension and interpretation. As we discussed in Chapter 1, effective communication is a two-way process, and in the case of Disney, the new cultural context shaped the message being conveyed. Such recontextualization, argues Brannen, provides an enhanced explanation of the basic communication model by taking into account both home and host contexts. Moreover, Brannen (2004, 605) contends that recontextualization is 'the process by which the consumer or transferee makes sense of the product, practice, or service transferred abroad into his or her own culture'. In other words, it is a form of localization of meaning in different national and language contexts.

We argue, however, that language involves more than recontextualization. It is a *reconfiguration agent* 'that affects the total system within which knowledge transfer takes place' (Welch and Welch, 2008, 354). As we identified in earlier chapters, the internal system-altering characteristic of language goes beyond the knowledge transfer process. Language has the capacity to change the way in which the internationalizing firm operates. It determines what the firm sees, hears and pays attention to.

Language alters the firm from within through its effect on information and communication pathways, types and quality of interactions, and critical networks. Many of the effects operate at an informal level but are still powerful, as we indicated with respect to organizational structure. In other words, language as a reconfiguration agent extends the idea of language beyond its role as a vehicle for transferring information and knowledge. A further aspect of reconfiguration is the constant movement it creates. Language is a fluid, dynamic force.

The concept of a reconfiguration agent is also apparent when one considers the dark side of introducing a corporate language. It is possible to identify four aspects: what we refer to as 'The Four Ss'.

Silencing Effect

The introduction of a CCL can reduce the amount and quality of interaction between individuals and units of the internationalizing firm. In a Danish study of 14 companies operating with English as the CCL, Lauring and Tange (2010) identified several negative consequences: a reduced amount of overall communication; stilted and constrained interaction, with less humour and irony; individual withdrawal from meetings and networks; and information loss. These authors refer to the 'silent organization' as a by-product of these aspects.

Sidetracking Effect

As we discussed in Chapter 6, lack of fluency in the CCL can affect career pathing, effectively limiting or sidetracking progression. Those without the requisite language competence may find themselves isolated, often with others similarly affected, in what have been called language pockets (Barner-Rasmussen and Aarnio, 2011). These pockets can become *language traps* from which individuals may find it difficult to escape without investing in appropriate language development. The alternative may be to exit the organization.

Stagnating Effect

Related to the above, the language barrier may be such that individuals and units can be so isolated that they effectively are at a standstill, potentially cut off from important developments within the company such as technology and marketing programmes, and training options. Opportunities could be lost, both within and outside the firm, for individuals as well as internationalizing firms.

Sifting Effect

In earlier chapters we introduced the concept of language as power. Those with relevant language fluency can control the flow of information. The result is a sifting effect – filtering, separating and sorting out what is to be translated or disseminated.

LANGUAGE AND THE CONDUCT OF ACADEMIC RESEARCH

One of the themes stressed in this book is the way in which language permeates all aspects of IB. Despite this somewhat obvious statement, it is surprising that much of the research conducted by IB scholars takes little account of the effect of language. Harzing et al. (2002) refer to the fact that the necessity to accommodate language is a necessary cost and inconvenience of IB research. It is not surprising, therefore, that there is a seeming predisposition to select top managers or expatriates as the target respondents as these individuals are most likely to be fluent in English, the language of IB (see Marschan-Piekkari and Reis, 2004). This approach neatly sidesteps the language issue from a research perspective and results in a preponderance of work that reflects a select managerial group comprising those with requisite language skills.

Language appears to be missing in discussions of the research process itself (Welch and Welch, 2008). This was borne out in a recent content analysis of the four main IB journals – *International Business Review, Journal of International Business Studies, Management International Review* and *Journal of World Business* – by Chidlow et al. (2014). 'In the time period under investigation (2000–2009), a total of 1440 articles were published in the four journals.' They identified '401 cross-language studies, of which 334 were quantitative (72 per cent of the total number of quantitative survey-based articles) and 67 qualitative (69 per cent of the total number of qualitative articles)'. These figures indicate the overwhelming influence of language boundaries, yet the analysis of the publications revealed a lack of transparency as to how the language issue was treated throughout the research process. Where language was discussed, there was a tendency to see it as a technical problem to be handled or minimized.

We now highlight the range of language decisions that cross-language researchers confront (see Figure 10.3). How translation is handled is obviously critical to the integrity of the research process. In whatever form, though, once language boundaries are encountered, the use of translation at different stages in the research process becomes important.

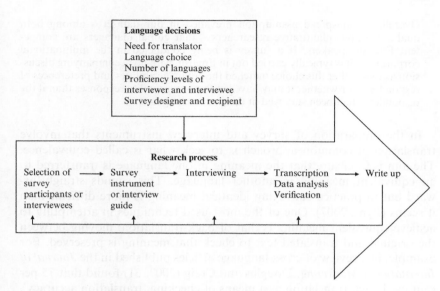

Language decisions

Need for translator
Language choice
Number of languages
Proficiency levels of
interviewer and interviewee
Survey designer and recipient

Research process

Selection of → Survey → Interviewing → Transcription → Write up
survey   instrument   Data analysis
participants or or interview   Verification
interviewees   guide

Figure 10.3   Language decisions during the research process

There is some awareness when studies involve the use of multiple language surveys due to the nature of the research. For instance, studies of multi-national subsidiaries operating in various countries may necessitate the use of several survey instruments in the languages of subsidiary targeted respondents.

The empirical starting point is the selection of participants. Daniels and Cannice (2004, 200, 202) recognized that language was a factor in conducting interviews. They admitted that they 'always asked if we can conduct interviews in English or whether we need to arrange for an inter-preter'; and 'restricted our interviews to high-level managers who tend to be cosmopolitan and English-speaking'. Of course, avoiding the need for a translator may restrict the pool of potential interviewees and may bias results as a consequence. There is also the possibility that translation can be part of data collection (Xian, 2008).

Scholars in non-English-speaking countries often undertake surveys of aspects of multinational activities in English and we have little idea of the way in which English fluency has influenced the composition of the survey questions. On the other hand, there is limited understanding of how the targeted respondents react to receiving English-language questionnaires. As Chidlow et al. (2014, 567) comment:

Overall, a widespread assumption prevailed in our dataset – among both qualitative and quantitative researchers – that global managers are competent English speakers. If a survey is being conducted in the multinational corporation, it is typically carried out in English, with no accompanying discussion as to whether this choice matched the language abilities and preferences of respondents, or whether it may have led to poorer quality responses than if the respondents had been surveyed in their native language.

In the preparation of survey and interview instruments that involve translation, a common approach is to seek what is called equivalence. The aim is to ensure that the meaning in one language is transferred to an equivalent meaning in another language. This sounds straightforward but in practice conveying identical meaning is more difficult than it seems (Pym, 2007). One of the most-used techniques in attempting to achieve equivalent meaning is that of back-translation: moving between the original and translated text to check that meaning is preserved. For example, in a review of cross-language articles published in the *Journal of International Marketing*, Douglas and Craig (2007, 31) found that 75 per cent used back-translation as a means of checking 'translation accuracy'. When discussing the findings of their content analysis, Chidlow et al. (2014, 269–70) remark:

> In our dataset of quantitative papers, back translation is regarded as in and of itself a form of quality assurance . . . We found back translation to be the technique most commonly mentioned in association with equivalence (or 'consistency', which is used as a synonym). Equivalence is in turn associated with (or even interchangeable with) accuracy, validity, reliability and quality. Authors assume that equivalence of meaning is achievable, although what constitutes equivalence is usually not made clear. Authors . . . portray back translation as a *guarantee* [sic] of equivalence.

The problem, though, is that equivalence assumes that all languages are comparable in terms of vocabulary, meaning and context. Chidlow et al. (2014, 574) comment: 'The equivalence paradigm is predicated on the possibilities of the translator-as-technician reproducing as close a copy of the original as possible and transferring meaning across languages and cultures without changing it.' As the international marketing literature has long pointed out, literal translation can lead to the types of blunders we list in Chapter 1, and the language issue around brands discussed in Chapter 7. What is striking here is that internationally operating firms are very aware of the issue, but this is not reflected by researchers.

The quest for equivalence through reliance on back-translation can mask the fact that the relationship between two languages is asymmetrical. This is simplistically demonstrated by word count. English has the richest vocabulary: in 1986, it was estimated to have 500 000 words, versus German with about 185 000 and French with fewer than 100 000 (McCrum et al., 1986). As most research in IB is published in English, the assumption that equivalence can be achieved is ripe for challenge.

A related issue is the role and background of the person undertaking the back-translation. According to Chidlow et al. (2014), the back-translator was invisible: 'It was rarely clarified if the translator possessed not just linguistic expertise, but also the necessary level of content knowledge and familiarity with the context being studied . . . few authors report on taking steps to check for or improve comprehension in the data collection or analysis phases.'

Whether the instrument is translated or not, another pertinent question is the respondent's language capability and its effect on whether and how the person answers questions posed in the questionnaire. Does the person answer them to the best of their language capability, which may inadvertently bias the response? Without being in the location personally, there is no way for the researcher to ensure that the target respondent actually answers the questionnaire. It may be that the person hands it on to a work colleague or subordinate more fluent in English to answer on their behalf. This individual may not have the requisite issue-related knowledge to answer the questions meaningfully. Alternatively, the target respondent may use a professional translator to go through each item. As mentioned above, literal translation is not always meaningful. Much depends on the translator's ability to accurately translate the question as intended. In each of these situations, the researcher is dependent on the quality of the translation. Answers may thus be compromised.

Another consideration that is virtually ignored is the potential effect of language on the response rate and the pattern of responses. Harzing's (1997) research on the issue of international mail survey response rates is one of the few that considers the possible influence of cultural aspects, including language. Her focus was on the then dominance of US-based research with its English language bias. She found that response rates differed between countries and nationalities. But Harzing did not consider that language fluency could be at the heart of the issue. If a mail survey arrived in a foreign language, it would be easy to ignore or delete it due to work pressures, rather than struggling to answer it, or find a translator to help with the task. As our work on translation revealed, work colleagues are important for on-the-job translation, but people are somewhat wary of imposing too much on their goodwill.

A growing body of IB research is based on qualitative methodology, which relies heavily on interviews. The above issues become even more pronounced in that language concerns may dictate: whom to interview;

the language to be used for the interview guide and in the interview; whether to use a translator; and the choice of language for data transcription and verification. However, Chidlow et al. (2014, 571) found that

> IB researchers conducting qualitative cross-language research largely do not account for their translation decisions in their reporting . . . This lack of sensitivity to language is rather paradoxical given Polkinghorne's (2005, 135) description of qualitative research as 'languaged data'. It also does not reflect the complexity of a qualitative research project, in which multiple translation decisions are faced: producing a target-language version of the interview guide, conducting the interview, transcribing the interview, analyzing the data and reporting interviewee quotations in the publication. (Welch and Piekkari, 2006)

The conduct of the interview is perhaps where language plays a particularly critical role. Differences in language fluency between the researcher/ interviewer and the interviewee may have an effect on how the interview is conducted, the information exchange and the power balance.

Language issues affect the transcription and data verification stage of the research process. The interview transcript may require translation at some point, usually into English for journal publication or thesis examination purposes. In the original KONE research, 33 per cent of the interviews were conducted in Finnish, Swedish or Spanish (Marschan, 1996). Interviews were transcribed in full, with relevant parts later translated into English. A similar approach was taken by Reis (2002), who conducted interviews in Portuguese, German and English. The non-English interviews were transcribed and subsequently relevant parts were translated into English. This process meant that the original data were preserved, allowing rechecking of meaning and themes for data integrity purposes. In Reis's study, as she was fluent in the three languages involved, she was able to cope with the fact that some interviewees switched languages during the interview. 'One German top manager, who had been on several foreign assignments during his career, replied using German, English and Portuguese' (Marschan-Piekkari and Reis, 2004, 234). However, as Reis relates, the multilingual interview generated what she referred to as a 'cocktail of languages' that posed a transcription challenge. In terms of data verification, there are language 'traps'. An interesting example is provided by Marschan-Piekkari and Reis (2004, 239). The transcript of the interview, which had been conducted in English, was sent back to the Italian participant, a top-level manager.

> To the researcher's surprise, his secretary, who had a good command of English but was not present in the actual interview, had reinterpreted the transcript, as she explained in her accompanying letter: I am sending you your interview with [Mr X's] corrections and my interpretation of the same. He has read it and

agrees with the clarifications I have made [to the English in the original]. This 'reinterpretation' was not very helpful in terms of the original interview content.

This example illustrates how well-meaning translators may tamper with the data in not necessarily constructive ways. This action was revealed only through a frank exchange during the data verification process. One could speculate as to whether this type of action is more common than researchers are aware of.

The above discussion focuses on the challenge of how to preserve meaning in the translation process. One of the practical solutions suggested is to incorporate back-translation alongside the use of a diverse group – monolinguals as well as bilinguals, who can assess the quality of the end-product. Pre-testing survey and interview questions on a target language audience, and then using bilinguals to assess similarity, is another suggestion. Of course, selecting translators who are conversant with the IB concepts and context of the empirical study is also a valuable step (see Chidlow et al., 2014). We recognize that these add to the time, cost and complexity of the research, but at the least, if this cannot be done, then the limitations of not having done so should be clearly acknowledged. The writing-up stage is where the researcher is communicating with a wider audience. It is incumbent on the researcher to be transparent about all aspects of the process.

Translation is integral to IB research that crosses language boundaries. Given that so few researchers report on how they handle the language issue in the research process, we recommend that it should become a standard aspect of the presentation of the research methodology – as important as the normal methodological aspects required by academic journals. Chidlow et al. (2014, 573) concur. They conclude:

> documenting and accounting for the choices that the researcher and translator have made becomes a central methodological task – something that we found to be rare among the articles we analyzed. These decisions cover both fieldwork and the writing up of the study, and include whether to translate, which language(s) to use in the study, what is the translation purpose, the approach to translation to be taken, and how to report on translation in the write-up of the study.

Where Does Language Fit?

The reaction of some colleagues from a communication and language department who attended one of our earlier seminar sessions on language was quite telling: 'Who are you from international business to talk about our area – language?' A spirited discussion followed. What was clear from this territorial reaction was that the issue of language crosses many academic disciplinary boundaries. Our sense is that, rather than

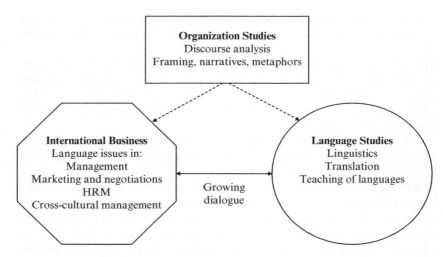

Figure 10.4   The language domain

maintaining this division, there has been increasing recognition of the contribution that different fields can bring to the study and application of language in internationalizing firms, as indicated in Figure 10.4. We see a growing dialogue between disciplinary communities in the united endeavour to explore and explain how and why language matters. Language in IB is not an isolated island. Rather, it is a domain in constant flux and influenced by continuing dialogue with colleagues from other disciplines.

The study of language in IB is showing where and how language fits – that is, its place and purpose in the business context. An important part of this work is its managerial focus: demonstrating that language resources have to be managed in a way that improves overall firm performance. There needs to be a return on the investment in language. Interaction with other disciplines can assist in dealing with the multilingual reality of global business expansion.

As Figure 10.4 illustrates, for those in language studies, the growth of interest in language as a factor in IB operations provides a stronger *raison d'être* for their teaching and research. Linguists have sophisticated techniques and methodologies that allow for the study of language at the micro-level. As we commented in Chapter 2, the training of professional translators is a vital aspect of IB. Perhaps the practical emphasis of both IB and language studies has prompted a growing awareness of what each brings to the language domain.

Organization studies could be seen as taking a more theoretical approach. As indicated in Figure 10.4, there is an emphasis on discourse analysis and associated concepts such as sense-making and sense-giving. There is a focus on the choice of words and how they are used to create meaning. At this stage, such work has had limited impact on the way in which language is studied in IB (hence the use of dashed arrows in Figure 10.4).

Foreign Language Teaching

As we outlined in Chapter 1, English as the *lingua franca* has had an inevitable impact on the interest in learning languages as part of a business or tourism degree. This is reflected in comments such as: 'The trend towards promoting higher education in English is accompanied by a growing assumption that understanding English is all that is needed for the global citizens of the future' (Cason and Rodríguez, 2013, 15). Such sentiments may help to explain the decline in interest in foreign languages other than English. However, this may be a short-sighted perspective given that other languages, such as Chinese and Spanish, are becoming more important in IB. Internationalizing firms that need employees with languages other than English for their various markets to cater for the localization of their operations will seek employees with requisite languages. In Chapter 9, we made reference to the way in which some students interested in a career in IB saw the value of investing in foreign language training.

Demand for language skills can come from various sources. For example, in Chapter 7, we noted that many jobs in the tourism sector have foreign language requirements in order to cater for international tourists. A study by Leslie and Russell (2006, 1405) of interest in language study by UK and non-UK tourism students found that UK students were far less interested than their equivalents on the Continent. It seemed that having English as a mother tongue had a tendency to desensitize UK students to the importance of being able to converse with international tourists in their own mother tongues. Leslie and Russell comment that 'the lesser commitment of UK students to developing FL [foreign language] skills is potentially placing them at a disadvantage to their Continental peers as regards employment opportunities'. They also point to the negative implications for UK tourism businesses. There is destination competition, and language skills are an aspect of competitive advantage.

A CONCLUDING NOTE

Language effects on IB are extensive, often subtle, but frequently overlooked in business and by researchers. What we have sought to do in this book has been to bring language to the forefront, to show that it matters. Long subsumed under the culture umbrella, it has been too easily ignored, a forgotten factor. We are not arguing that language is everything and affects every aspect of international operations. For example, the Portuguese retailer, Jerónimo Martins, failed in Brazil in spite of its language advantage. According to *The Economist* (2014, 62), Brazil was 'too big, the company too small, and despite speaking the right language, Brazilians proved too different'. Nevertheless, the pervasive effects of language need to be taken more fully into account in explanations of IB activity.

Language too readily can be seen as an individual issue, but we argue that it is too important to be left at the individual level. Rather, it is a multi-level issue. While language as a resource is person-bound, management actions can influence individual action. As we detail, targeted policies – such as training, financial incentives and language-driven appointments – can assist in encouraging individuals to contribute to building organizational language capital. To be effective, managerial action needs to be in concert with individual action in order for language to be seen as a distinctive part of the firm's international capabilities. However, in order to manage language, firms need to manage people as the repositories and carriers of this important resource.

REFERENCES

Barner-Rasmussen, W. and C. Aarnio (2011), 'Shifting the faultlines of language: a quantitative functional-level exploration of language use in MNC subsidiaries', *Journal of World Business*, **46** (3), 288–95.

Boussebaa, M., S. Sinha and Y. Gabriel, 'Englishization in offshore call centres: a postcolonial perspective', *Journal of International Business Studies* (2014), doi:10.1057/jibs.2014.25.

Brannen, M.Y. (2004), 'When Mickey loses face: recontextualization, semantic fit, and the semiotics of foreignness', *Academy of Management Review*, **29** (4), 593–616.

Cason, J. and P. Rodríguez (2013), 'Why English?', *Forum*, **14** (Winter), 14–15.

Chidlow, A., E. Plakoyiannaki and C. Welch (2014), 'Translation in cross-language international business research: beyond equivalence', *Journal of International Business Studies*, **45** (5), 562–82.

Daniels, J.D. and M.V. Cannice (2004), 'Interview studies in international business research', in R. Marschan-Piekkari and C. Welch (eds), *Handbook of Qualitative Research Methods in International Business*, Cheltenham, UK and Northampton, MA, USA: Edward Elgar, pp. 185–206.

Douglas, S.P. and C.S. Craig (2007), 'Collaborative and iterative translation: an alternative approach to back translation', *Journal of International Marketing*, **15** (1), 30–43.

The Economist (2014), 'A Portuguese explorer', 1 March, 62–3.

Fiol, C.M. (1989), 'A semiotic analysis of corporate language: organizational boundaries and joint venturing', *Administrative Science Quarterly*, **34** (2), 277–303.

Harzing, A.-W. (1997), 'Response rates in international mail surveys: results of a 22-country study', *International Business Review*, **6** (6), 641–65.

Harzing, A.-W., M. Maznevski and country collaborators (2002), 'The interaction between language and culture: a test of the cultural accommodation hypothesis in seven countries', *Language and Intercultural Communication*, **2** (2), 120–39.

Lauring, J. and H. Tange (2010), 'International language management: contained or dilute communication', *European Journal of International Management*, **4** (4), 317–32.

Leslie, D. and H. Russell (2006), 'The importance of foreign language skills in the tourism sector: a comparative study of student perceptions in the UK and continental Europe', *Tourism Management*, **27** (6), 1397–407.

Marschan, R. (1996), *New Structural Forms and Inter-Unit Communication in Multinationals: The Case of KONE Elevators*, Doctoral Thesis A-110, Helsinki: Helsinki School of Economics.

Marschan, R., D.E. Welch and L.S. Welch (1997), 'Language: the forgotten factor in multinational management', *European Management Journal*, **15** (5), 591–8.

Marschan-Piekkari, R. and C. Reis (2004), 'Language and languages in cross-cultural interviewing', in R. Marschan-Piekkari and C. Welch (eds), *Handbook of Qualitative Research Methods for International Business*, Cheltenham, UK and Northampton, MA, USA: Edward Elgar, pp. 224–63.

McCrum, R., W. Cran and R. MacNeil (1986), *The Story of English*, London: Faber and Faber.

Piekkari, R., L. Oxelheim and T. Randøy (2014), 'Internationalization of the corporate board and change in its working language', competitive paper, Vancouver: Annual Meeting of the Academy of International Business, 23–6 June.

Polkinghorne, D.E. (2005), 'Language and meaning: data collection in qualitative research', *Journal of Counselling Psychology*, **52** (2), 137–45.

Pym, A. (2007), 'Natural and directional equivalence in theories of translation', *Target*, **19** (2), 271–94.

Reeves, N. and C. Wright (1996), *Linguistic Auditing: A Guide to Identifying Foreign Language Communication Needs in Corporations*, Clevedon, UK: Multilingual Matters Ltd.

Reis, C. (2002), *The Private and Public Lives of Men Managers in a European Multinational Company: A Feminist Cross-cultural Analysis of England, Germany and Portugal*, Doctoral Thesis, London: University of London.

Vaara, E., J. Tienari, R. Piekkari and R. Säntti (2005), 'Language and the circuits of power in a merging multinational corporation', *Journal of Management Studies*, **42** (3), 595–623.

Welch, C. and R. Piekkari (2006), 'Crossing language barriers: qualitative interviewing in international business', *Management International Review*, **46** (4), 417–37.

Welch, D.E. and L.S. Welch (2008), 'The importance of language in international knowledge transfer', *Management International Review*, **48** (3), 339–60.

Welch, D.E., L.S. Welch and R. Piekkari (2005), 'Speaking in tongues: the importance of language in international management processes', *International Studies of Management & Organization*, **35** (1), 10–27.

Xian, H. (2008), 'Lost in translation? Language, culture and the roles of translator in cross-cultural management research', *Qualitative Research in Organizations and Management: An International Journal*, **3** (3), 231–45.

Index

Printed and bound by CPI Group (UK) Ltd, Croydon, CR0 4YY

12/10/2023

08129864-0001